A Mind in Prison

To Jennifer
with love
Perette M.*

June '02
& greetings from Bruno M.

A MIND IN PRISON

The Memoir of a Son and Soldier

of the Third Reich

Bruno Manz

BRASSEY'S

Washington, D.C.

First paperback edition 2001

Copyright © 2000 Brassey's

Published in the United States by Brassey's. All rights reserved. No part of this book may be reproduced in any manner whatsoever without written permission from the publisher, except in the case of brief quotations embodied in critical articles and reviews.

Library of Congress Cataloging-in-Publication Data
Manz, Bruno, 1921–
A mind in prison : the memoir of a son and soldier of the Third Reich / Bruno Manz.—1st ed.
p.   cm.
Includes bibliographical references and index.
ISBN 1-57488-242-2 (alk. paper)
1. Manz, Bruno, 1921–   2. Soldiers—Germany—Biography.
3. Antisemitism—Germany—History—20th century.
4. Scientists—United States—Recruiting—History—
20th century. 5. National socialism—Influence. 6. World War,
1939–1945—Personal narratives, German. I. Title.
D811.M342 2000
943.086'092—dc21
[B]   99-086468

Paperback ISBN 1-57488-342-9

Printed in the United States of America on acid-free paper that meets the American National Standards Institute Z39-48 Standard.

Brassey's
22841 Quicksilver Drive
Dulles, Virginia 20166

10 9 8 7 6 5 4 3 2 1

This book is dedicated
to the victims of the Third Reich.

The author is deeply indebted to Albert Noyer,
who suggested this book and
supported it from start to finish.

CONTENTS

The truth will make you free.

Gospel of John

A MIND IN PRISON

Prologue

This is the story of my life in Germany between 1921 and 1957—a life that was dominated almost from its beginning by Adolf Hitler. I am telling my story because I believe it has to be told. There is presently much discussion about how much Germans knew regarding the concentration camps, and how readily they condoned, or were actually involved in, the atrocities committed. I do not claim to have a simple answer to these questions, but I do believe that my testimony can make a valuable contribution to the verdict of history that is now evolving.

I was not, nor am I now, a "typical German," because there is none. But my fate was typical of the disastrous ways in which Nazi propaganda, in conjunction with the German culture of the time, affected Germany's youngest minds. My mind was imprisoned by this fateful coalition for more than fourteen years, somewhat longer than the duration of the "Thousand Year Reich." My body was never in prison, but my mind was and it had to do the

Führer's will. When I was ten years old, I was already poisoned with anti-Semitic hatred. At the age of eleven, half a year before the Nazis came to power, I joined the Hitler Youth. And in the New Year's night of 1939–40 I became a soldier in Hitler's army.

I admitted my mental imprisonment neither to myself nor to others but, rather, accepted the gloomy mood of my teenage years as my natural state of mind. I never had consciously experienced spiritual freedom. Even before the imprisonment began in earnest, I had already been conditioned by slogans such as "You Are Nothing, Deutschland Is Everything." It did not occur to me that the "pursuit of happiness" is a human right; it would take a quarter of a century before I read this truth—to my utter amazement—in the American Declaration of Independence.

Growing up in Nazi Germany, I was not used to relying on my own judgment in social and political affairs. Whenever my thoughts conflicted with the official ideology, I sacrificed my right of sovereign thinking on the altar of patriotism. At the young age when a person tests his or her intellectual wings, my mind was already in chains, as was the will that might have broken them. Instead of using my own brain and conscience, I followed orders. Until the end of the Third Reich, I was not my own but the Führer's creature.

Evil works two ways: it harms either your body or your soul—or perhaps both. Its favorite tool has always been the prison. This tool was also the Nazis' chief instrument of tyranny. When they wanted to recruit someone for their evil deeds, they imprisoned his mind. When they wanted to destroy him, they threw him in a concentration camp.

I do not for a moment compare my suffering with that of the victims in Hitler's prisons and concentration camps. Only the few who survived that ordeal know the suffering of the many who died there. My suffering was of a different kind—not as brutal as theirs but longer lasting. It was more subtle and insidious, like a creeping sickness or a gradual poisoning, drop by drop. I do not say this to complain or to solicit sympathy, but to expose the stealthy ways of evil when it masquerades in the guise of virtue.

Whoever wants to testify in this ongoing trial of history must speak the absolute truth. He owes this not only to the victims, but to humankind as a whole, for this is not the trial of one nation, but the self-analysis of humanity. Any attempt to veil the truth would be a sin against the victims and a crime against the future of the human race. If there is one place where humankind needs the truth, then it is here.

Therefore, while bearing witness before the tribunal of history, I shall spare none, neither my father nor myself. It will be painful to describe how my father fanned the flames of hatred and seared my eight-year-old soul with the brand of anti-Semitism. And it will be unpleasant to confess that I had several warnings that I did not heed. But if I lacked the courage or the self-criticism to speak the truth now, I should better remain silent.

I believe that every German of my age and older who lived in Nazi Germany during the Holocaust has to answer these questions:

- Where were you?
- What did you know?
- What did you do or not do?
- What have you now to say?

This is the spirit of my book. To make it as authentic as possible, I have written directly from memory without consulting any other sources. And yet, despite its autobiographical form, this book is not about me. It is about the barbarism of Nazism. It is a document about one of the darkest chapters of human history. And it is the repayment of a debt long overdue.

CHAPTER I

In the Crucible of Despair

I was born in 1921 in the city of Dortmund, one of the big industrial towns of the Rhine-Ruhr District of western Germany. In the years of my childhood the city was cloaked in the smoke and soot from its two main industries, coal-mining and steel-making.

I was the second of four children. My father was a self-employed architect who was often out of work. At the beginning of World War I in 1914, he had been seriously wounded and lost control of one leg. A grenade exploded next to him and sent its fragments into his body. He fell into horse manure and contracted tetanus, whereupon he fought for his life for the next four years. My mother was also disabled by an eye injury she experienced during her childhood.

It was a difficult time for parents to raise children, a time of economic hardship, high unemployment, and political chaos. I still remember when the bailiff confiscated a cherished piece of furniture because my parents could not pay the rent. In spite of these hardships, my parents provided us children with a home in which we felt loved and secure.

I loved and respected my parents, and I still do. Yet my father was that fateful person who, when I was less than ten years old, initiated the insidious process of my mental imprisonment, which was later completed with even more efficiency by Nazi institutions and propaganda. My father was a German chauvinist, who soon fell into Hitler's wide-open arms. His nationalistic conceit is perhaps best exemplified by his favorite saying, *Von deutschem Wesen wird dereinst die ganze Welt genesen* (The German character one day will cure the whole world). He spoke of Germany as the nation of poets and philosophers, and implied, as did the Nazis, that Germany was the cradle of culture (the word "civilization," interestingly, was out of favor). I wholeheartedly embraced this hubris because it presented itself so cleverly as age-old wisdom in poetic form. Little did I know that collective pride is a narcotic for the mentally homeless.

In 1929, the year of the Great Depression, my father became a member of the Nazi Party. From then on he relentlessly tried to win others over to his course. I still remember his incessant proselytizing and his penchant for blaming other groups and nations, and the Jews particularly, for Germany's troubles. What I recall most vividly were his outbursts of hatred, which were essentially directed against three groups: the Jews, the French, and the so-called November criminals who had negotiated the Treaty of Versailles. At the same time he hailed Nazi crimes, such as the assassination of Walther Rathenau (a German statesman), as deeds of patriotism and historical justice.

Had my father been aloof or cold to us children, his preaching might not have influenced me as strongly as it did. But he was loving and caring, and he made for us wonderful toys that were the envy of our friends. Once he built a Black Forest peasant house with people and animals, which attracted visitors from all over town. For my younger brother he tailored the uniform of a grenadier of the Prussian army under Frederick the Great, complete with helmet and wooden rifle. On Christmas Day he took the six-year-old boy to town to show him off to young and old.

For me, he built a miniature workshop mounted on a large board, featuring an electric motor, a transmission, a generator, a steam engine, and a dozen special tools such as a circular saw and a lathe. He also supplied fine woods and showed me how to make chess figures. Unfortunately, since I did not share his talent, I disappointed him by simply cutting the wood to pieces.

My fondest memories are the little walks on which he took me in spite of his physical handicap, on warm summer mornings. There, he forgot his anti-Semitic hatred. Instead, he talked about his work, the houses he built, and how they fitted into the landscape. These were the happiest moments of my childhood. I suppose they were also some of my father's happier moments.

The conversation at the dinner table, when it did not deal with political subjects, was often substantive, constructive, and educational. My father had two favorite maxims that I took to heart. One was "Do right and fear nobody"; the other was "Be more than you pretend to be." I believe that he sincerely tried to live up to these principles, but never realized how seriously he violated the first one by preaching his hatred. As to the second motto, I believe that he truly adhered to it. Had it not been for his disastrous political hatemongering, I think he would have been an ideal father.

My family was essentially non-religious. My father considered himself a free-thinking man, and my mother had suffered in her childhood at the hands of Catholic nuns because she was the child of a "mixed marriage" between a Protestant father and a Catholic mother. On Monday mornings, if she had missed the Sunday Bible school, she had to stretch out her hands to receive a blow with a ruler across the fingers. Today the story helps me to appreciate the wisdom of the separation of church and state in the American Constitution.

Although my parents did not favor religious education, I had the good fortune of having a teacher in the Evangelical grammar school who had an extraordinary talent for telling Bible stories, such as Joseph in Egypt or the Flight of the Holy Family. My father must have felt how much I loved this Biblical instruction, for he did not interfere, except that he disparagingly referred to the teacher as a *Sozi* (a slang word for a Social Democrat). But his clerical animosity was directed not so much against Protestants as against Catholics, whom he called bigots. He referred to the annual procession of the Catholic faithful through the streets of our town as "a triumphal march of stupidity."

My father had been born and raised in a small village directly at the border with France. In the town, anti-French feelings ran deep, and he had adopted the chauvinism of his father, the director of a coal mine. Though my grandfather had a reputation as a tyrant, both at home and on his job, he saw to it that his twelve children received a decent high school education. Yet he hated the French and the Jews and passed his hatred on to my father, who then passed it on to me.

Yet my father's antipathy against the French was not the hatred that transfused his anti-Semitism but, rather, a presumptuous contempt. He portrayed the French as unmanly, despite his experience with the bravery of French soldiers during the First World War. One of his favorite shibboleths was: "A good German likes no Frenchman, but he loves to drink his wines." He still smarted from the lost war, as did many Germans of his generation. They deeply resented the 1919 Treaty of Versailles, which they called "The Dictate of Versailles" and which, it is true, was an instrument of vengeance. With its humiliating provisions, such as Germany's loss of sovereignty over its rivers and some of its territories, the treaty contributed considerably to the revisionist sentiment of most Germans and, in the end, to World War II.

Though my father had suffered terribly during the war, he spoke in fond terms of his service in the Imperial army. He particularly raved about the thick pea soup in which, as he put it, the spoon would stand upright. When I joined Hitler's army in World War II, I found to my disappointment that neither the pea soup nor most other things were as topnotch as my father had described them. Indeed, I doubt that he really liked his service in the army as much as he claimed. Rather I believe that he was motivated by a nationalistic ardor and desire to stimulate the same fervor in me. In this regard, he was extraordinarily successful.

Both of my parents had suffered greatly during the difficult period at the end of World War I and immediately thereafter. My mother told us horrible stories of people dying of starvation in the streets. One of the victims was her brother. What Germans resented most was that the food blockade continued even after Germany had surrendered, and that it did not end until the emissaries of the Weimar Republic had signed the Treaty of Versailles. But even then the punishment did not end. When Germany was unable to pay the astronomical war reparations, the French invaded Germany's Ruhr district and took coal and steel in place of money.

An immediate consequence of the unreasonable war reparations was the great inflation of the 1920s. Since the German government was unable to come up with the billions of marks demanded by France, it printed more money, creating an inflationary spiral. My mother told us the story of how she received the wages my father had earned as an employee of a large industrial company in Dortmund. Because of the rapid devaluation of the money, the employees were paid daily. My parents would meet at the company gate, where my father dumped the paper money into my mother's apron. She then rushed to the closest bakery to buy a loaf of bread before the price doubled. She also showed us one of the billion-mark notes printed on only one side in order to save time and printing costs.

I do not recall sensing any hatred when my mother told us these stories, only a desire to lament the suffering. It was her nature to suffer, but not to hate. In World War II, when Dortmund was burning from Allied bombing raids and her home was destroyed, my mother showed the same penchant for hateless lamentation. Her favorite dictum was Goethe's words, "If you wish to know what is proper, ask well-bred women."

When my father talked about the hardship of the war and its aftermath, it was different, particularly when he spoke about the Treaty of Versailles. Ironically, he blamed the Jews even more than the French. According to him, the Jews were responsible for everything: for inciting anti-German feelings all over the world, for starting the war, for the punishment of Versailles, for the starvation, and for all the misery and humiliations that were still visited on the German people. He was convinced that the Jews were leading a world conspiracy against Germany, and he preached his irrational hatred with an almost religious zeal. Rothschild, Morgan, Rathenau, and Trotsky were some of the Jewish leaders whose names he pronounced as if they were the scum of the earth.

A good example of my father's proselytizing was a family that lived in the apartment beneath ours. They were churchgoing Catholics who rejected Hitler—until he came to power, that is. They also were friends of ours, in spite of my father's persistent attempts to bring them into the Nazi fold. The brunt of my father's zealotry fell on the family father, who was no match for him. Sometimes it seemed that my father had won the politically unsophisticated gentleman over to his side, but after another church attendance the poor devil, as we called him, had rekindled his doubts and reinvigorated his anti-Nazi feelings. When my father noticed his relapse, he would say that it was time to give him another "head wash."

Eventually, repeated "head washes" produced results. After every "grooming," that family moved a little closer to the Nazi movement. And when the Nazis came to power in 1933, the family discovered, to our surprise, that they had sympathized with Hitler all along. To prove it, the old man asked my father to sponsor his oldest son for the SS. A few months later when the young man presented himself in his new black uniform, my childish soul was filled with envy.

My father's anti-Semitism invaded even provinces as serene as music. He loved classical music and sometimes whistled familiar tunes or played them on the violoncello. I still remember when he was whistling a melody, which I later identified as the second theme from the *presto* of Beethoven's Seventh Symphony. After he had finished the tune, he asked with unfeigned amazement, "How can anybody invent such a beautiful melody?" However, in spite of his undeniable music appreciation, he would never listen to the works of Jewish composers such as Mendelssohn or Mahler. I am not sure whether this was because he was afraid the music would poison his Aryan soul or because he was convinced that it was not worthwhile listening to.

He displayed the same obstinacy in other fields, such as science. Though he clearly lacked the education to understand Albert Einstein's theory of relativity, he declared with the arrogance of the ignorant that every schoolteacher knew the "trivialities" that Einstein tried to sell as profound scientific discoveries. It took fifteen years until I had the opportunity to acquaint myself with the theory of relativity, and another fifteen years until I could truthfully claim that I understood it. My father's favorite term for Jewish accomplishments in science was "a typically Jewish attempt to stupefy." With distortions like this he denied every achievement of German Jewry from Heinrich Heine to Sigmund Freud.

Most of my father's preaching reached us children at the family table. I was barely old enough to understand it all, but the primitive slogans were hammered into my mind, particularly the ever-repeated lie "The Jews are our misfortune." After he had talked himself into a rage, my father would use language that shocked all of us, particularly my mother. On one occasion he raved about "The Night of the Long Knives," which apparently he considered the remedy for "The Jewish Question." At another instance he shouted that there would be no peace in the world until all Jews were dead. When my mother cried out in anguish, "My God, they are human beings, too!" he countered with the contemptuous phrase, "Lice are animals, too."

While I abhorred the violence that these outbursts seemed to suggest, I was convinced that the underlying cause was just and patriotic. And patriotism was a cause close to my heart. The nation, the flag, soldiery, sacrifice on the altar of the Fatherland, these were the ideals I nurtured in my childish mind. I had adopted them from my father and the people with whom he socialized, and also from some of the teachers at high school. Not all of these elders were anti-Semitic hatemongers; some were well-meaning patriots who entertained nostalgic dreams of national glory.

One of the more innocent dreamers was a teacher who organized the Boy Scouts at high school. His idol was Walter Flex, a hero from the First World War who had written the book *Wanderer Between Both Worlds.* Sometimes the young teacher read to us from this book, which touched me deeply with its purity and sincerity, as did a song from the same author. It dealt with a column of young volunteers marching to the front in Flanders in 1914 and beholding a formation of gray geese flying overhead. Anticipating early death on the field of glory, and fearing that the migrating birds might share their fate, the young men ended the somber song on the refrain, "Oh restless journeyer, beware, beware, the world is full of murder!" Today this artless poetry still touches me as an island of patriotic innocence in a sea of political deprivation.

Most of my father's business acquaintances were either Nazi sympathizers or party members. In fact, I recall only one unmistakable anti-Nazi, the owner of a prosperous carpenter shop whom my older brother called Herr Geheimrat (*Geheimrat* means privy councillor or confidential advisor) because he was a Freemason and had a certain air of distinction. He also had a predilection for satire, which my father admired as long as it was not aimed at Hitler. A few years later, when criticizing the Nazis had become dangerous, Herr Geheimrat proved that he also had courage, as I shall report later. In spite of his affiliation with the Freemasons, he and my father were close friends, as were his wife and my mother. He also entertained a splendid army of play soldiers from the time of Frederick the Great, with horses and cannons, which I sometimes was allowed to review but never to touch.

What I recall most vividly about this enigmatic man were the political discussions in which he engaged my father. When they touched upon Hitler and the Nazis, the debate became quite loud and sometimes bitter. "You will see," I recall my father shouting, "Hitler will save us." "No," retorted Herr Geheimrat, "he will get us only deeper into trouble." In my childish judgment, this man was the only person who could stand his ground against my father. I liked to listen to him because he seemed to support his arguments with historical examples. Unfortunately, the unscheduled lessons from the *Geheimrat* came to an early end, when his wife came crying to our house claiming that he had beaten her. Since she also had a black eye to prove it, my mother got so enraged that she banished Herr Geheimrat from our house. When he returned years later, I was already fully indoctrinated with Nazi ideology.

A decidedly negative influence on me was another of my father's business acquaintances, who was the owner of a building company. My father called him *Haudegen* (literally "hitting saber," meaning "old champion"). He surpassed my father both in age and years of Nazi Party membership. I believe it was this old champion who had recruited my father for the party in 1929. His trademarks were a curved pipe of the kind foresters used to smoke and a large brimmed hat that concealed a conspicuous scar across his skull. At about this time, I saw a picture from Wagner's opera *Siegfried*, in which the god Wotan appears as a "Wanderer on Earth," wearing a brimmed hat of the kind Old Champion wore. Unfortunately, the picture from German mythology filled me with more respect for the man than he deserved.

According to rumor, Old Champion had received a blow on his head in a brawl with the Communists and suffered some brain damage. From this dubious source I heard for the first time the grisly tales of Jewish ritual murders. Such tales were routinely fabricated by the notorious Nazi propaganda organ *Der Stürmer.* While this ugly mouthpiece of German anti-Semitism would have an even more deplorable influence on our lives in the years to come, its venom reached me already at this early age.

Once, the man with the brimmed hat took me aside and taught me an anti-Semitic rhyme of calculated offensiveness. He wanted me to sing the verse to one of my playmates who was Jewish, but I resented it because it exuded the smell of the gutter. I was so embarrassed that I delayed the provocation from day to day, but Old Champion kept pressuring me until I finally obliged. The vulgar words pained me so much that I rattled them off rather quickly, hoping the poor boy would not understand them. But I was mistaken. The lad must have heard the insulting verse before, for he turned around without a word and avoided me after that. I can still recall the feeling of shame. The rhyme is so ugly that I would not repeat it here if it were not so symptomatic of the hateful atmosphere in which I grew up. Thus, I present it with an apology for its vulgarity.

Jude Itzig	Jew "Itzig"
Nase spitzig	Nose pointed
Augen eckig	Eyes angular
Arschloch dreckig.	Ass-hole dirty.

In summary, the atmosphere in which I grew up was a mixture of national glory and misery, pride and humiliation, hope and despair, devotion and hatred, beauty and ugliness, romantic tales and infamous lies. Though I learned history in school, I did not understand that history is more than battles and victories, glory and conquest. It did not occur to me that there are values such as historical responsibility, historical merit, and, alas, historical guilt. I was a guileless, gullible romantic who blindly accepted the nationalistic rhetoric and anti-Semitic canards of the elders. By the time I was ten years old, my soul was already thoroughly poisoned with a dull, collective hatred.

Yet all of this was talk, not action. I believe my father was as incapable of physical brutality as I am. I do not know whether he ever witnessed any of the more serious atrocities of the Nazis, or whether, had he seen them with his own eyes, he would have condemned them. But I do know that he was incapable of committing such acts, though he sometimes talked as if he was only waiting for an opportunity to carry them out. He was a highly excitable rabble-rouser who, in the heat of debate, would say things of inexcusable irresponsibility. Had he been physically brutal, and had I found out, he would have lost me that very instant. But I stayed in the mental prison he had prepared for me because I loved him and believed that his cause was just, even noble.

Of course, preaching hatred is a particular kind of destructive action. It can have consequences as harmful and irreparable as any deed of violence. I doubt whether my father understood this, for even after the Second World War, when he was old and demoralized, he did not show any sign of regret or atonement, but went right on blaming the new misery of the defeated nation on the Jews, as he had done before. My sister told me that, at the time of the Nuremberg trials, she played a record with music of Felix Mendelssohn. My father probably had never heard it before, but listened so attentively that my sister hoped he might have been converted to the truth. However, after it ended he murmured the word *Klaubacke*, which is a colloquialism for plagiarist. He could not believe, or did not want to believe, that a Jew could have composed the beautiful music he had just heard. It still pains me that his destiny had not granted him redemption from his pernicious hatred.

A Whirlwind of Seduction and Doubt

In 1931, when I was barely ten years old, I had my first encounter with the Storm Troopers. Not far from where we lived was the Nazi Party headquarters. Next to it ran a wide, tree-lined street, built on former city walls, which played a fateful role in my early childhood. This pleasant avenue was the scene of heated debates and bloody fights between Nazis and Communists, for at the time the Communists still had a larger following in Germany than the Nazis, particularly in this town of miners and steelworkers. My father took me to that street a few times and soon became engaged in the ongoing discussions. He was a furious debater, and I admired him when he got the upper hand, though I barely understood what it was all about.

Eventually I went to the avenue on my own. With a childish mixture of agitation and admiration, I watched the brawls between the Brownshirts and the Communists. What impressed me most was the brawn of the Nazis, which I mistook for heroism.

Today I am surprised at myself, for I despise brutal force and naked power. I suppose what attracted me to the ugly scene then was my naive belief that might is right. Most of all, it was the hope, nourished by my father, that Hitler and his Brownshirts would eventually come to power, and that would be the end of such lawlessness.

Sometimes the Communists demonstrated in front of the headquarters to provoke the Nazis. The Storm Troopers, who were already lying in wait, would suddenly rush out with clubs and knives. Before I knew it, a bloody street battle would be going on. Usually the police were also on alert and scurried to the scene in special trucks marked "Riot Police." Waving their formidable riot clubs, they beat down anybody who stood in their way. Although they were mainly after the Nazis and the Communists, they sometimes hit innocent bystanders. Since I was quite young and also rather quick, they never hit me.

My father did not participate in these brawls, not only because of his handicap from war injuries, but also because they were against his nature. Nevertheless, he admired the Brownshirts and their supposed acts of bravery, as did I. My father's specialty was the word of mouth. He considered it his mission to convert as many people as possible to the cause of Nazism and anti-Semitism. He was a born proselytizer, who pursued his avocation with an almost religious ardor.

My own political activity at this early age consisted mainly of pasting little swastika labels onto house walls and advertising columns. I bought the labels at the party headquarters and paid for them with the money I earned from a little part-time work, which brought me some fame among my playmates. The work was a cart service that I provided to drunks who emerged from a pub across the street from where we lived. When a drunkard emerged from the tavern, unable to walk, I loaded him onto my cart and drove him home. Most of the time, I earned more abuse than money, but, once in a while, I got a dime with which I hurriedly bought ten more labels. My mother did not like this activity and tried to persuade my father to forbid it, but he thought it was funny. From the ranting and raving of the drinkers I knew that most of them were Communists, which was no problem as long as they did not know that I was a Nazi. However, thanks to my own cockiness, my affiliation would not remain a secret for long.

On every first of May the Communists held their traditional May Day Parade, which always led them through our street. They came with men, women, and children waving huge banners, singing the Internationale, and bellowing their slogans. My father and I watched from the window of our third-story apartment and pooh-poohed them from this harbor of safety. Curiously, the women, who appeared enormous to me, were clad in bathing suits. This mode of attire stirred me up to ever more wanton ridicule, to which the demonstrators responded with threats. At that point, my mother angrily pulled me from the window and forbade me once and for all to provide cart service to "this kind of people."

Two highly emotional experiences from that time are still fresh in my memory. The first concerns "The Horst Wessel Song." Set to a North Sea folk melody, the text is credited to Horst Wessel, who was a leader of the SA in Berlin around 1930. Wessel was killed by a rival over his mistress's affections. True to form, the Goebbels propaganda transformed his unseemly end into a martyr's death at the hands of the Communists, and elevated "The Horst Wessel Song" to the status of the official party anthem.

Of course, I was not aware of the unsavory origin of the text, nor would I have understood it. It was the melody that took me under its spell. Today I would say that it has a serious flaw, for the tune goes down when it should go up. The first line of the text says, *Die Fahne Hoch!* (The flag hold high!). However, the melody to these words goes down, placing the word "high" on the lowest note. This did not bother me at the time because the melody does have a certain ring that is quite rousing. In fact, it reminded me of the national anthem of another nation that I had learned in school.

Nevertheless, when I heard the song for the first time, it made on me an impression far out of proportion to its musical quality. The fateful moment came unexpectedly when I was about to enter my grandparents' apartment. The entry path led through a long hallway in which every sound was amplified. In this acoustically enhanced environment, I suddenly heard some singing that struck me with an intensity I had never felt before. I rushed out into the street to see what was happening, and there I saw a truck with the swastika banner waving from the rear, moving slowly down the street. As I trained my eyes on the flag, I spotted the Storm Troopers behind it, singing "The Horst Wessel Song."

I was mesmerized! I still recall my feeling at that moment, the exhilarated impression that their faces were glowing with inspiration—while they probably were quite ordinary. I felt that their singing was a euphony of animation, while it more likely was an unrestrained vociferation. I saw gracefulness where, in all probability, there was crudeness, and I heard melodiousness where there was stridency. Thus I stood motionless and mentally defenseless, all too willing to drink in the singing like a magic potion, while chills of rapture traveled down my spine. As the singing slowly faded in the distance, I felt that it was the most inspired chanting I had ever heard. I don't know how long I stood there in my childish euphoria, but in the following days, I reconstructed the mediocre melody in my musical memory, and I still felt the same unenlightened exaltation. It took years for the enchantment to wear off.

The second experience was far more negative although, unfortunately, not negative enough to awaken me from my youthful romantic slumbers. Up to this time I had never seen a portrait of

Hitler. I had heard his name a thousand times, and it was always pronounced with a reverence that bordered on adulation. Voices were lowered whenever people spoke the name of the Führer. To my childish mind, he was like a coming messiah.

Though I had not seen the Führer's likeness, I did have some visual expectation. In school I had learned about the people's rebellion of 1848 against feudal regimes in France and the German principalities. The leaders of these uprisings were often highly idealistic university students. The young Richard Wagner was one of them. Thus, I had formed a mental picture of these rebels, which portrayed them as youthful, idealistic, and handsome. And that was also the semblance of Hitler that I had formed in my unsuspecting mind.

I was to be disappointed. It happened, of all places, at the toilet, which in those days was not on the same level with our apartment, but one flight of stairs lower. There was a stack of newspapers in that room, and the top one displayed the Führer's likeness. It was one of those drawings based on photographs that one can still see in newspapers such as the *Wall Street Journal*. The picture, which was quite small, was part of a promotion for his book, *Mein Kampf*. However, instead of a youthful hero, an aged wretch with a little mustache stared back at me. I was dumbfounded! "This can't be the Führer," I muttered with disbelief; "this must be somebody else." But, undeniably, there was his name and the swastika in the claws of an eagle. There could be no doubt: this pathetic man, who was later impersonated by Charlie Chaplin, *was* the Führer.

For a moment I was painfully sober and almost ready to use the newspaper for the purpose for which it was intended. But my reverence for the Führer took the upper hand, and I cheerlessly placed the paper with his picture at the bottom of the pile, so that the dreary face would no longer stare at me. This was the only time I treated the Führer disrespectfully. It was also the only time

I doubted his almost godlike qualities. Unfortunately, I soon forgot this episode that should have been a warning to me. Slowly and subconsciously I restored in my mind the glowing picture of the Führer that I had already formed years before I received this subtle warning. Why did not angels keep the slender flame of doubt alive in me!

CHAPTER 3

Violation of a Defenseless Mind

In high school I had a friend who was two years my senior and more developed than I was, both physically and mentally. While I admired this friend for his self-assuredness, his nonchalance, and his worldly experience, I disliked his cynicism and dirty jokes. This schoolmate was a member of the NS Student Federation (NS is the abbreviation the Nazis always used for National Socialist), which was a branch of the Hitler Youth. When he suggested that I join, I asked my father for permission, which he gladly granted. Thus I became a member of the Hitler Youth in the fall of 1932, six months before the Nazis came to power.

That's when all the marching began that dominated my life for the next thirteen years. During those years, I was always in a uniform colored either brown or gray, except in the very early days when brown shirts were difficult to come by. We wore white shirts then instead. But the red armband with the swastika was already there. Also, in the early days, we wore our colored school caps which, however, would soon be banned as relics from the class society of the past. In this makeshift uniform we marched with the Storm Troopers through the cold and rainy streets of Dortmund, wet and freezing, shouting their mindless slogans, and singing their unsavory songs.

One particularly ugly song stuck in my mind. It had the refrain "And when the Jewish blood spurts from the knife, yes, then things go twice as well." I was horrified but, unfortunately, not for long, for I did not take these words at face value. I certainly did not consider them as a declaration of intent, but as a rhetorical overstatement in the heat of the political campaign. The thought that, one day, some of those who uttered these ugly threats might carry them out was far from my mind. I rather thought that the loathsome song was a typical soldiers' song, as rough and rowdy as soldiers are supposed to be.

Once a week my group gathered for one of our "home evenings," dreary gatherings that were, ironically, anything but evenings at home. These took place in an unheated, dimly lighted shack, which was furnished with a small table and a few crude benches. The only decoration was the swastika flag behind the leader's table. Most members were older than I. The leader, who was already in his forties, preached with a strident voice and intimidated me with his blatant show of political savvy.

At the first home evening the leader talked about one Gottfried Feder, whose name I had never heard before and would not often hear thereafter. Apparently, this man was a party leader who had developed a plan to break, as he called it, "the Jewish monopolistic capitalism and interest slavery." I had only a foggy idea of what he meant by that, but one thing came through loud and clear: The economic monster this man attacked in his book was an instrument of the Jews, and its purpose was to subjugate my people. Hunger and poverty were the generals who had brought Germany to its knees before, and now the country's enemies intended to apply the same tactic again. My father was right; the Jews, indeed, were our misfortune.

I was always freezing at these home evenings, physically as well as mentally. The leader, who seemed to be as cold as the shack, preached mainly to the older members, paying little attention to me. His disregard almost turned me off, but his strident preaching eventually persuaded me that he had an important message, if not for me, then for the others. I did not blame him for the neglect; I blamed myself, for I was ashamed of my political inactivity and inexperience. Chastened by the leader's arrogance, which I mistook for depth, I promised myself to make good for my deficiency by faithfully attending the unpleasant home evenings and learning from the unsympathetic man as much as I could.

Another home evening dealt with the "Jewish World Conspiracy Against the Aryan Race." This time, the leader targeted the Jewish-Polish revolutionary Rosa Luxemburg, who was one of the leaders of the German Communist Party. Together with Karl Liebknecht and others, Luxemburg allegedly had engineered the collapse of Imperial Germany at the end of the First World War. This historical lie was part of the "dagger legend" with which the Nazis tried to explain the defeat of 1918. In retaliation for the alleged act of treason, the Nazis murdered Luxemburg in Moabit prison in Berlin and threw her body into the Landwehr Kanal. This criminal act was portrayed to us as a deed of patriotic duty. To celebrate it, we squalled out another ugly song that began with the words "A corpse is floating in the Landwehr Kanal." Thus the satanic lie of the Jewish world conspiracy sank ever deeper into my eleven-year-old soul. In my unsuspecting mind the murder of Rosa Luxemburg was an assassination worthy of a Brutus or Wilhelm Tell.

I did not like the marching, the shouting, or the home evenings, and that would remain so for the next twelve years. However, I thought these unpleasant activities were a small price to pay for the privilege of helping the Führer in his gigantic struggle against the Jewish world conspiracy. I knew that I would have to go through many more hardships until I lived to see the Third Reich, and I hoped that one day my toils would earn me the gratitude of the Fatherland. Little did I know that they would earn me only disgrace in the eyes of the rest of the world.

In my school at the time—one of three high schools for boys in the city—the teachers tried to be neutral toward Nazism and did not admonish me for being a member of the Hitler Youth. They avoided the name of the Führer, probably in a futile attempt to make him a non-entity. I had the feeling that most of them were equally afraid of Nazism and Communism, and that their mistrust was the motivation for their lukewarm support of the Weimar Republic. They did not love the young democracy, yet considered it their only guarantee against the twin threats from the Right and the Left.

But one teacher was different. This teacher sincerely cherished the Weimar Republic and tried to inspire us students with his allegiance to the Constitution. He was one of several mathematics and physics teachers at our school, but he had not yet taught in our class. Later, when he became our class teacher, we endearingly referred to him by his first name, Theo, though we always addressed him respectfully as Herr Studienrat (*Studienrat* means study councillor), as was the custom in those days.

This teacher, who was a practicing Catholic and a Social Democrat, had the longest-lasting beneficial influence on my life. If it is true that a teacher may earn himself eternity, then it is true of this unforgettable man. Fifty years later and long after his death, his spirit still guided me when I was standing in front of my own class and trying to pass on to my students what I had learned from him. I shall return to Theo several times. At the moment I want to recount only my first encounter with him. As with so many others I still have to report, it should have been a warning to me. Unfortunately, and to my lifelong regret, it was drowned by the deafening noise of the Nazi propaganda machine.

This story deals with Constitution Day, which Theo initiated at our school and which we observed every year until the Nazis put an end to it. For it, students gathered in the schoolyard, while Theo stood on the balcony. First we listened to his speech about democracy and the Constitution, and then we sang the national anthem while he slowly raised the flag. The colors were black, red, and gold, as they are in the new Germany. I loved these colors, and I still believe that they form an exceptionally harmonious triad. Whenever I see them today, they fill me with nostalgia for this brief period of political innocence.

I admired Theo for his dedication to the course of democracy, and even more so for the way he expressed it. Although I rejected the idea of democracy, Theo made me feel that there was something about it worthy of support by a good and honest man. What impressed me most were the sincerity and unpretentiousness with which he communicated his conviction.

Once, I secretly observed Theo in the schoolyard while he was talking to a boy who was in some kind of trouble. Though this was definitely not a political affair, I noticed on Theo's face and in his gestures the same conviction I already knew from his political activities. It seemed to come from a rare combination of serenity and intensity. Although he was completely calm, he was so animated that he forgot to take a bite from the sandwich that was dangling from his hand. I loved his face with the rimless glasses. The receding forehead, which was almost bald, and the pointed nose gave his face a bird-like shape. It was not handsome, but it bore an expression of unswerving goodness. When, fifty years later, I saw a picture of the American composer Aaron Copland, I was reminded of dear Theo. Curiously, at that unforgettable moment when I spied on him, I was filled with envy. I wished that this man were talking to me. The unpleasant leader from the NS Student Federation came to my mind, and I pain-fully felt the contrast between his boisterous hustling and Theo's simple being.

When Theo delivered his annual speech about the sanctity of the Constitution from the balcony of the school building, I was completely convinced of his sincerity. I even liked the mental picture of the Weimar Republic that he projected. And yet, something was wrong. Something was out of balance. There was another side to the picture that I deeply resented. It was not he whom I resented, not the way in which he stated his conviction; it was the object of his conviction! It was the Weimar Republic. Obviously my cherished teacher was ignorant of its origin as well as its purpose. Did he not know that the Weimar Republic was a creation of the Jewish world conspiracy? Did he not realize that the Constitution was dictated in Versailles and designed to en-slave the German people? Had Theo never wondered who had destroyed Bismarck's legacy, the Second Reich, and why? To me, the very name "Weimar Republic" was a lie. This monstrosity neither breathed the spirit of Weimar (home of Goethe and Schiller), nor was it a republic. How could a man with Theo's intelligence fail to see this glaring truth?

I heard his voice, but I closed my mind, while the clarion call of the Führer was ringing in my soul. It was an uneven contest: here the lonely voice in the desert, there the siren song of the Thousand Year Reich. With a heavy heart and an inflamed mind, I ignored the second warning of my life and missed an irretriev-able chance of freeing myself from the invisible chains of mental servitude.

CHAPTER 4

Imprisonment of Seventy Million Minds

The fateful day was January 30, 1933. Germans would always remember this day as "The Day of Power Seizure." In the political chaos of the Weimar Republic, the nearly senile *Reichspräsident* Paul von Hindenburg appointed Hitler *Reichskanzler* of Germany. In a few weeks the *Reichstag* would burn and the first Jews and Communists would march to the concentration camps. It was the end of freedom and civilization in Germany, and the beginning of a turmoil that would soon engulf Europe and, eventually, the whole world. Never before in human history have more people suffered and died than during the terrible developments that began with this day.

But my father and I thought otherwise. Believing that a new era of national glory and happiness had begun, we were downright euphoric. Spending the whole day before the radio, we breathlessly listened to the events in Berlin. In the evening, my father and I went our separate ways to participate in the local celebrations. I rushed to the NS Student Federation to march in the torch parade that paralleled the parade in Berlin and in thousands of other German cities. My father went to the Nazi headquarters to watch the parade from there.

The streets were lined with jubilant people. Flags were in almost every window, most showing the hastily made swastika emblem, and some displaying the Imperial colors of black, white, and red. The sudden availability of all of these flags was a mystery to me, but I considered it a good omen for a strong and united Germany. The noise from the marching bands and the incessant shouting of Heil was deafening. In all that turmoil, I imagined my father standing somewhere in the crowd, seeing me marching by and being proud of me. The thought filled me with a happiness I should not feel often in the years to come. As usual I was freezing in my white shirt and shorts, but the ecstatic crowd, the sweet smoke from the torches, the military music, the incessant Heil chorus, and the image of my father warmed my heart and kept my feet marching.

The parade led to a rally at the town square, where the local party leaders addressed the huge crowd. But this was no longer a party rally; it was a people's rally. The speeches were again and again interrupted by roaring applause, which was now expressed in endless repetitions of Heil. This word had suddenly become a synonym for *Ja* (yes) in the German language. In the following years it would become the favorite word of the *Mitläufer* (fellow-travelers, or me-tooers), as the newly converted *Volksgenossen* (people's comrades) were called. But this night, Heil was everybody's monosyllabic, unending mode of expression. This was not applause, this was not acclamation, this was madness! It was a wave of mass psychosis that carried everybody away, including myself. I don't know how often I yelled the idiotic word that night.

I was physically exhausted, and so must have been others, for the infernal noise gradually abated. Nature took its course, and slowly, slowly, the exaltation cooled down. Eventually, the band intoned the "Deutschland Lied," and the crowd joined in singing the first verse. Then the band started "The Horst Wessel Song." That was new. Only a few days ago most of these people would have professed unfamiliarity with the song. But now, everybody suddenly knew the melody and even the text. This was another mystery to me, as was the sudden presence of swastika flags everywhere. After the last note was sung the crowd started yelling again, but a voice from the loudspeaker announced, "the rally is closed." This was the signal to disband. Tired but cheerful, I started my long walk home.

The streets were still filled with people and excitement, flags were still flying, and patriotic music was blaring from radios in the windows. I was in a dream-like state of euphoria and expectation. This was the beginning of paradise! Germany would break the chains of Versailles and the Jewish conspiracy. Everybody would find work. Nobody would go hungry. My mother would never again weep while the bailiff carried our furniture away. The Führer would change everything for the better, and a new Germany would arise from the ashes of defeat.

I don't know how I got home that night or how late it was when I went to bed. Instead of going to school the next morning, I went to the Nazi Party headquarters, where I saw the first Storm Troopers acting as police officers. They were identified by makeshift armbands with the inscription "Auxiliary Police." Most of them carried arms and some led dogs on leashes. The Communists still tried to demonstrate, but the Storm Troopers used their new weapons ruthlessly, and the crowd was overwhelmingly on their side. One could smell the exultation of the Nazis and the despair of the Communists. That the Jewish community was in even deeper despair did not enter my mind. To me the only reality was what I saw and heard and smelled.

In the coming months everything changed: the people, the government, the *Reichstag,* the party system, the Nazi Party itself, youth organizations, the police, the armed services, newspapers, radio, unions, schools, teachers, even the churches. Most people were filled with a strange mixture of relief, hope, and trust, along with some remnants of doubt. The exceptions were the Jews, the Communists, and the few brave souls who had the strength of character to oppose absolute power. The local governments quickly fell in line with the new government in Berlin. Storm Troopers soon penetrated the police and converted it into an instrument of Nazi policy. Eventually, the SS created an entirely new kind of police, the Gestapo. Radio and newspapers were tuned to the directives from the newly appointed Reich's Minister for People's Enlightenment and Propaganda, Joseph Goebbels. The schools and the youth organizations enjoyed the Nazis' particular attention because, as Goebbels proclaimed: "He who has the youth also has the future."

What evolved from all of these changes was an entirely new culture. Forgotten was the venerable tradition of German humanism. Abandoned were the ideals of Beethoven and Goethe, although we still knew their names. In fact, the Nazis exploited them to prove the superiority of the Aryan race. But they didn't say that Beethoven rededicated the "Eroica" when he heard of Napoleon's conversion from a liberator to a dictator, and they conveniently forgot that Goethe always warned his devotees about the crowd, particularly the German crowd. Who had now the strength of character to remind us of Immanuel Kant's admonition "Act such that the maxim of your action may serve as a general law of society"? And who had now the guts to join in Schiller's chorus "All men are becoming brethren"?

It was a strange transformation of a nation. On the one hand, it was extremely radical and had the direst of consequences; on the other hand, it faded almost without a trace when the Third

Reich collapsed. This transformation had all the attributes of a psychosis, though it engulfed a whole nation, rather than an individual. The Nazis called it "revolution," but it was national insanity! It gripped almost everybody. Only the wisest and bravest could resist.

I was neither wise nor brave. Not yet twelve years of age, and long infected with the germs of national hubris and anti-Semitism, I was the ideal victim of this mass psychosis. It carried me away like a tidal wave.

No Escape

My father's career in the Nazi Party was anything but brilliant. In spite of his longtime membership and his fanatical zeal, he never held any position in the party hierarchy, nor did he ever wear a uniform. He only served temporarily as an administrator for the local Nazi charity organization that was called "NS People's Welfare." The Nazis had a knack for appealing to the instincts of the people, the basest as well as the loftiest. The suffering and hunger brought on by the First World War were still painfully alive in everybody's mind, and the Nazis exploited the experience by seducing the minds with the slogan "Nobody shall go hungry or freeze."

My father ran the NS charity organization in our part of town. I don't think he understood that the Nazis took advantage of him. He simply wanted to help and, for once, not to proselytize. His function was to distribute the food and clothes donated by wealthier people to the less fortunate. The distribution center was his architectural bureau, where the volunteers picked up the donated items and delivered them to the needy. I still remember the smell of frozen fish in my father's office.

Of course, the whole thing was a façade, as was the second word of the party name, "Socialist." The Nazis were anything but socialists, yet the name was an effective propaganda trick. Under it, they continued the farce of the NS People's Welfare for a few years until they could claim more or less truthfully that nobody was any longer hungry or freezing. The financial means for this charity came from the national money collections that occurred almost every Sunday when literally thousands of boys and girls from the Hitler Youth were in the streets, rattling their collection cans. It was a familiar sound and picture. For me it was an unpleasant duty that I performed perhaps a hundred times. Of course, most of the money went into arms and war preparations, but I did not know that at the time, nor did I care.

My father soon withdrew from the fake philanthropy and turned to a relatively innocent pet project, which had been his dream for some time. He called it "The House Altar." It was essentially a rectangular arrangement of the photographs of the Nazi leaders around the swastika banner. The Führer's likeness was on top, flanked by the portraits of Göring and Goebbels. Göring's picture was quite flattering at the time. Still slender, handsome, and dressed in the uniform of a fighter pilot of the First World War with the order *Pour le Mérite* dangling from his neck, he certainly conformed better than Hitler to my mental picture of a youthful hero. His notorious brutality escaped me, and his legendary girth was still a thing of the future.

Occasionally, my father had to remove the picture of a crony who had fallen out of favor with the Führer. These embarrassing dismissals were always like little funerals. Only if the expulsion of a party leader had been publicly announced with great fanfare was the removal of his picture less ceremonial. I still remember when SA Chief Ernst Röhm was shot on Hitler's order, and my father dropped his likeness like an effigy of the devil.

Also displayed on the house altar were my father's war decorations, the Iron Cross Second Class and the medal for war injury. My decorations from the Second World War never made it to this place of honor because, by that time, the house altar and the entire house had already been destroyed by Allied bombs. My older brother, who was not as close to my father as I was, laughed about the ersatz icons. When I carped at his lack of loyalty, he replied that he had no taste for such idolatry. I sometimes had my doubts, too, but I respected the contrivance out of devotion to my father and the Führer.

There was one more person who had the guts to ridicule the house altar: Herr Geheimrat, who recently had returned to good grace with my father. When Herr Geheimrat reentered our house, he approached the silly display with feigned deference by extending the Hitler salute in mockery. My father was so enraged that he almost banished him again. But Herr Geheimrat calmed him down by telling a little story he had heard in a meeting of the Freemasons. A famous revue artist, the story goes, had recited the following rhyme to his audience:

Ein Bäumlein steht im Walde
A little tree stands in the forest
Es hat sich organisiert
It has joined the ranks
Es gehört der NS-Baumschaft an
It became a member of the NS Tree-Organization
Damit ihm nichts passiert
So that nothing will happen to it

Of course the humorless Nazi authorities frowned at the clever poem and ordered the satirist to retract it. The next day the witty man offered an edited version that went as follows:

Ein Bäumlein steht im Walde
> A little tree stands in the forest

Es hat sich NICHT organisiert
> It has NOT joined the ranks

Es gehört NICHT der NS-Baumschaft an
> It did NOT become a member of the NS
> Tree-Organization

Damit MIR nichts passiert
> So that NOTHING will happen to ME

My father laughed heartily at the little joke, though he considered the Freemasons an enemy of the Third Reich. He even allowed Herr Geheimrat on further visits to extend his mock salute, though their debates went on as heatedly as ever. Had my father informed on the man, he might have sent him to the concentration camps. But whistle-blowing was not my father's style. A little later I shall add an appendix to the story of the house altar which, if it were not so sad, would be amusing.

At about the same time, in the spring of 1933, Hitler came to Dortmund to speak at a rally in the Westfalen Halle, a huge covered sports arena which was an architectural landmark at the time. My father took me there, and we watched the spectacle that was unfolding at the bottom of the pit from seats high up under the ceiling. Everybody down below looked ridiculously small, but I was old enough to understand that. Only with regard to the Führer I must have expected a miracle, for I still recall my disappointment when he appeared as tiny as everybody else down there. Nevertheless, I had no problem recognizing him by his prominence and entourage.

As puny as the visual spectacle was, the acoustical drama was truly impressive. The hall was filled to capacity and the noise was deafening, even before the Führer arrived. When he finally entered the hall, the uproar was unbelievable. I knew that the mili-

tary band would now play the "Badenweiler Marsch," for Hitler had adopted this martial music as his personal air, but I could not discern the sound of it among the thunderous Heil chorus. This went on for several minutes, occasionally interrupted by a few words from a local party leader. Eventually, the Führer's signature tune, which by that time the band must have repeated many times, penetrated the abating noise.

Finally, the Führer spoke. At first he uttered only one word—*Deutsche*. That was all he could say before the crowd started yelling again. So he made a second attempt, only to be interrupted again. Thus he repeated the word five or six times until, finally, he was able to complete the salutation: *Deutsche Volksgenossen und Genossinnen* (German People's Comrades and Female Comrades). Now the crowd became rapturously silent while the Führer, as usual, indulged in reminiscences. In a very low voice and with an air of thoughtfulness, even serenity, he spoke of the dismal time when, as he wrote in his book, he decided to become a politician.

The crowd was now as quiet as a congregation in church, while the Führer reflected on his rise from a poor unknown to the leader of a great nation. Very gradually, almost cunningly, he raised his voice and emotional temperature. Now the crowd was no longer quiet, but responded with applause. Its fervor grew in proportion to the thunder of the speech. One could virtually feel the rising heat from one sentence to the next. After about ten minutes Hitler screamed at the top of his voice, while the crowd greeted each sentence with frantic applause. Then came the climax. A few simple words, rather primitive, but irresistible, infectious, messianic, absolutely convincing. This was the truth! Nobody could doubt it, nobody could deny it. People jumped to their feet, gesticulated, cried, screamed, and howled in ecstasy. The huge hall was transformed into a cauldron of deranged minds.

I report here partly from the experiences of the following years when I heard Hitler many times on the radio. It was always the same ascent from an acoustical and emotional low to the high pitch of orgiastic rapture. He ruled over the crowd like a mass hypnotist, like a Savonarola or Cromwell. But his effect on me was even stronger. Not only was I preconditioned by my father, but even more so by my own nature. I had always hungered for spiritual fulfillment, and now it came to me in the form of this messianic man, who had the power to change the minds of millions from despair to hope, from misery to national glory. For me the Führer's message was an evangelistic truth. He was the Germanic messiah, and his vision of the Third Reich was a covenant of national glory and happiness.

This was the only time I saw Hitler with my own eyes. In the following years I made several attempts to get closer to him, but there were always those millions between him and me, those who later claimed they had never been his followers. I heard him on the radio perhaps a hundred times, mostly in school where listening to his speeches soon became mandatory. We also were marched to the movie theaters to watch newsreels that showed Hitler as he addressed the *Reichstag* or the party cadres at the Reich's Party Congress in Nuremberg. The visual impression of him on me was as strong as the oral effect.

Today I believe that the whole Nazi movement would have been impossible without this demagogue of unprecedented proportions. Goebbels, the master of propaganda and no mean orator himself, did not make anywhere near the same impression on me. Indeed, little Göringses and Goebbelses are always around, but the evil genius of a Hitler comes only once in a thousand years.

The drama in the Westfalen Halle had an aftermath, which, if possible, had even more dire consequences than the Führer's sorcery. On our way out of the huge arena a man in a black uniform handed my father an extra copy of the notorious weekly *Der Stürmer*. This was the worst thing that could have happened to us, for it drove both of us to actions that, many years later, filled me with shame, and my father with fear of retribution.

In the following days, my father and I feverishly read the sordid stories served up by the ugly journal. They all dealt with the Jewish world conspiracy, of which we already had heard so much. But these reports topped everything. They "exposed" a systematic scheme of subversion that was much more lethal than we had expected. I particularly remember three of the tales that dealt with the alleged murders of three great Germans: Luther, Mozart, and Schiller.

Of course, the *Stürmer*'s version was that the Jews were too cowardly to commit these murders with their own hands. But they had money, so they hired other Germans who did their dirty work for filthy lucre. In this way, the story went, Luther was killed by paid Jesuits, and Mozart was annihilated by hired Freemasons. In both cases the "blood money" came from the Jews. In Mozart's case, the gruesome tale described in detail how a brave man, who suspected foul play, descended into the mass grave where the composer had been buried, and how he poked about the mass of bones in search of Mozart's skull. Suddenly, he saw something glittering in the light of his torch. This was the mercury poison that had been administered to Mozart by one of his brethren from the Freemasons, who was a paid servant of the Jews. When the vigilant man reported his finding to the authorities, an investigation was launched. But a few days later he died under suspicious circumstances, probably by the same poison that allegedly had killed Mozart. Thus, the whole investigation came to naught.

Most "revealing," however, according to this journal, was the "tragic" death of Schiller. His murderer, of all people, was his good friend Goethe, who was also a Freemason. Goethe sin-

cerely loved his friend, but when he received the order from the
Jewish conspirators through his Masonic superior, he carried it
out with an aching heart. A few years later, when he held
Schiller's skull in his hands, he silently asked his friend for forgiveness.

From later editions of the trashy paper we learned that Goethe
was not the only lackey of the Jewish conspiracy. There were others such as Thomas Mann, Woodrow Wilson, Lloyd George, and
even Lenin. Whole institutions such as the League of Nations
and the Communist International were infiltrated by the Jews.
Even art forms such as Cubism, twelve-tone music, and the international language Esperanto were instruments of the worldwide
collusion. No allegation was too absurd for us to accept. To the
contrary, the wider the defamatory magazine drew the circle of
the alleged conspiracy, the more plausible it appeared to us.

A little corollary to this episode that would be amusing in any
other context has to do with the house altar I mentioned earlier.
The picture that represented the Führer was a technically inferior photograph of his profile that my father had bought at Nazi
headquarters. From the very beginning my father was unhappy
with this picture, but he put up with it for want of a better one.
The stumbling block was the Führer's shaggy hair, which was
dotted with mysterious spots that looked quite unnatural and created the impression that the photograph had been tampered with.
Of course, the objectionable picture was eventually replaced by a
better one, but that was *not* the problem, nor was it the end of the
story.

Apparently the Goebbels propaganda was also unhappy with
the Hitler photograph, for it suddenly ordered the picture to be
withdrawn from all shops and showcases. But no explanation was
given, and that's when the rumors started. The *Stürmer,* we heard
by the grapevine, had launched an investigation, yet its findings
were so sensitive that they could not be printed. They could only

be transmitted by word of mouth, and then only to the most trustworthy. In this way, we eventually learned the "truth." The pathetic photograph of Hitler was a sinister fabrication of the Jews. With great technical skill, they had woven all sorts of Jewish faces into Hitler's shaggy hair, thus putting him on notice that they were still calling the shots. Now our eyes had been "opened." Turning the picture around and viewing it from all angles, we "saw" a whole array of Jewish faces laughing and scoffing at us.

I was stunned. I am not sure whether my father took the affair as seriously as I did, but it was he who dug even deeper into the sinister plot. As the commotion was already cooling down, he surprised us at the dinner table with a view that tingled my spine. Turning Hitler's profile upside down, he showed that his ear became a Jewish nose, his lower jaw turned into a bald forehead, a strand of hair was transformed into puffy lips, and so on. Now I was really frightened. If the Jews could penetrate the inner sanctuary of the National Socialist Party, was there anything they could not do?

The immediate effect of these "discoveries" was that my father subscribed to the magazine that fabricated these tales. One of the most disgusting aspects of the gazette were the caricatures of Jewish faces provided by a man who called himself Fips. The drawings were so loathsome and grotesque that they defy description. For a while I resented these repugnant grimaces, but my father told me they had to be that ugly to reveal the ugly truth. That argument made sense to me and persuaded me to defend the revolting caricatures to a classmate of mine who cautiously had expressed his revulsion.

For my twelfth birthday my father gave me a little air gun complete with target board. First we had our innocent fun with it, but after a while, the amusement took an ugly twist, as we pasted the cartoons from the *Stürmer* on the target board. Thus we used human faces, however distorted, for target practice. My mother, who was handicapped by her eye condition, at first did not realize what our targets were. But my older brother, who did not take part in this practice, eventually told her that we were shooting at Jewish faces. The next day the air gun had disappeared.

As if this was not enough, my father now publicly displayed the *Stürmer* in a glass-covered showcase he called *Der Stürmer Kasten* (The *Stürmer* Shrine). He hung the large box at the iron fence of the State Court that was adjacent to the house to which we recently had moved. I suppose some of the judges of the court did not like what they saw, but none of them protested, and the red box remained there until Allied bombs put an end to it. This unsavory undertaking was the prime reason why my father never returned to Dortmund after the war.

In our new house lived a Jewish family with one daughter, a plump girl with long black hair. She was about my age, but taller and stronger. Her father, whose first name was Sally, was a division chief at a department store. This family, which lived in the upper story of the house, became the target of our hatred. It was the only time my mother got involved, if only slightly, because she had heard a rumor that Sally had brutalized some children for misbehavior in his store.

The disturbing story was reported by one of my father's cronies, who served as a helper in the NS People's Welfare organization. This man, whose first name was Walter, ran a hardware store next to Sally's department store. The incident is so fresh in my memory because Walter topped off his story with the crude remark: "Oh, it's raining. That's fine with me, but where Sally walks, it should rain shit." As young as I was, I had the distinct feeling that the man wanted to ingratiate himself with my father by winning my mother over to the cause of anti-Semitism. I doubt whether he succeeded in that regard; I only know that he gave me the last push I needed to commit two of the most shameful deeds of my life.

One occurred when I met the young girl on the staircase and rudely asked her to step aside, uttering something about Jews having no rights in our country. She probably could have knocked me down, but she only reacted with a haughty expression on her face. Her dignified silence took me completely by surprise. I didn't know what to say or do. My arrogance and stupidity filled me with shame. Having learned a lesson, I silently stepped aside and never harassed the girl again.

But this lesson was not strong enough to quench the hatred that was continuously fomented in me by the unrelenting anti-Semitic propaganda. Instead of directing it against the family's daughter, I now turned it on their property. The house had a cellar in which each party had its own compartment. Sally's compartment and ours were separated by a lattice fence through which I could reach the overseas luggage he had piled up there. So virulent was my hatred that each time I went to the cellar I used a small hatchet to knock little holes into the suitcases. I justified this action to myself as a kind of compensation for the damage the Jews allegedly were inflicting upon the German people. In the years to follow I used this mendacious logic several times to defend the violent anti-Semitism of the Nazis, until I slowly came to recognize that the Jewish conspiracy was fiction.

Nevertheless, at the time of my childish acts of hatred I did not feel pity for the defenseless family whose anguish was all too obvious. That came a few years later, when the war had already started, and Sally and his family were grievously insulted by my father. Little did we know at that time that the family probably was only months away from the concentration camp.

In the early years of the Third Reich most Jews were still free and relatively unharmed. But the Jewish intelligentsia was already imprisoned, as were the Communists and the members of the small German opposition. The existence of concentration camps was well known in Germany. The people even had a nickname for them. Instead of saying *Konzentrations Lager,* they said *Konzert Lager* (Concert Camp), thus giving the institution a certain ring of harmlessness. The Nazi propaganda was aware of this linguistic twist and used it to its advantage. But first the lie machine taught the German people that a concentration camp, indeed, can be a scene of horror.

In a report from South Africa the Nazi press alleged that concentration camps were a British invention. While that may be technically true, most of the stories and pictures of the report were fabrications. I mention only one picture that made a great impression on the German public and also on me. It showed a soldier from the Boer army bound to the mouth of the barrel of a British cannon.

But the masterpiece of the Goebbels propaganda was an amply illustrated report in the official picture magazine, *Illustrierter Beobachter* (Illustrated Observer), which convinced me that the German concentration camps were, indeed, as harmless as the sobriquet "concert camp" implied. The report depicted the prisoners of the Dachau concentration camp and their living conditions. They were shown at their daily routine such as washing up in the morning, singing on their march to work, or receiving their wholesome evening meal. These rosy pictures were confirmed by numerous printed interviews with the prisoners. One could hardly imagine happier or healthier inmates. Since the report from the British concentration camps had given the institution a bad name, the report from the German camp was a great relief to me.

Of course, the whole thing was a farce, but a farce that worked. It fooled me and millions of other Germans. Even my mother praised the concentration camp as a place that promoted order, cleanliness, and useful work, without doing harm or injustice to anybody. At about the same time, the first young Germans were already drafted into the Labor Service, a paramilitary organization without weapons that built roads, drained swamps, and so forth. Now the soldiers of peace were joined by the Jews and the Communists from the concentration camps. Could there be anything more just and reasonable?

When I was about fourteen years old, I felt duty bound to study Hitler's book, *Mein Kampf*. When I started reading the book, I soon found it to be rather tedious. There was not a trace of the personal magnetism that Hitler exuded in his speeches; there were no stirring ideas, not even a single memorable phrase. Everything was drab and uninspiring. When he spoke, it was different! Hearing his magic voice, every word convinced and excited me, and the exuberance of "ideas" overwhelmed me. And yet, when the same ideas were put in print they appeared stale and tired. I was quite disappointed, but I attributed my disappointment to my immaturity rather than to the author and his book. With hindsight, I must say that I was not that far from the truth—I only reversed the order. It was not his book that my immaturity misjudged; it was his speeches, his actions, his whole personality. Unfortunately I did not understand this at the time, and I brushed the negative impression of Hitler's opus aside with the intent to study it again when I was older. With this lame decision I missed another chance of breaking out of my mental prison.

There is a little story that deals with the same dichotomy, Hitler the person and Hitler the writer. It tells of a young submarine commander who first read Hitler's book and then met him in person. The book had disgusted the officer so much that his opposition to the Führer was no secret among his comrades. However, one day Hitler visited his boat and shook his hand while looking him straight in the eyes. From that moment on the young man was an ardent follower of the Führer. The story may be apocryphal, but it suggests that other people shared my problem with the phenomenon of Hitler.

I also read other Nazi books such as Alfred Rosenberg's *The Myth of the Twentieth Century* and Houston Stewart Chamberlain's *The Foundations of the Nineteenth Century*. While Rosenberg's book was too confused to make any lasting impression on me, Chamberlain impressed me with his knowledge of ancient Greece, which he portrayed as the first blooming period of the Aryan race in world history. The presentation stimulated me to go to a bookshop and buy a few picture postcards of Greek sculptures. I selected an Aphrodite and an Apollo, but after the saleslady asked me how old I was, she let me have only the Apollo. Nevertheless, I thought I recognized in these beautiful figures the Aryan men and women Chamberlain so glowingly described in his book.

My father, who was not an avid reader, had enough trouble making his way through Hitler's book, not to mention Rosenberg's tome. But he proudly presented me to his friends and comrades as an example of a well-educated member of the new generation. My mother, whose eye condition allowed her merely to peruse the newspapers, was essentially an apolitical person. While she was immune to Hitler's personal magnetism, she respected him out of devotion to my father. On the other hand, she denounced "the wenches who pursue him." Though she sometimes displayed the Mother's Cross, which the Nazis had conferred on her, she never joined the NS women's organization.

Once, when we children had done something that had upset my mother, she said, "Now I am going to tell you something you will not like." After a while, she continued, "There was a Jew among my ancestors! Your father will not tell you that, but he knows it." At the time, the unexpected disclosure upset me greatly, while my older brother only shrugged his shoulders. Eventually, however, I forgot the incident. After the war, my mother refreshed my memory and told me that the ancestor she was referring to was a Jew who had emigrated from Spain to

Germany. I tried to find out more about this heritage, but my grandfather, who could have supplied more information, was no longer alive. Fifty years later I learned that I was a carrier of the Gaucher's disease, which is a hereditary disorder that primarily afflicts Ashkenazi Jews.

My older brother was the one in our family whose spirit was the least infected with the Nazi bacillus, but whose life was the most affected by Nazi policy. Since my brother did not perform well in high school, my father took him out of classes when he was about sixteen years old. He then entered his name into a Nazi program for boys to work on farms for room and board. Thus my brother was sent to a peasant in Pomerania (now part of Poland), where he was supposed to be well treated and fed. But, apparently, the farmer exploited my brother, prompting the boy to send wailing letters in which he begged my father to take him back. I remember my mother and grandmother sitting on my brother's bed, reading his letters and weeping. After more than a year, my father relented and let my brother return home. He then found him a clerical job with one of his business acquaintances. During this brief period, my brother was a member of the NS Corps of Motorists.

In 1936 my brother was drafted into the Labor Service, where he spent the next six months. After that came the army, which was supposed to claim "only" the next two years of his life. But when the two years were over, the war was approaching, so his service was extended indefinitely. Nine months later the war began and deprived him of six more years of his life. He first served in the campaign against France, then on the Eastern front against Russia, and finally on the Western front against the Allied invasion forces. But when the war was over, he still was not a free man. The next three years he spent in a French coal mine as a prisoner of war. When my brother finally returned home, after having lost thirteen years of his youth, he was embittered, physically ruined, and without an adequate education or a marketable skill.

I was more lucky in this regard, but I was also more exposed to Nazi ideology, for the river of poison from the *Stürmer* flowed unabatedly. Some of the most grotesque distortions were the supposed quotes from the Talmud, which were never verbatim, of course. Unfortunately, I was so young and inexperienced that my mind was virtually defenseless against this onslaught of lies and fabrications. The more horror stories I read, the more I became convinced that the ancient book of Jewish law and wisdom was nothing but a compendium of satanic instructions for performing the rape of Aryan women and the ritual murder of their children. Almost every issue of the scandalous magazine showed a cartoon of a rabbi grinning with devilish satisfaction over a bowl dripping with the blood of a murdered child. Most nauseating was the allegation that the blood was mixed into Jewish bread.

I was so horrified that I sought comfort wherever I could find it. My mother merely said, "Look into the regular newspaper. Do you see those stories there?" But my father went into more detail. He said that the ritual murders had been going on for more than a thousand years, but since the Jews controlled the printing press, the truth had never leaked out. The embodiment of the satanic Jew, he said, was "Ahasva" (probably Ahaz, king of Judah, 700 B.C.). He portrayed him as a kind of Jewish Macbeth, who restlessly wandered all over the globe, driven by lust and guilt.

At about the same time my father received a few anonymous letters that apparently were written in protest against the *Stürmer* box. At first he did not show us the letters but merely stated that they were an attempt to drive a wedge between the Führer and Julius Streicher (the publisher of the *Stürmer*). That was the first time I heard the infamous name, as I had not yet acquired the habit of looking for the names of publishers and reporters or, for that matter, for the times and places where the reports had been filed. I asked my father who Streicher was, whereupon he opened one of those anonymous letters he had kept under lock. It was a single page showing a caricature of Streicher that matched the cartoons of his magazine in repulsiveness. Above the picture was a cutout from the front page of the magazine, reading in Gothic letters "Der Stürmer." Below was the handwritten sentence: "The Führer does not know about this!" Pointing at the ugly face, my father said: "This is Streicher. The Jews of Dortmund are trying to silence me. But I shall rather die than be silent."

CHAPTER 6

The Master Jailer

One of the first actions of the new regime was to consolidate the multitude of youth organizations from the pre-Nazi era into one NS organization, the Hitler Youth. It consisted of two echelons for the two age groups: the *Jungvolk* (Young People) for the twelve- to fifteen-year-olds, and the Hitler Youth proper for the fifteen- to eighteen-year-olds. The NS Student Federation to which I belonged had always been considered part of the Hitler Youth. To avoid any appearance of social discrimination, the NS Student Federation was now completely absorbed by the two echelons of the Hitler Youth. Though I was not quite twelve years old, I was automatically transferred to the *Jungvolk*.

During my first year in the *Jungvolk,* I was fortunate to have a leader who came from the Boy Scouts and reminded me of the teacher who promoted this movement at school. The young leader, who was four or five years older than I, always wore the gray tunic of his father, who had been an officer in the Imperial army. He also blew the *Fanfare,* a kind of trumpet. Attached to it was the black ensign with the white victory rune that was the official emblem of the *Jungvolk.* He marched ahead of us, blowing his *Fanfare,* while we followed with drums and pennants.

It was a happy time, but a brief one. Once, the leader took us to a summer camp on the premises of a farmer in northern Germany. We slept in the barn and ate the simple but wholesome food the farmer's wife prepared for us. In the evening we gathered around the campfire and sang Boy Scout songs, which our leader accompanied on a guitar-like instrument that was popular in the youth movement. I looked up to this young man as an example of everything that was decent and romantic about the youth movement.

Apparently, the leader had also taken a liking to me. One day, during a home evening in the inhospitable cellar of an industrial building, he presented me with a little green book that showed the victory rune on the outside. It was a membership booklet that was carried by the lower leaders. This was his way of saying that I had been appointed *Jungenschaftsführer,* which was the lowest rank in the *Jungvolk.* Thus I became the proud leader of some fifteen boys whose names were listed in the green booklet.

The idyll was not to last for long, for the cherished leader was soon replaced by someone who came fresh from a training course for Hitler Youth leaders. This young man, who was about eighteen years old and whose first name was Heino, was almost the exact opposite of our former leader. Of all the people with whom I was personally acquainted during the Hitler era, he was the most typical Nazi: fanatical, ruthless, and cynical. His rank was *Stamm Führer,* which corresponds to battalion commander, as was indicated by a white shoulder strap. This leader was the only official in the whole Nazi establishment I was genuinely afraid of.

Heino completely changed the atmosphere in our *Jungvolk* unit. He trained us in all sorts of military skills, such as small cal-

iber shooting or throwing hand-grenades. Under his leadership
we performed war games such as smuggling a suitcase, which was
supposed to contain a bomb, into the railway station. We were
always divided into two parties battling each other, and Heino
pushed us to ever more aggressive fighting. Once my group had
to storm a steep embankment that was defended by another
group. When I had made it almost to the top, one of the defend-
ers hit me with his infantry spade so hard under the nose that I
needed medical attention. The scar is still visible today.

Heino also taught us those Nazi songs that shocked the world,
songs like "Today we own Germany, tomorrow the whole world."
But even this arrogant song was not militant enough for Heino,
who was always searching for even more belligerent strains. Once
he came up with a Cossack song, of which I remember only the
line "We carry calluses from the sabers on our hands." The source
selection was not incidental, for Heino was fascinated by the East,
particularly the vast plains of Russia. His heroes were the knights
of the *Deutsch-Ritter Orden* (Order of German Knights), who conquered and settled the Baltics during the Middle Ages.

Once Heino put me to a test by ordering me to conduct a home
evening about knighthood. Undoubtedly he had the *Deutsch-
Ritter Orden* in mind, but I misunderstood him and innocently
recounted the saga of Siegfried slaying the dragon. I took the
story from one of my schoolbooks that stemmed from the pre-
Nazi era. In this version of the epic, Siegfried dug a hole that
enabled him to stab the monster from below, into his soft under-
belly. At that point Heino indignantly interrupted me. "That's
how cowards fight, not knights!" he carped, and added, on a
more ominous note, "You will never be a fighter." It meant that I
had failed the test. That was the beginning of the end of my
career in the *Jungvolk*.

Everything Heino said and did was designed to foster our
fighting spirit. That's why he taught us songs like "We love the

sea and the surging waves, the gray face of the icy storms." He said it was a Viking song and we should pronounce the *"heijo, heijo"* of the refrain so that it sounded Scandinavian, rather than German. His signature song went like this:

The mightiest king in the realm of the air is the eagle,
    begot by the winds.
The birds, they are trembling whenever they hear the
    powerful beat of his wings.
When the lion's roar through the desert resounds, the
    crowd of animals shudder.
O yes, we are the lords of the world, the rulers over the seas.

Today I believe that Heino really understood what Hitler wanted him to do—that is, mold us into fearless conquerors. His favorite word was "ruthless," which also happened to be Hitler's preferred adjective. Fifty years later, in America, I was amazed how often I heard or read a very different expression: "human decency." It struck me then that I had never heard this expression in Nazi Germany. Today I believe that it could have saved my soul from being enslaved by the evil of Nazism, had I heard it spoken once or twice by a person of authority. Instead, all I heard were words such as "ruthless" or "merciless."

Along with the *Deutsch-Ritter Orden,* Heino's heroes were the Vikings who pillaged England and conquered the Atlantic coast of North America, and the Vandals who ransacked Rome. Thus, most of Heino's songs dealt with piracy, conquest, and plundering.

Of course there were more moderate songs, which Heino did not favor. One that I had learned from my former *Jungvolk* leader was more of a choral than a marching song: "Holy Fatherland, surrounded by perils, your sons are gathering around you. Encircled by enemies, holy Fatherland, look, we are standing here, hand in hand." I liked the words and the solemn melody, but when I intoned the song in Heino's presence, he ridiculed it. He barely tolerated the official youth hymn that had been composed by the Reich Youth Leader Baldur von Schirach. It first boasted, in true Nazi fashion, "Yes, through our fists will fall whatever stands against us," and then went on babbling of "the flag of the Youth for freedom and bread."

"Freedom" was a big word with the Nazis, particularly when coupled with the word "bread." In my naivete, I thought that this combination incorporated the very essence of the National Socialist *Weltanschauung* (worldview), unaware as I was of the sinister program hiding behind it. I simply refused to realize that my own freedom was already severely reduced. Of course, I was often unhappy with this situation and even depressed, but whenever that happened I blamed it on the Jews. At such times, Heino's terror regime appeared to me a necessary but temporary hardship in the struggle against the Jewish world conspiracy. Thus, I persuaded myself that Germany needed fighters like Heino, whether I liked him or not.

Heino's main objective was to forge us into ever tougher fighters, both physically and mentally. In his fanatical drive for physical fitness, he even exceeded the ambitious sports program of the Reich's Youth Command, by pushing us ruthlessly to our limits or even beyond. Although he had a heart condition, he applied the same reckless pressure to himself. Since I am physically not particularly ambitious or skillful, I soon became the target of Heino's special attention. He pushed me so hard that I barely escaped injury. Yet he never resorted to violence against me, probably because he knew that I had joined the Hitler Youth almost a year earlier than he had.

Heino showed his true face in the execution of the official program to integrate the religious and non-political youth organizations into the Hitler Youth. For a while, the Federation of Catholic Young Men was reluctant to join. Hence they needed some "persuasion," which nobody could provide better than Heino. On a dark winter night he led us to their headquarters to smash windows and showcases. When that did not produce the desired result, he summoned their leader to his headquarters and beat him so brutally that the young man needed hospitalization. I was not privy to this incident, but I could read every detail of it in the bulletin that Heino proudly issued the next day. He even showed us the victim's demolished spectacles that he kept as a souvenir. A week after this incident, the Federation of Catholic Young Men was fully integrated, and their brutalized leader timidly reported for duty.

This was not the only time Heino terrorized members of the former non-Nazi youth organizations that were known under the slightly derogatory name "Federated Youth." When the young men tried to sing their cherished songs from times past, Heino either beat them up on the spot, or had a surprise coming for them later. Once, he summoned the leadership of his *Stamm* (equivalent to battalion) to a special training course in a youth hostel. I was a member of this group, and so were a few former leaders of the Federated Youth. This was for Heino the long-sought opportunity to enforce the "complete integration" of the young men into the Hitler Youth. Every night I heard their screams as they were beaten by Heino and his cronies. He referred to these visitations as "the coming of the Holy Spirit." In the morning at breakfast, their swollen faces bore testimony to their nightly brutalization. There was no escape for them. They had to submit to these abuses because membership in the Hitler Youth was a condition for attending high school.

As time went on, Heino's reign became more and more oppressive. He tried to keep away from us everything that was gentle and tender. Literature, the arts, religion, folk songs, even Christmas celebrations, were banished. And when he suspected somebody of indulging in these "decadent" pursuits, he persecuted him with verbal and physical abuse. "I shall tear your ass open" was one of his favorite affronts.

What I hated most were the war games, which were essentially a fight of boy against boy in a contest of physical strength. Before Heino took command, a boy was considered defeated when his opponent had captured his neckerchief. But Heino dispensed with this rule and decreed that the way to defeat one's opponent was to choke him until he surrendered.

I had much to suffer from this directive since most boys of the leadership corps were older and stronger than I. Encouraged by Heino, they missed no opportunity to beat me up. To top it all off, Heino poked fun at me. There was a deep mistrust between him and me. Neither one of us thought that the other was a good National Socialist. He believed that I was too weak and decadent; I felt that he was too brutal and cynical. I knew he was itching to send the "Holy Spirit" to me, but he shied away from it because he knew that my father was an "old party champion."

Nevertheless, Heino made my life in the *Jungvolk* ever more uncomfortable. Frustrated that he could not lay his hands on me, he used other tactics to bring me in line. By purely bureaucratic manipulations he deprived me of three items I coveted with all my heart. The first was the Golden Hitler Youth Emblem, to which I was entitled because I had become a member of the Hitler Youth before the power seizure. This badge was so prestigious that it was the only Nazi ensign that the armed services allowed to be displayed on their uniforms. High officials like Albert Speer exhibited it on their tunics. The second item was the green shoulder strap, which would have indicated the position to which I had advanced in the meantime. All of the leaders in Heino's battalion wore one or the other shoulder strap according to their ranks. I was the only one completely without insignia. The third item was called *München Ausweis* (Munich identification card, issued by the Hitler Youth command in Munich).

The ID card was long overdue. Every time new insignias arrived from Munich, I longingly waited for mine, but they never came. Instead, the treatment Heino afforded me became ever more brusque and contemptuous.

Today I wonder what Heino's profession might have been had he lived in normal times and in an ordinary society. Significantly, I always come to the conclusion that he did not fit any conceivable job. He was of normal height with a powerful build and not bad looking, though his face always bore an expression of contempt and anger, particularly when he laughed, and his manner of speaking betrayed a frightful arrogance. The eyes had some of the mercilessness that distinguished Reinhard Heydrich's icy stare. He also shared the Gestapo chief's lack of humor and obsession with physical cleanliness. I do not go so far as to say that I could imagine Heino as one of the henchmen in a concentration camp—like Heydrich, he did not like to get his hands dirty—but I do say that he could have planned the systematic genocide as efficiently as Heydrich did. After the war, when I was faced with the gruesome pictures from the concentration camps, Heino's image helped me to believe my own eyes.

My ordeal from Heino's reign lasted until 1936. One cold winter night, on my way home from a leadership meeting, my immediate superior informed me rather unceremoniously that I had been deposed by Heino. That was the end of my career in the *Jungvolk*. I could have asked my father for help, but I was too ashamed. Thus I told him that I had been transferred to the Hitler Youth proper because I was now fifteen years old.

While I was happy having escaped Heino, I was also dispirited, so much so that I postponed reporting for duty to my new Hitler Youth leader from week to week. But the day inevitably arrived and, as had happened so often before, it was another disillusionment. While the atmosphere in the Hitler Youth was quite different from that in the *Jungvolk*, I was not sure whether I liked it

better or worse. These young men showed nothing of that ideological conviction that was so characteristic of Heino and his
companions. Instead, they exuded a certain skepticism that, for
my feeling, bordered on cynicism. For example, they openly joked
about Nazi leaders, except, of course, the Führer. But Göring
and Goebbels were the butt of their jokes. In the *Jungvolk,* this
would have been unthinkable.

Another surprise to me were the songs. Out were the offensive
anti-Semitic or ultra-national songs from the NS Student Federation and the *Jungvolk,* and in were songs from the youth movement, soldier songs, even folk songs. One in particular caught my
fancy. It dealt with the love between a German girl and a Gypsy
boy, and it began with the verse "Yonder in the valley stood their
tents." Whenever we were on a march and somebody started that
song, a murmur went through the column: "This song is forbid-
den." Apparently, the Reich's Youth Command and Propaganda
Ministry had put this song on their list of prohibited books and
songs, because it celebrated the mortal sin of love between a German and a member of an inferior race. Of course, the *Verbot* (pro-
hibition) made the song all the more tempting to me. As beautiful as it is, I thought, it must contain a certain venom from which
our leaders want to protect us. I still joined in singing the melo-
dious ballad, but with a mixture of guilt and excitement as if I
were smoking my first cigarette.

The atmosphere of the Hitler Youth reminded me of the terse
account my older brother had given me of his brief membership
in the NS Corps of Motorists. "We mainly drink beer," he said,
and that seemed to be the custom in other NS organizations as
well. The SA in particular had become a refuge for all those who
were not quite "one hundred percent." Even the NS Party had
accumulated too many *Mitläufer* (hangers-on) and beer drinkers.
And the Hitler Youth, it seemed to me, was merely a training
ground for future members of those clubs of philistines. My feel-

ing was that the true spirit of National Socialism was alive in only two organizations: the SS and the *Jungvolk*. I would have quit the Hitler Youth altogether, but I knew that my father would have objected and that membership in this tired club was a condition for attending high school.

In all those three years of my membership in the Hitler Youth, I did not meet one remarkable figure, with the possible exception of one leader whom they called "Old Grouch." His position in the Hitler Youth was equivalent to Heino's in the *Jungvolk*, but he was far less dangerous. He was about forty years old and an engineer by profession. His trademarks were a motorcycle along with hood, goggles, boots, and a long leather coat always stained with street grime. This fantastic outfit gave him the appearance of a canal worker, which prompted my older brother to refer to him as "The Sewage Worker." I had the impression that Old Grouch was unable to manage even the faintest smile. When the local groups had their home evenings, he traveled on his motorcycle from one group to the next to see that everything went according to his unimaginative instructions. His main concern was pre-military training, such as using a compass or reading a map.

On one of these nightly visits to our group, Old Grouch was faced with a peculiar problem he didn't quite know how to handle. Somebody had the audacity to break wind in his presence, whereupon he angrily demanded that the culprit step forward. But nobody did. That incident initiated a series of harsh measures against our group. Every night we had to assemble, whereupon Old Grouch asked that the miscreant give himself up. Since nobody ever surrendered himself, he drilled us for one hour in a schoolyard. This went on for a few weeks until we left town for summer camp. There, in our tents by the lakeside, we thought we were safe from Old Grouch.

But it was not to be. After we had spent a few days in the camp, we were awakened in the middle of the night and ordered to line up by the campfire. Nobody thought of Old Grouch, but there he stood with his grim face and filthy leather coat, asking the same old question and theatrically stating the date, the time of day, and the place of the smelly offense. "Who had the impudence to do that in *my* presence?" Needless to say, nobody answered, whereupon he sent us back to our tents with the express order to fall out in the morning before breakfast. There he stood again, angrily demanding that the culprit step forward, only to meet with the same stubborn silence. Now he changed his tactics and appealed to our sense of honor. "A German boy always stands by his deeds," he told us. When that did not help, he resorted to a vulgarity that could have come from the *Stürmer:* "This shitty guy probably has Jewish blood in his veins." Now the silence was deafening. The stupid line did not resonate with anybody, the least with me. It was evident that Old Grouch had stepped into a trap he had set himself. After a long pause came his final word, "No breakfast this morning." With that he turned around, stomped to his motorcycle, and drove off.

CHAPTER 7

Professors of Propaganda

I attended one of the three high schools in Dortmund. It was a splendid building next to the east-west railroad artery. In the years of the Weimar Republic, the elevated railway embankment had been the scene of a particularly obnoxious Nazi assault. The French statesman Aristide Briand was on his way to Berlin to meet his German colleague Gustav Stresemann. Both men were European peacemakers who sought an accord more reasonable than the Treaty of Versailles. But the Storm Troopers were already lying in ambush, and when the railroad car of the French statesman passed by, they bombarded it with rotten eggs and tomatoes.

I was not privy to this event because it happened at a time when I was still attending grammar school. The man who told us the story was the new director of our school, who was appointed to this position by the Nazis a few months after they had assumed power. He recounted the shameful deed of the Storm Troopers with undisguised gusto, and portrayed it as an act of patriotic duty. My father also recalled the incident, which apparently had caused a great stir at the time. He said that Stresemann was "not much better than the so-called November criminals, who had delivered Germany into the hands of the avengers of Versailles."

In the early days of the Nazi regime, religious instruction in school was not yet completely banished. We still could elect this subject in lieu of a third foreign language. And since my favorite fields were music, history, German literature, and religion, I selected Protestant religious education. The teacher was fairly young, which was unusual because only confirmed Nazis could then enter a teaching career. I liked the debates with this gentle and thoughtful emissary from the clergy, and he seemed to reciprocate, even though I was sometimes combative and arrogant. But the young man seemed to have made it his mission to free my mind from the chains of Nazism.

I liked this man and his cautious teaching because I had the impression that he was sincere. I even had the feeling that he cared for me, but I also thought that he was behind the times. Did he not know that Christianity was a product of the Jews? Was he completely unaware of the Jewish conspiracy? And had he never heard that Luther was killed for Jewish blood money? At first, I tried to articulate my disagreement as gently as the young man voiced his opinions. But when he seemed to be completely unimpressed by the supposed weight of my arguments, I got more and more strident. Eventually, I used his class mainly as a trial run for the political and religious arguments I had learned in the *Jungvolk*. One of these arguments was destined to ruin the precarious relationship between me and this conscientious man.

I had absorbed this argument from a higher Hitler Youth leader who was Heino's superior while on a visit with my *Jungvolk* unit to the ruin of an old castle in the beautiful countryside south of Dortmund. The leader, who wore a red shoulder strap, was fielding a question and answer session when I asked him what was wrong with Jesus Christ. His answer surprised me. "While Jesus obviously was *not* a Jew," the leader sermonized, "he nevertheless ordered his disciples to teach *all* nations." Here he quoted the passage "Go ye, and teach all peoples," which, I believe, is from the Gospel of Matthew. "But how can that be?" he continued. "How can Aryans share the same God with Jews, Negroes, and other inferior races?" After a rhetorical pause, he turned his full authority to me and exclaimed: "That's what's wrong with Jesus!"

As stupid as this argument was, I used it in my oratorical battles with the gentle clergyman. At a critical moment, when he felt the time had come to really challenge me, he exclaimed, "What is wrong with Jesus?" That was the signal for me to echo the dumb argument of the Hitler Youth leader. Hardly had I done so when I saw the sadness in his dear face, and fervently wished that I had said something more thoughtful. It was too late. The teacher withdrew from me, probably because he felt that my case was hopeless. Perhaps he would have made another attempt, and maybe I would have responded more congenially, but the moment never came. Religious instruction was soon abolished, and the kind teacher left the school for good.

We had a music teacher who was almost the exact opposite of the gentle clergyman. Even though I loved music and longed for inspiring music education, I intensely disliked this man. He dispirited me so much that, later in my life, I missed the opportunity to become a musician, as I always had wanted. The mutual antipathy between the music teacher and me already dated from the days before the power seizure. It began the very instant we met for the first time in his special classroom he called the music hall. This spacious chamber was easily the most illustrious classroom of the school building. It was adjacent to the *Aula* (great hall), where the school festivities took place, and it opened to the memorable balcony from which Theo used to raise the Republic's flag on Constitution Day. But as prestigious as the room was, I detested it as much as its occupant.

What I despised was the music teacher's method of teaching.

It was essentially an artless cramming of technical trivia into our memories, occasionally accompanied by boxes on the ear. I thought this was the antithesis of music, and he seemed to sense my criticism. After the power seizure, this teacher and I soon found additional reasons for our mutual antipathy. One was that he became a Nazi overnight, a fact to which some of my classmates and I reacted with contempt. To express our feelings, I scribbled a verse on the blackboard, *Tretet ein, tretet ein, in den Konvertit Verein!* (Enter, enter the club of the converts!). When the teacher read the message, he confronted me, and I readily confessed. Fortunately I was wearing the Hitler Youth uniform that day, which saved me from his notorious boxes on the ear. Nevertheless, he called me a "little ringleader" and documented my inordinate behavior in the class record.

The music teacher soon became the stage manager of the Nazi festivities at our school that occurred now with ever-increasing frequency. His academic field and the closeness of the music hall to the *Aula* made him the natural choice for this position, but I think he also lusted for the opportunity to demonstrate his devotion to Führer and Reich. As the principal music teacher of the school, this man ran the orchestra and the chorus. Though I played the violoncello, I boycotted the orchestra whenever I could. When I was old enough, I also avoided the chorus by feigning that my voice was breaking. Once a young substitute teacher took the music teacher's place and played to us the second movement of Mozart's E-flat Major Symphony on the piano. That was the happiest moment of my entire music education, and the E flat major symphony is still one of my favorites among the composer's symphonic works.

The music teacher soon returned and continued what I called "musical oppression." By now he had concocted a "New German Music Book," which showed both flags, swastika and black-white-red, on the front cover. At the time the Nazis had not yet attained absolute power, which is why they still tolerated the Imperial colors. Some people took advantage of this interim period by showing both flags, thus demonstrating that they were, as the saying went, "110 Percent Nazis." Apart from the usual patriotic and Nazi songs, the music book contained one song with his own text and music. It began with the words "We want a strong and united Reich, in which to live is a pleasure. For that we march, I and you, and hundred thousands more. Sieg Heil to you, our Führer!" I choked with disgust when he asked us to sing this botched composition.

Equally offensive to my taste were the speaking choruses that we had to intone under his direction. They were performed at the national holidays, which now followed in rapid succession. One of the choruses thundered, "Either black or white, but not gray; either warm or cold, but not tepid." Another rumbled, "Hard like Krupp steel, tough as leather, quick like greyhounds." Perhaps the most typical Nazi slogan was "Führer, give the order; we follow!" During the war, this acclamation, which sounded almost like a credo, was displayed on millions of posters. While I did support what the words said, I intensely disliked the manner in which we had to speak them. This teacher had a unique talent for turning me off, both as a music lover and as a National Socialist.

Soon after the Nazis' power seizure, the director of our school, a gentleman of the pre-Nazi era, was removed from office. His position was taken by the teacher who promoted the Boy Scouts at our school. The young man was a politically naive romantic, who accepted the Nazi regime without criticism. Apparently, however, the harmless yes-man was not sufficiently aggressive and fanatic for the Nazis, for they soon replaced him with the zealot who had portrayed the attack on Briand as an act of patriotism. In personal unpleasantness and servitude to the regime, the new director rivaled the music teacher.

The new director, who proudly displayed the Nazi Party emblem on his lapel, taught history and religion. The story of the Storm Troopers who bombarded the railroad car of the French statesman was only his opening gambit. His next move was to characterize Briand and Stresemann as "stooges of international Jewry." Blanket statements of this nature were the general tenor of his lessons. Officially, he was only our history teacher, but he claimed that, "implicitly," there was "a lot of religion" in his history lessons. The facts are that his history lessons were essentially tirades against the Jews, and his religious instructions were diatribes against Catholics.

Having been brought up in an environment where anti-Semitism was rampant, I did not reject the substance of the director's attacks on the Jews, but I disliked the manner in which he conducted them. Most emphatically, I resented the jokes with which he peppered his harangues, because they were frequently obscene. My instinct told me that the implied sexual depravity of the Jews could not be true. Yes, I believed in the Jewish conspiracy, but I failed to see how these people could be so different with regard to a human trait as common and basic as sexuality. My suspicion was strengthened by the director's unpleasant laugh. There was a certain uncleanness about it that offended both my eyes and ears. When he was particularly pleased with one of his cracks, he hissed and snickered while he fingered his goatee.

Once the director asked us, "Who is the greatest religious founder of all times?" Naturally, one of my classmates named Jesus Christ, but the director scolded him for implying that a Jew could have achieved something as creative as founding a religion. Another boy suggested Buddha, only to draw a yawn from the man, who claimed to be a teacher of religion. Suddenly, I had a hunch. "Zarathustra," I yelled. "That's already better, but still not good enough," replied the director. "Come on, think again," he rumbled, but we were at our wits' end.

The guessing game went on for several minutes. Eventually, the director became annoyed. "It's a shame that I have to tell you the answer," he declared. "Here it is, and don't you forget it: The greatest religious founder of all times is Adolf Hitler." We were flabbergasted. Nobody doubted the Führer's greatness. I, for one, considered him Germany's greatest statesman—but religious founder?

When the director noticed our bewilderment, he momentarily left the classroom, and when he returned, he waved Hitler's *Mein Kampf* in his hand. "Here is the Führer's credo," he yelled. And then he read:

Wer leben will,	He who wants to live,
Der kämpfe also.	Let him fight.
Und wer nicht kämpfen will	
	And he who does not want to fight
In dieser Welt des ewigen Ringens	
	In this world of eternal struggle
Verdient das Leben nicht.	
	Does not deserve to live.

"This is Aryan religion, not Jewish cabalism or Catholic pietism," declared the director. "This is more religion than you will ever find in the Bible," he cried while waving Hitler's book above his head. I was not so sure.

Although I substantively agreed with the director's anti-Semitism and even with some of his anti-Catholicism, I soon started to boycott his history lesson, mainly because of his stridency and unpleasantness. It was my second boycott at school. Now I was deprived of three of my favorite subjects—music, history, and religion. The director did not seem to notice my withdrawal, or he conveniently overlooked it, for he knew that I was, as the saying went, an "old champion" of the Hitler Youth. He also might have felt that I did not need instruction in Nazi doctrine, as I did not make a secret of my conviction. But the director's primary reason for letting me go so easily was somebody else.

This was a classmate of mine whose first name was Heinz. He was a practicing Catholic whom I admired for his faithfulness and courage. Though he was not directly opposed to Nazism, he occasionally voiced some mild criticism. We were good friends, even though I was deeply convinced of Nazi ideology whereas he was skeptical. Our friendship continued when we became soldiers during the war until he was killed in action. Naturally, we exchanged our thoughts about our director, and neither one made a secret of his disapproval.

At one of our chats, Heinz told me in confidence that the director was really a turncoat who was despised in church circles. "Before the power seizure," Heinz disclosed, "he was known as the most zealous churchgoer of St. Reinoldi [Dortmund's finest church]. He joined the party only after the power seizure." Thus, the director was Apostle Paul in reverse, preaching hatred not before, but after his conversion, while exchanging the Bible for the party book.

Now this man was our school director. It didn't take long before things changed for the worse. While he still lacked the authority to replace teachers such as Theo, he did hire new teachers who were young and had been trained in hastily arranged short courses on Nazi ideology. The doctrine they had absorbed there suffused all of their teaching, from history to physical education. One of them introduced a new history book, which had the horrible title *Volk Werdung der Deutschen*. The phrase is so clumsy that it sounds equally awkward if translated into English: "People Becoming of the Germans."

The book began with Charlemagne, who was praised as the founder of the First Reich, the Holy Roman Empire of the German Nation. Two other heroes of the First Reich were Frederick Barbarossa and Frederick the Great. The villains were mainly the

Jews and, to a lesser extent, Louis XIV and Cardinal Richelieu. They all seemed to have come into this world for one purpose only, the destruction of the First Reich. After its collapse, Bismarck forged the Second Reich. According to this book, the Weimar Republic was not a Reich at all, but a cesspool of traitors and perverts. Needless to say, Hitler was the greatest statesman of all time. That he was also the greatest general of all time was not yet known.

Our class teacher at the time was a gentleman of the old school who taught history and German literature and whom we addressed as Herr Professor. He was an environmentalist and a nature lover, and he tried to instill in us the same spirit. Though he was cautious not to run afoul of Nazi ideology, one could feel that it was alien to him. His attire, his deportment, his vocabulary, even his Hitler salute—which was compulsory—were strikingly out of style with the new movement. We called him "The Eternal Civilian," because his clumsy posture was the exact opposite of the stiff military pose. Nevertheless, the old-fashioned gentleman tried to play by the rules, such as extending the Heil Hitler salute and joining in "The Horst Wessel Song" when it was required.

When we went to summer camp, the professor wanted a formal flag-raising parade every morning. Since he lacked any military skill, he needed somebody to conduct the affair. The natural choice would have been a big boy who was two years my senior and proudly displayed the green shoulder strap, which identified him as one of Heino's lieutenants. Yet, strangely, the professor selected me instead of the older boy, though I was bare of all insignia. "You are mature enough," he told me, "to know what you are doing." And to the older boy, he summarily said, "Hermann, you cannot think." I was not sure what he meant by that, but I took comfort in assuming that the professor did not care much for military decorations.

Once, the director ordered a contest for the "best decorated" classroom of the school. Of course, the adornments should reflect Nazi ideology. When my father heard of this, he donated a huge copy of a drawing of Hitler, based on a famous picture postcard that showed the Führer at the beginning of the Nazi movement. He was standing in front of his Mercedes with a trenchcoat hanging from his shoulders. Underneath the picture, the postcard displayed the propaganda slogan "Hitler is Germany, and Germany is Hitler."

I hung the picture on the back wall of the classroom and intended to complete the decoration with the slogan from the postcard, which I wanted to arrange in a huge semi-circle above the picture. The professor did not object to the picture, but when he read the slogan, he flatly disapproved. I then remembered the maxim of the NS welfare organization: "Nobody shall go hungry or freeze." When I suggested this motto, the professor was greatly relieved and approved almost joyfully. Though he did not state his reason for the rejection of the first choice, he did make me realize how preposterous the slogan was.

Everybody liked the decoration and the gentle motto, except the director, who said that it reminded him of the Salvation Army. Today I think he was not entirely off the mark, since the hypocritical motto of the NS charity organization gave the Führer the air of a saint. All that was missing was the halo.

Of course, Theo did not participate in any of this. He simply ignored the new developments and comported himself with his usual cheerfulness. Soon he became our class teacher and taught us mathematics, physics, and chemistry. He practiced the Socratic method: never providing the answer to a question or the solution to a problem but, rather, asking questions designed to stimulate our thinking and guide us to find the answer ourselves.

Once Theo said he wished that our desks were arranged in a circle, and that he was sitting at the center. "It would be a perfect democracy," he added with a smile. But in the absence of such an arrangement, he took his seat at a desk in the rear of the room, thus shrewdly avoiding the view of the huge Hitler picture on the wall behind him. In his stead, one of us stood in front of the class next to the blackboard, addressing the mathematical problem at hand and trying to implement a solution. If this suggestion did not work, another boy came forward with another suggestion, and so on, until we found the solution.

These were the happiest hours of my school years, nay, of my entire youth. If I ever learned anything, it was then. By asking his cleverly designed questions, Theo led us to discoveries that had taken humankind hundreds of years to achieve. Under his guidance we deduced one of the Keplerian laws of planetary orbits. We also reinvented the proof of Greek mathematicians that the square root of two cannot be represented as the ratio of two integers, no matter how large. In chemistry, we inferred from the fixed weight relations in which the chemical elements combine to form compounds that they are composed of indivisible particles, called atoms, which display the same weight relations.

Once we talked about the Pythagorean theorem, and I claimed that it did not need a proof because it was obvious. My blunder was that I had a special case in mind, namely a right-angled triangle with two equal sides, in which case the proof, indeed, is obvious. But Theo drew a general right-angled triangle with unequal sides on the blackboard and challenged me to prove the theorem in this case, which, of course, I could not do. He then said with his characteristic blend of gentleness and earnestness, "You see, the truth lies sometimes deeper than you think. When somebody claims that he alone is in possession of the truth, you should be suspicious." That's when I decided to become a mathematician and a physicist.

Today I wish that Theo also had taught me political lessons. But he did that only twice, once rather early in my high school years, as I have already recounted, and once almost at the very end, as I still have to report. Of course, had Theo opened my eyes so that I could see the truth—the whole truth—I might not be alive today. At the time I did not regret Theo's political reserve; indeed, I felt subconsciously relieved that he did not push me into conflict with official Nazi doctrine, which touched me from all sides. Today I am inclined to believe that my personal welfare was the motive for Theo's restraint. He did not want to hurt me. Be that as it may, I lived a double life: one that was mainly mathematical, and another that was predominantly political. The first one I lived with all my heart; the second one, with a misguided sense of patriotic duty.

To my chagrin, mathematics and physics played only a minor role in the education program of the Nazis. Today I know why. Uneducated as most of the Nazi leaders were, they had not the slightest inkling of the awesome potential residing in budding new sciences such as rocketry and nuclear energy. Hitler and Goebbels understood only too well the power of propaganda and physical force, but they had no idea of the almost unlimited potential of modern science. Accordingly, they considered physical fitness and history, or what they called history, the most important disciplines of education. One shudders if one imagines what would have happened had they been smarter.

Needless to say, the director pursued the education program even more efficiently than the official guidelines required. With fanatical zeal, he hired ever-younger teachers who had passed NS training courses. Most of the young men, who proudly wore the uniform of the NS teachers organization, were history or physical education teachers. Their entrance changed the whole climate at our school.

I had considerable trouble with physical education. The new standards were so high that we spent an inordinate part of our time meeting them. One of the new sports we had to learn was boxing. The teacher was a brute who reminded me of Heino. Even though he was not supposed to do so, he sometimes challenged one of us to a match and gave him a bloody nose.

An additional drain on our learning capacity and our time was the frequent visits to movie theaters, where we watched Nazi films from the Reich's Party Congress or the Berlin Olympics. Being children, we loved these digressions and did not mind that they shortened our education, which was already compromised by too many other activities. Once we saw a newsreel of the match in which Max Schmeling defeated Joe Louis. Of course, the film of the rematch showing the African American defeating the German was not shown. The young Nazi teachers hired by our director accompanied us on these visits. Back at school, they commented on the propaganda features and tried to glorify Schmeling for his victory. The physical education teacher even demonstrated in great detail how the Aryan systematically ground down the black fighter. Theo never attended these tendentious movies.

The propaganda films were made especially for young people with impressionable minds. With hindsight I must say that they were quite effective, particularly the pictures from the party congress and the Olympics produced by Leni Riefenstahl. One of their effects was that they strengthened my belief in the superiority of the Aryan race. Inexperienced as I was, I took these films for living proof that values such as creativity, bravery, and honor were the prerogative of the master race and its torchbearer, the German nation.

I still remember one episode that made a particularly strong impression on me. At the beginning and end of one of the propaganda films, a deep voice recited a phrase from Hitler's *Mein Kampf:* "The Aryan has always been mankind's Prometheus." Though the phrase is so primitive that it is almost bereft of meaning, it reverberated through the dark movie theater with the convincing power of a fundamental truth. Still under the influence of my father's chauvinism, I took these words for gospel. Far from noticing their idiocy, I thought they were the revelation of genius.

When, as an American, I look back at these years, I am amazed and perplexed that I accepted the prefabricated stories of the Nazis almost without mental reservation. Of course, it was not one single phrase or speech or movie that overwhelmed me, not one person or medium of information, but a never-ending hail of lies, half-truths, clichés, historical distortions, and misrepresentations. They affected me day in and day out, at home, from the elders, in the Hitler Youth, at school, on the radio, in the newspapers, at the movie theaters, everywhere. Worse, the primitive propaganda slogans seemed to be supported by the more thoughtful arguments of respectable patriots such as a few teachers, elders, public figures, and Boy Scout leaders.

Still a teenager, I stood at the confluence of powerful movements, ranging from the inflammatory teachings of the Nazis to the glorification of the Fatherland by harmless patriots. They persuaded me that creativity, bravery, honor, and even gentler values such as love and beauty had an unadulterated existence only in the land of Aryans. Today, whenever I witness bravery in other societies, or behold the beauty of other countries, or feel the love that other people are capable of, I am reminded of the dark time in my life when I believed the preposterous lie that these mores were the exclusive achievement of the Aryan race.

The Nazis also exploited the heroic music of Beethoven and Wagner for their propaganda purposes. They played it at every opportunity, from Hitler's speeches to extra bulletins to state funerals. Bach was never performed, because his deeply moving religiosity was an embarrassment to the Nazis. Mozart was treated with a strange mixture of mistrust and fear. I believe the Nazis felt in their bones that Mozart was the Shakespeare of music, who had a troublesome knack for revealing human frailty, as had the author of *Hamlet*. The rebellious spirit of *The Marriage of Figaro*, which already had displeased the emperor at Mozart's time, was also not to Hitler's liking. Schubert was another case of Nazi embarrassment. On the one hand, they did not want to let a candidate for the pantheon of Aryan creativity slip through their fingers; on the other hand, they simply didn't know what to do with him. His soulful songs were as alien to their mentality as was the St. Matthew Passion. That a commandant of a concentration camp listened to Schubert songs while the chimneys of the crematories were smoking—as was reported—I simply cannot fathom. Nevertheless, my early music appreciation was distorted by the slanted selection of the Nazis.

Other favorites of the Nazi propaganda were certain cultural events, some especially created for this purpose, others hijacked and refurbished for the same insidious purpose. One of these propaganda tricks was an exhibition showing mainly photographic documents from the terror regime of Béla Kuhn in Hungary after the First World War. The gruesome pictures offered the Goebbels propaganda machine the chance of catching two flies with one stroke. On the one hand, they made us shudder from the atrocities of the Communists; on the other, they fostered the sanctimonious sentiment that such ugly things were impossible in the Third Reich.

Equally effective was the traveling exhibition *Schaffendes Volk* (A People at Work), which exploited creative achievements such as the Volkswagen and the Autobahn for cheap propaganda effects. I attended the exhibition with my class in Düsseldorf. It was one of the rare occasions when Theo praised an accomplishment of the Nazi regime. I can still see him leaning over the model of an Autobahn crossing shaped like a cloverleaf. "Here you can see," he remarked in his thoughtful manner, "that the perfect solution of a genuine problem always has beauty."

We also attended the world-famous Shakespeare festival in

Bochum. Although we had read *Julius Caesar* in school, we were not allowed to see the play in Bochum because the Nazis did not like *Tyrannenmord* (assassination of a tyrant). For the same reason, Schiller's *Wilhelm Tell* was banished from the curriculum.

The most effective—or destructive—propaganda tool of the Nazis was the color film *Jud Süss*. Here *"Jud"* is a derogatory name for Jew. *Süss* is the alleged miscreant's family name and means "sweet." Until the Second World War, such names were typical of German Jews. They were a legacy of Frederick the Great, who had decreed that all Jews in his kingdom give up their Jewish names and adopt German names.

The movie depicted the life of a Jew who had risen from poverty to power by financial intrigues. Of all the crimes he was accused of, I remember most vividly the rape of a beautiful German girl. Particularly impressive to me were the words of her aggrieved father, spoken by one of Germany's best actors: "Sorrow does not speak justice. However, it is written in the law, though a Jew carnally intermixes with a Christian woman, he thereupon shall be put to death by the noose." Needless to say that the "law" either had never existed or had been a perversion of justice during the darkest Middle Ages. Of course, the execution was also shown, complete with the villain's begging for mercy, as he was pulled up in a cage to the top of the church tower from which he was hanged.

The mendacious movie affected me exactly as the producers had intended. It persuaded me to believe the old *Stürmer* canard that the Jews were trying to subjugate the German people by debauching their women. What our school director was unable to prove with his salacious jokes, the movie demonstrated with irresistible persuasiveness. Indeed, it convinced me that the alleged Jewish conspiracy was much more than a purely political plot. To my unsuspecting mind, it now appeared a systematic attempt to destroy the Aryan race by defiling their women and "polluting" their blood.

In retrospect, I must say that the film was a masterstroke of propaganda. Directed by one of Germany's most skillful film-makers, and acted by some of its best performers, the picture showed the alleged sexual depravity of the Jews in living colors. Moreover, it strongly suggested that the story of Jud Süss was by no means an isolated incident, but the general rule of Jewish behavior in Aryan societies. I was too young to discern the lie or to see the intention behind it. In short, the movie was the perfect dupery, and I was the perfect dupe.

This was one of the rare occasions when I actually felt collective hatred. The fate of the young girl, who allegedly had been driven to suicide, pursued me for several weeks. My agitation deepened when one of the young history teachers discussed the movie with us in school. He produced the facsimile of an "old document," allegedly a contemporary account of the sexual conquests of Jud Süss. Holding the bogus paper high above his head, he proclaimed, "On this document the movie is based." Then reading from it, he "informed" us that the villain had actually disgraced dozens of Aryan women. As if that were not enough, he declared, with the authority of a government-appointed history teacher, that thousands of other Jews had committed the same crime ever since the first Jew had set foot on German soil. To top it all off, he read from another "source" that the Jews behaved the same way in Spain, France, and England. "Small wonder," he mused, that these countries occasionally experienced "justifi-able" anti-Semitic riots. (The word "pogrom" was not used in Nazi Germany.)

One of these justifiable riots lay still ahead. The Nazis were only waiting for an excuse. The opportunity offered itself when a Jewish assassin killed a member of the German embassy in Paris. It happened a few days before the ninth of November 1938, which was the highest Nazi holiday. What better time for taking revenge than the night before the emotionally charged anniversary of the November coup in Munich? And what a surprise!

"Spontaneous" reprisals occurred all over Germany. That was the infamous Kristallnacht of 1938.

On the morning following that fateful night, I was riding my bicycle on my way to school. The route took me almost diagonally through town. As we were required on these national holidays, I was dressed in my Hitler Youth uniform, yet I had not the slightest inkling of the atrocities that had occurred during the night. But I soon discovered the first traces of violence. Here broken glass, there demolished furniture, here strewn clothes, there plundered showcases, and even traces of blood. It took a while before I understood that this had been a concerted action by the SA against the Jews, but when I arrived at school there could no longer be any doubt. Most of my classmates had observed similar things, and all were agitated, though we weren't sure whether we should approve or disapprove. Rather, we exchanged information with the strained objectivity of people who had just witnessed an accident.

However, one person was deeply troubled: Theo. We were still stirred up while gathering in the auditorium of the physics laboratory for our first lesson of the day. Everybody was dressed in his Hitler Youth uniform, for those who had not joined had long been expelled from school. We were waiting for Theo, and the thought that he might break his long silence about the political events heightened our agitation. We were required to rise when he entered, and he was supposed to extend the Heil Hitler salute. Today we had to wait longer than usual.

Finally, he arrived, and we saw right away that he was highly disturbed. His face was pale and his familiar smile was missing. Thus he stood before us, motionless, while covering his face with his hands. After a long pause he took his hands off and said slowly and distinctly, in an urgent tone of voice, "Boys, the things that happened this night in our country will be to the shame of our nation for a thousand years to come. Heil Hitler. Sit down."

We were stunned! I don't know what we had expected, but not this. Most of us were convinced that some action against the Jews was justified. After all, one of them had spilled German blood, so it was time to teach them a lesson. Theo was wrong. He was well meaning, but woefully uninformed. He was a Weimar Republican, but we were Hitler Youths. He represented the past; we were the future.

I remember only vaguely how the lesson continued. One of us was reading his report about the previous lesson, but nobody listened. Everybody pondered Theo's shocking words. "How can he say something like this?" I asked myself. "Why does this man, whom I respect more than anybody, try to dispirit us in this hour of national renaissance. How can self-defense be a shame to our nation?"

We were about twenty boys, and all of us, except Heinz, disagreed with Theo. If only one of us had informed on him, he would have gone straight to the concentration camp, but none did. We cherished him too much for that. But I wished he had not spoken those frightful words. They pained me, they reverberated through my soul with an almost Biblical austerity. Little did I know that, one day, I would consider them the most fundamental truth a living person had ever spoken to me. Why did I fail to recognize this truth when there was still time to change my life?

Kristallnacht had several other consequences. When I returned home, my father was as agitated and as surprised as I was. I also noticed that he was slightly disappointed because he had not received any advance notice of an action that was obviously well planned. This was another sign for him and me that he was not as trusted in party circles as he thought he deserved.

The most remarkable reactions on the part of my parents came a few days later. My mother had returned from one of the shopping trips that she still undertook in spite of her semi-blindness. We all noticed that she was quite upset, yet she did not say a word. This went on for several days, as if she were brooding about some very unpleasant news she had received on that shopping trip. Eventually, at the dinner table, she broke into tears and told us the story of an old Jew who tried to escape the Storm Troopers who were pursuing him. In his anguish the old man entered one of those narrow patrician houses that have many stories and a round window at the top. Once inside, the helpless man hastened up the stairs, higher and higher, while the thugs followed him. Eventually he reached the highest point with the round window. That's where the murderers caught up with him. As he was begging for mercy, they threw him out of the window.

When my mother finished her story, everybody was painfully silent. My father did not say a word, but it was obvious that he went through one of those rare moments in his political life when he felt some guilt. I choked with emotion. This was the first time I felt pity for a victim of the hatred that my father and I had entertained for years. A few days later my mother told me, in tears, that every night she thought of the old man who, in his heart rending distress, climbed the stairs to his death. And I confessed to her that I was haunted by the same painful vision.

In school the horrifying events of Kristallnacht drew even wider circles of reaction, ranging from support to indifference to disgust. One of the young Nazi teachers who taught German literature made us write a report under the headline "Do we do injustice to the Jews?" We had a few days' time, and I had to think of the defenseless Jew who had been killed without trial and without guilt. But then I told myself, "This is war, and in every war things do happen that I cannot morally justify. However, that does not mean that the war itself is unjust." In this spirit, I wrote and delivered my report, as did all of my classmates with one exception.

Heinz—the exception—had the sense of justice and the civil

courage to write, "Yes, we do injustice to the Jews, and that is a shame to our nation." The punishment was swift and harsh. First, Heinz was suspended indefinitely. But Theo intervened and demanded a teachers' conference to decide what his punishment should be. It took weeks until the conference convened; all the while I saw Heinz only in the home of his parents. Finally the conference took place and we waited anxiously for the outcome. The next day Theo entered the classroom with an impish smile on his face. "Well," he said slyly, "reason has prevailed." Then he opened the door and cried, "Come in, young rebel!" With that, Heinz entered the classroom to our unanimous applause.

But that was not the end of it. In the following days, Heinz was slapped in the face by three different teachers. The first was our music teacher, who administered one of his infamous boxes on the ear. The second and third were two of the young Nazi teachers. Their blows came at the airfield of our city. The Führer's deputy, Rudolf Hess, was expected for a visit. Thus, all schoolchildren were lined up to greet him. While we were waiting there, Heinz was slapped twice in his face within the span of a few minutes. We all felt that this was a concerted effort ordered by our director, and we were so outraged that we protested, whereupon our boxing teacher threatened us with even harder blows.

In the aftermath of Kristallnacht, the Jewish community of our city went into almost complete hiding. The synagogue had been burnt down, and all Jewish shops had been plundered and were now closed. My father used the opportunity to urge one of his Jewish clients, who had been in arrears for years, to pay his debt. The man owned a furniture store, and my father had planned and conducted the remodeling of his building. Now he summoned the shopkeeper to his architectural bureau. After an hour of haggling he came into our living quarters with a fistful of money. Though I don't know what transpired during that conference, I am sure that my father did not ask for more than was his due.

By early 1939 the war was only a few months away, but I was convinced that peace would prevail, as were my father and most of the teachers at school. We relied on the deceptive words with which Hitler had concluded one of his last speeches, a few months before he dropped his mask: "I, however, believe in a long-lasting peace." Nevertheless, war preparations were under way everywhere. In the Hitler Youth we were trained as fire fighters. In case of a war, the main job of a Hitler Youth was to stand guard under the roof of a house against incendiary bombs. But when the war finally came, I did not serve in this capacity, for I soon became a soldier, and so did my older brother. Only my younger brother served as a fire fighter in the bombing raids to come, until he too joined the army.

In school now there was talk about an emergency graduation. That all members of my class would become soldiers was a foregone conclusion. Thus our director and his cronies now treated us with more respect than they had afforded us only a few weeks before. We also had reached the age at which we were to be addressed with the formal *Sie* instead of the intimate *du*. All teachers abided by this rule except Theo, who seemed to have some difficulties in changing the habit. Most remarkable was the respect with which the young Nazi teachers now treated Heinz. They had a good reason, for it was he, their former whipping boy, who now suggested that we all should volunteer to become fighter pilots in the Luftwaffe. When the director heard of this, he came to our class and congratulated us. Suddenly all animosities were forgotten. Only Theo observed an uneasy silence.

Since I would not complete my eighteenth year of age before June 1939, I could volunteer only with my parents' written consent. My father was no problem, but my mother was. I knew how much she worried about my older brother, and how fervently she wished that she would not have to worry about me, too. That made it difficult for me to ask for her signature. When I finally placed the paper in front of her, I almost felt guilty. But she signed it quickly because she did not want to disappoint me.

In the meantime the war propaganda became ever more strident. My father and I were now convinced that hostilities were inevitable, yet we had no idea that they might escalate into another world war. Even though hostilities had not yet started, the school went ahead with the emergency graduation. There was a superficial exam and a pompous celebration. Our music teacher had a field day, and the director gave a speech about bravery and dying for Führer and Fatherland. The stupid phrase induced me to imagine how it would feel to stick my bayonet into somebody's stomach, or vice versa. The thought made me so sick that I sought comfort in the song of the German column marching through Flanders in the spring of 1914 and seeing a swarm of wild geese overhead. While the director was still ranting, I whispered, "We are like you a gray cohort and move in the Emperor's name. And should we travel without return, do rustle us in autumn an Amen."

A few more days of peace were still granted us, so the family, except for my older brother, spent a happy week on vacation in southern Germany. When we passed through Munich, we visited "The House of German Art" and saw the exhibition *Entartete Kunst* (Degenerate Art). Since I had no appreciation of fine art unless it was strictly naturalist, I had no trouble rejecting almost the entire collection of denounced pictures and sculptures, nor did I fail to notice that this "junk" was primarily the product of Jews. Nearly sixty years later I saw the same exhibition, or what was left of it, in Washington, D.C., and I went through an inner turmoil that was surpassed in severity only by the shattering experience of the U.S. Holocaust Memorial Museum.

My father was an ardent admirer of Paul Troost and Albert Speer, the two architects whom Hitler had entrusted with the realization of his dreams of pomp and splendor. Thus, my father always wanted to see the new chancellery, which Speer had built in Berlin, but when that was not possible, he urged me to visit the building at the first opportunity. I did this during the war, but it proved to be one of the many disappointments that nevertheless failed to awaken me from my youthful dreams of national glory.

A few days after our return from vacation, the war began. Hitler's voice thundered from the radio, "Since 4:30 this morning, fire is being returned." The phrase was a blatant attempt to create the impression that the Poles had started the shooting, and it was quite successful as far as my classmates and I were concerned. We firmly believed that this was a war of defense.

We now had to report for labor service at Dortmund's airfield, even though we had volunteered for the air force. The trouble was that the armed services could not immediately handle so many volunteers. But they also did not want them to be idle. Thus, they made us dig, which was now more important than learning. After I had earned a few pennies from digging, I rushed to a bakery to buy some chocolate, only to learn that the Reichsmark I held in my hands could no longer buy such luxuries.

The war did have some effect on my political views. The anonymous Jewish conspiracy now moved almost imperceptibly into the background, and enemies of flesh and blood moved into the foreground, enemies that could shoot at us or drop bombs on our cities. At the beginning of the war these were mainly the French and the British. The Poles were so quickly defeated that they were not counted as enemies but considered, rather, the war's clumsy originators. As to the Jews, the jury was still out. If they were really behind this war, then surely the Russians and the Americans would have to enter it, for we believed that Moscow and New York were the true strongholds of international Jewry. But there were not the slightest indications that these nations were interested in a war with us.

The Nazi propaganda was the supreme author of public opinion. Even the images of other nations were prefabricated by the official propaganda mill. The French were portrayed as decadent and perverse. The English fared somewhat better. Although they supposedly suffered from an excessive instinct for mercantilism, they had the true sense of the master race as they had proved in Egypt and India. If the British had not been in the pockets of the Jews, and if they were not so inflamed by this warmonger, Winston Churchill, they would have been our ally instead of our enemy. The Russians were of an inferior race. If they were not so numerous and their country not so vast, they would not pose a problem at all. The Americans were plain silly and incapable of producing anything of value, as was amply demonstrated by the junk they offered in the Woolworth store! Nor were their soldiers any better. All the Americans had in mind was to find out who could spend the longest time atop a telegraph pole, or which girl had the biggest bosom.

The big question was the Jews. So far, they had mobilized only the French and the British against us, and these nations would be defeated or drop out of the war in a matter of a few months. Only if the Jews succeeded in mobilizing Russia and America would this war escalate into another world war. But if that happened, Hitler had warned in one of his last speeches, "then this war will lead to the annihilation of the Jewish race in Europe." I heard the Führer's words, but it did not occur to me that he meant precisely what he said. Systematic genocide was the farthest thing from my mind; even the word was unknown to me.

My classmates and I eventually got our marching orders. We had to report for military duty at midnight on New Year's Eve of 1939. This was for Theo the signal for the farewell party he had promised us. Each of us received a written invitation to his house on the outskirts of the city, and each attended in civilian clothes. We were about twenty boys and, as it turned out, only three of us would survive the war. But this night we were all in high spirits, except for Theo, who was strangely subdued. Though he had always warned us against tobacco and alcohol, he now served a punch containing traces of wine, which lifted our spirits even higher. Theo did not sermonize, as he sometimes had done in school, nor did he try to dampen our boundless optimism. He even managed an occasional smile when the wave of our euphoria reached a new high. But his anguish did not escape Heinz and me, for Theo seemed to single us out this night with his kind attention. The further the party progressed, the more bittersweet it became for the three of us.

It was past midnight when we parted. In school Theo had always avoided physical contact, but now he placed both hands on my shoulders and looked me in the eyes with a sad smile, unable to utter a word. My classmates were already walking ahead, and I hastily freed myself to follow them. As I looked back, I was able to see him once more in spite of the blackout against air attacks. He was standing on his terrace, as he used to stand on the balcony at school. When he noticed that I was looking back at him, he waved his hand. My classmates were singing, but I was choked with emotion, for I had suddenly discovered that I loved this man.

I never saw him again. After the war I inquired about him, but all I could find out was that he had "disappeared."

CHAPTER 8

Long on Obedience, Short on Purpose

On December 31, 1939, shortly before midnight, I left my parents' home to report for military duty. My father and I were convinced that the war would be brief and relatively bloodless, but my mother was a worrywart by nature and nurture. In the First World War she had agonized over my father's life-threatening injury. The Second World War began with anxiety about her oldest son. Now I exacerbated her worries, and a few years hence her youngest son would do the same. She always bore the brunt of the family's hardships, be it sickness, poverty, or danger. I often watched her helplessly when she suffered, and now I wished I could save her this agony. But I knew no better way than to request that she stay inside and only my father accompany me to the streetcar that stopped in front of our house.

It was pitch-dark because of the blackout; even the streetcar was without lights. When it arrived my father probably felt that he had to comfort me and said, "It will soon be over." I was so touched by his helplessness that I could not utter a word. Thus, we parted in darkness and silence.

Several hundred young men had gathered at the assembly place. Most of them were draftees, some were volunteers, but only Heinz was a classmate of mine. Soon we were marching through the dark city streets to the railroad station. I did not see Heinz during the rail transport, but we met later. The journey took us to a basic training camp of the Luftwaffe at Neu Brandenburg, west of Berlin. Though this was a trip of only 450 kilometers, it took about twenty-four hours because of all the troop movements that were going on.

These hours were a somber prelude to the nearly six years of military service that lay ahead of me. I don't think I entertained any social bias, except that I was infected with the insidious racial conceit of National Socialism. However, after a few hours of travel in the company of these men, who were supposed to be my comrades, my sense of solidarity was severely tested. They came from an area of Dortmund that had the reputation of being a slum, and it showed in their language. They used vulgar expressions and metaphors I had never heard before. Every second word was an obscenity. I was utterly disgusted and bewildered. If they were my comrades, I didn't want to see my enemies.

This experience was another of the many warnings that I always brushed aside before they could get hold of me. However, during those twenty-four hours, the thought did occur to me that some of my German compatriots were as ugly as the grimaces in the *Stürmer*. Moreover, these people were real, whereas the contortions of the gazette were cartoons. Eventually, however, I became hardened against this kind of company and against many other annoyances of military life. In fact, I suffered only one more blow of comparable intensity. This happened two days later when we received our uniforms. I had the audacity to complain to the sergeant who handed me my steel helmet that it was too large, whereupon he yelled something unfit for quotation. After that experience I quickly learned to consider, but not condone, the vulgarities of military life as an inevitable evil.

Basic training was hard and unpleasant, particularly because the weather was unusually harsh. I felt that most of the drill was superfluous and mainly designed to forge us into obedient puppets rather than competent fighters. *"Jawohl, Herr Unteroffizier"* (Yes, will do, Corporal Sir) was our daily mantra. *"Bitte Herrn Unteroffizier die Nase putzen zu dürfen"* was a twisted nonsense that was supposed to mean "I am asking Corporal Sir for permission to blow my nose," but could also mean "I am asking for permission to blow Corporal Sir's nose." I had to take care to suppress laughter when I used the stupid phrase, for any sign of disrespect would have made my life at basic training even more unpleasant. But I thought that such stilted language was fitting for a bunch of genuflecting courtiers, not for a nation that prided itself to be socialist.

Most of the trainees were draftees who were not allowed to choose their future military career. Volunteers like Heinz and I were mainly high school graduates and soon became the special targets of the drill sergeants. When we shouldered the rifle, we had to hit the butt with such force that a loud crash was heard. One of the drill masters put his ear close to my rifle butt and cried each time I hit it, "I don't hear anything!" Such was the service to Führer and Reich.

The barracks were brand-new and almost luxurious, except that the heating system was turned off most of the time. The food was edible, though I had a hard time getting used to it. Eventually, however, I learned to appreciate the German saying that hunger is the best cook. The pea soup of which my father had raved was so-so. Only the army bread, which was not rationed in the early war years, lived up to expectations. Today the wholesome bread is one of the few pleasant memories of my military service.

After a few weeks of basic training the volunteers were sent to a military hospital to be inspected for aviation fitness. At the time the Luftwaffe had more volunteers than aircraft, which led to the rather high physical standards that many could not meet. Those who were rejected had forfeited their privilege to make choices and were returned to the training camp. Heinz and I were part of this group. After finishing basic training, we were transferred to the Neuruppin air base, north of Berlin.

The trip from Neu Brandenburg to Neuruppin led us through Berlin, where we had to switch trains. On this short trip I had two more of those experiences that could have been a warning to me, if I had not encapsulated myself in a protective shell. While this defensive coating provided me with some shield from the unpleasantness of military life, it also dulled my sensitivity to the truth. The first abortive warning came from the Führer himself, more precisely, from his new Reich Chancellery, which Albert Speer had built for him.

We had to proceed from Berlin's Potsdamer train station to the city's Stettiner train station, using the S-Bahn (*Stadt Bahn* means city transit). That's when I remembered my father's behest to see the new chancellery at my first opportunity. Thus I left the Potsdamer station, crossed the Potsdamer Platz, and entered the Voss Strasse, where Hitler had the palatial residence in which (more precisely, *under* which) he would spend his last days. To my right towered an old-fashioned building, the department store Wertheim, which, as far as I knew, once was in Jewish hands. To my left, somewhat further down the street, extended the marble palace of the Reich Chancellery.

I wanted to concentrate on the Führer's mansion, but the Wertheim building didn't let go of me. It was a remarkable contrast. Here the structure of a worldly business, rather tall, functional, and unassuming, and there the Führer's celebrated edifice, extravagantly broad, but surprisingly low. Like a Greek temple, the chancellery glorified the horizontal, but unlike a Gothic cathedral, it denied the vertical. Something was missing, some undeniable ideological truth like the message of the Statue of Liberty (which I did not know at the time). Yes, the architect had met some of the challenges that came with the nature of the building. It was imposing and simple at the same time; it had clear lines and was remarkably bare of superfluous ornaments and stucco; and it truly reveled in the illustrious materials. But it could not overcome the unpretentious Wertheim building! How could the Führer and his architect allow a commercial building to tower over the Reich Chancellery?

I was so bewildered that I forgot to salute the two SS men who flanked the imposing marble stairs, which looked oddly out of place at a building that had nothing to climb. The street was strangely deserted and did not strike me as the center of the world I had expected to see. The scene was as paltry as Number 10 Downing Street, the residence of the British prime minister that I once had seen in a press photograph. Where was the grandeur, where was the splendor? This was the nerve center of the Third Reich! And there, of all places, I suffered a minor crisis of my faith. I was so bewildered that I decided not to mention this crisis in the letters to my parents.

The other warning came while I was riding the S-Bahn. Since this encounter concerned human beings rather than a monument of marble, it was far more serious. At one of the train stops, a few careworn figures wearing yellow Star of David badges sneaked into the car. They did not dare enter the cabin, but stood on the small platform next to the door. Their entire behavior seemed to be dictated by only one wish—not to be noticed.

The cruelty against these defenseless people struck me as painfully as the story of the old Jew whom the Nazis had thrown out of the window during Kristallnacht. These weary figures, I thought, must have lived in this state of anxiety ever since that fateful night. This was worse than murder, this was violation of the soul, this was torture! It was the first time I witnessed a Nazi barbarity with my own eyes, and it plunged me into a whirlwind of contradictory feelings and thoughts. Desperately, I tried to understand the conflict raging through my mind. While my feelings were unambiguous, my thoughts were ambivalent. While I felt the mental pain of the aggrieved, I did not comprehend the shame to my own people who allowed this to happen.

Yet, I was still too wrong-headed and misguided to understand the essence of this disgraceful scene. The anti-Semitic venom I had absorbed in the formative years of my life had dulled my sensitivity to the truth that now stared me in the face. I lulled myself into believing that this mental cruelty was necessary for the protection of the German people. I found excuses and comfort in the very ideology that had spawned this disgrace. Bewildered and ashamed, I turned my eyes away and wished that the denigrated figures would disappear. At the next stop they obliged and glided out of the car as discreetly as they had slipped in. Still ashamed, but greatly relieved, I diverted my mind all too willingly to the trivia of the day.

Life at our new military station was even less pleasant than it had been at basic training. Upon arrival we expected to be treated, if not more respectfully, then at least more reasonably, for we had been told that we were a scarce commodity that was to be handled with care. But the corporals and sergeants at the new station would have none of it. Immediately after our arrival they made us scrub the floor of their quarters and do their laundry until late into the night. We had volunteered to defend the Fatherland, I said to myself, not to wash somebody's dirty clothes. But then, I rationalized that this was just another case where the spirit of the Führer had not yet penetrated to the remotest cell of society.

Most surprising to me was the almost apolitical atmosphere of the armed services. I hardly ever heard the word "Jew," not to mention "Jewish conspiracy." There was no collective hatred of any sort, but only a moderate vigilance against concrete enemies, the French and the British.

Today I know why the armed services were so remarkably apolitical. They had been formed from the echelons of the *Reichswehr* (the miniature army allowed by the Treaty of Versailles), which was the successor of the old Imperial army. Since the Imperial army was traditionally non-political, so was the *Reichswehr*. Attempting to politicize the coming army, the Storm Troopers (the SA) under their leader, Ernst Röhm, demanded in 1933 that they be commissioned to build the army. They wanted the future armed services to be a "people's army." But Hitler had a different idea. Not trusting his rebellious party comrades, he wanted the *Reichswehr* to create the new army. What he needed was a cadre of competent generals rather than a bunch of undisciplined rowdies. That is why he staked his future career as the conqueror of Europe on the *Reichswehr* rather than the SA. To forestall a potential rebellion, he conducted a massacre in 1934 in which the leaders of the SA, including Röhm, were executed.

I was thirteen years old when the massacre happened. The Goebbels propaganda represented it as an attempted coup by the SA, henceforth called the Röhm Putsch (*Putsch* means coup). The propaganda machine portrayed the leaders of the SA, Röhm included, as a bunch of depraved homosexuals. As usual, I believed the official version, though I did not know the meaning of the word "homosexual." I still remember asking my mother, who was washing the dishes, what a homosexual was. "Child," she sighed, "that is too terrible to explain."

When I joined Hitler's army, I did know what a homosexual was, but I had not the slightest inkling of the bloody power struggle that had preceded the army's creation. I expected a National Socialist Army, something like the "people's army" Röhm had in mind. Instead, I found a completely apolitical service fashioned after the model of the old Imperial army. Thus, I was equally surprised by the absence of anti-Semitism and the almost clinical fear of homosexuality. While we received no anti-Semitic indoctrination, we were warned almost weekly of the high penalties on homosexuality. The underlying theory was that homosexuality weakens morale and the fighting spirit.

The apolitical atmosphere was reflected by the songs we had to bellow while marching. To be sure, some of these soldier songs were stupid or tasteless, yet others like "The blue dragoons, they are riding"—which I knew already from the Hitler Youth—had a certain redeeming quality. But none had the hateful and arrogant spirit of the songs I had learned in the NS Student Federation and the *Jungvolk*. There was nothing yet of the ideological indoctrination that Hitler ordered in 1944 after the attempt on his life. There was no focus on the enemy, no stated goal of the war, no purpose except obedience. One sometimes got the impression that these corporals and sergeants considered the high school graduates their real enemies.

Every morning, before we fell out, we had one hour of indoor instruction. Although I was so sleepy that I hardly heard what the sergeant was saying, I was grateful for the respite before being exposed to the unusually cold weather. Most of the instructions dealt with tedious subjects such as handling of weapons, care of uniforms, rank emblems, names of superiors, arrest and use of weapons, and so on. However, two subjects caught my attention, namely comrades' theft and grievance regulations.

Before I joined the military, theft among comrades was inconceivable to me, but after the first twenty-four hours of military service I had no longer any illusions. What surprised me, though, was the obvious concern of the higher-ups, which showed itself in the frequent instructions and warnings against comrade's theft. There were relatively harsh penalties not only for the thieves, but also for victims who had failed to observe proper precautions. Here the underlying theory was that the man who failed to safeguard his possessions was tempting his comrades to steal, and that theft among comrades corrupted morale. One of the mandatory safeguards was to keep the cabinet locked at all times and to carry money in a bag worn around the neck. Failure to observe these preventive measures was a serious offense.

The grievance regulations were an attempt to temper the military system of command and obedience with some fairness and reasonableness. They provided a soldier with the right to file a written complaint when he felt offended by a superior. I took an early interest in these provisions because I foresaw that I should have to use them someday. Interestingly, a superior could call a subordinate, with impunity, all sorts of insulting names. But he could not call him a coward or a liar without risking some sanctions. The theory was that a vulgar expression was not an offense as long as it was used without malice and addressed to a private rather than an officer. Etiquette and politeness were a prerogative of gentlemen, and only the commissioned officers were gentlemen. I felt that this gentlemen cult was inconsistent with the second word in "National Socialism," and I had an uneasy foreboding that someday I would conflict with this relic of the past.

The Neuruppin air base was a school for aviators. My company provided ground support, such as standing watch and defending the facility against supposed attackers. The imaginary raiders were British paratroopers who were to land under cover of darkness and commit acts of sabotage. They never came, but in those early days of the war there were still enough soldiers for such a military circus. In the later war years, the Luftwaffe could no longer afford such luxury, because all able-bodied foot soldiers were transferred to the army.

There were about a dozen high school graduates in my company. We formed a small circle of an innocuous "conspiracy" against, as I expressed it, "military nonsense and abuse." I was the undeclared leader of this group, and that must also have been the impression of the sergeants who showed it by making me their favorite object of attention.

One of the circle members was Heinz. When I presented him to the other members as "my old friend from Dortmund," he declared that he could accept as a friend, without reservation, only a believer in Jesus Christ. But even though I was a non-believer, he hastened to add, I was as close to being his friend as God would permit. I was slightly surprised by this announcement and also thought it a little sanctimonious, but I valued Heinz too highly to take offense. A devout Catholic, he was unswervingly devoted to the defense of his country and, to a lesser extent, Führer and Reich. Though he sometimes voiced some mild criticism of Hitler's policies, he never spoke disrespectfully of him as a person. In 1943 Heinz revived his old spirit of volunteering, which he had already demonstrated at high school, by signing up as a paratrooper. A year later he was killed in action at the front against the Allied invasion forces.

Another circle member was Paul, who was also a high school graduate but from another city. He wrote poetry and acquainted me with a writer named Kolbenheyer, whose novels were infused with a romantic spirit of civilized nationalism. Since I shared Paul's idealism and propensity to romanticize the life of the soldier, we became close friends. However, our idealism drove us in opposite directions. I felt that the volunteers deserved to be treated with more respect, whereas Paul closed his eyes to their shabby treatment and tried to be an exemplary soldier. I contended that he was dreaming of an ideal brotherhood of knights. "That may be what the Führer has in mind," I preached to him, "but reality is a far cry from this noble dream." With anti-military speeches like that I tried to infuse Paul with my own rebellious spirit, but he would have none of it and steadfastly followed his chosen path of being an exemplary soldier.

Our friendship continued even though Paul was the favorite of the company chief, whereas I was the man's declared irritant. Eventually, the chief rewarded Paul's positive attitude by conferring on him the status of an "officer candidate." I believe Paul was the only member of the group who eventually became a commissioned officer.

Paul also was the only one who was sent on a study leave, which was granted in rare cases to students of medicine, engineering, rocket science, and so on. He was allowed to study one semester of physics at the University of Bonn. When I was on my second leave at my parents' home in Dortmund, Paul came from Bonn to visit me. This was the last time we saw each other.

When we were both fighting on the Eastern front against Russia, Paul in the extreme south and I in the extreme north, we exchanged dozens of letters about literature and philosophy that must have kept the military censors busy. In these letters we completely ignored the military and political events of the day, though Paul still wrote romantic poems about the life of the soldier. Eventually, Paul's letters stopped. After the war I learned from his parents that he had died in a Russian prisoner of war camp in Siberia.

Another "conspirator" was Karl, who was a high school graduate from Dortmund. He once told me that he admired me for my "strength of character in combining love of the Fatherland with opposition to the *Barras*" (the German soldier's slightly derogatory name for the Wehrmacht). Karl was the most congenial of all circle members. He was an entirely non-military person who hated every minute of his military life. Ten years after the war I met Karl again in a city close to Dortmund. He had been mentally destroyed by the hardships of a Russian prisoner of war camp. Most shocking to me was Karl's report of his arrival from Russia at the German repatriation camp. He said he was so mentally disturbed and violent that the German authorities put him in a straightjacket and kept him there for almost a year. But now he said he had regained his mental stability and was ready to marry. A year after the wedding his wife called and told me that Karl had hanged himself.

The group of conspirators had one extraordinary member who did not belong to our company but to the aviator school. Being about three or four years older than we were, he had the rank of sergeant and was almost ready to become a bomber pilot. He completely disregarded the difference in military rank between us; in fact, he treated the whole of military etiquette with contempt. Although he had to observe some caution, it was obvious that he did not like the Nazi hierarchy, including Hitler. When I told him that I had read Chamberlain's *Foundations of the Nineteenth Century*, he laughed and said that it was not worth reading. He then recommended some other literature that I can't remember. In the summer of 1940 he was transferred to a bomber squadron, and about ten months later we received the message that he had been killed in action in the Battle of Britain.

And then there was Helmut. He did not belong to the conspirators but became a friend of mine. He was born and raised in a province of west Poland that was inhabited mainly by Germans. After Poland's defeat the Nazis annexed the province and called it Warthegau. Helmut's father had a farm there on which he employed about a dozen Polish farmhands. One of them killed the old man after Germany's defeat.

Helmut spoke fluent German, but with a Polish accent. I mention him for several reasons. One is that he and I were comrades during the four years we spent at the northern end of the German front in Finland against Russia, right at the shore of the Arctic Ocean. Another reason is that, on a visit to Helmut's parents during the war, as I relate below, I heard one more of those warning bells that always tolled for me in vain. And still another reason is that Helmut is now a neo-Nazi.

There was a certain stubbornness and clumsiness in Helmut's deportment that was heightened by his Polish accent. Because of these personality traits he had much to suffer from the sergeants and some of his comrades. I felt sorry for him and tried to protect him, particularly later when I had become a corporal. As members of the military—though perhaps not as soldiers—we were both failures. That was certainly one of the reasons why we became friends. But Helmut suffered more from military abuse than I did because he remained a private during the entire war.

We conspirators soon came to the conclusion that the only way to escape the constant abuse of the corporals was to become corporals ourselves. Thus, we volunteered once again, this time for an instruction course for future corporals. It was worse than basic training. The only objective of the instructors was to drill us, as the saying went, *bis zur Vergasung* (till we vaporized).

Once, during the noon recess, when I was tired and covered with mud from head to toe, I passed by the open window of the instructors' barrack. From the radio sounded the Romance in F by Beethoven. Time was pressing, for I had to clean up so that I could cover myself with new mud after recess. And yet, I stood motionless and listened until the last note died away, oblivious to the ugliness of my surroundings and heedless of my own misery. This was one of the most intense sensations of beauty I have ever experienced.

After returning to the company, the conspirators became corporal candidates, with the result that they now performed corporal's duties. Thus, the time of chicanery had essentially ended, with one brief exception. The conspirators were now sent to the Air War College Wildpark Werder near Potsdam.

We traveled partly by rail and partly on foot. I shall never forget the walk. It was a beautiful day in May 1940, and we were moving at a leisurely pace through an enchanting landscape dotted with villages, orchards, pine woods, and lakes. I wanted to enjoy this happy time to the fullest extent, knowing that it would end soon. But some of my comrades had something else in mind. They were constantly quarreling with Karl, who, they claimed, had caused the group to fall into disrepute because of his blatantly non-military deportment. Now he was the butt of their jokes. I was so annoyed that I broke out in a rage, whereupon Karl made the remark that he admired me. Nevertheless, it was an unforgettably beautiful day. The whole earth seemed to be in bloom, and the war with all its ugliness appeared to be miles away. And yet, it was so near. When we arrived at the war college, the misery of military life struck us with renewed fury.

The air war college was a luxurious building complex that resembled a modern resort hotel, complete with swimming pool and tennis court. But the instructors were neither luxurious nor modern. They were age-old sergeants who charged at us like a pack of dogs. The yelling and barking was indescribable. At the mess hall, where we were served by beautiful women and supervised by ugly instructors, we had to learn how to eat again. Every manipulation, every action, every bite had to be performed on command. The food had to be gulped down in a sequence of rectangular motions.

An equally ridiculous scene was the inspection by the college commander. Today, I would say that this man was an invention of Hollywood. Dressed in white from head to toe, with a bronzed face and a small waist, he gazed at us in complete silence as if we were from Mars. When one of us blinked, he silently pointed him out with his swagger stick for the instructor to take note. To blink while standing at attention was a serious offense at the war college, and it would have had unpleasant consequences if we had stayed there. But it was not to be.

On the third day of our ordeal we were summoned to sign up for the career of an active officer. This new twist took us completely by surprise. None of us had ever entertained any plans of becoming an active commissioned officer. Reserve officer, yes; active officer, no. As it turned out, the whole assignment to the air war college was a blunder by some military bureaucrat. We should never have been sent there in the first place, and now we were quickly returned to the Neuruppin air base. "Thank God in heaven!" yelled my instructor as I marched out of the sumptuous place that now reminded me of Dante's Inferno.

In June 1940 I was granted my first military leave. This meant that I now could spend one week with my parents in Dortmund. When I read the direction sign on the railroad car at Berlin's Potsdamer train station saying "Berlin, Dortmund, Köln," I thought it a message from heaven. This time the trip took only six hours. When I rang the bell at my parents' home, my father opened the door and his face lighted up with joy. But a few days later, at a family outing, he caused all of us some grief that almost ruined the last days of my leave.

It was a beautiful summer day, and everybody was happy that the campaign against France and Britain was drawing to an end. My mother, who had recently received a reassuring letter from my older brother, was particularly grateful that everything went so well. Soon the killing would end, and my brother would come home. In this elated mood the family decided to spend the afternoon at a popular garden restaurant in a beautiful water castle south of Dortmund. My younger brother and sister were still children who took pride in me and my uniform.

The garden was a large park with tall trees, water wheels, brooks, and ponds that were populated with white swans. The tranquil setting was enjoyed by about a hundred guests, who were happy with anticipation that peace was around the corner. It was a festive atmosphere. The waiters were coming and going, cake was still available on ration cards, the coffee was imitation but drinkable, and cheerful music sounded from the loudspeakers. Then came the extra bulletin that everybody was waiting for. France had surrendered, peace was at hand. People embraced each other, my mother burst out with tears of joy, and even my father's eyes were moist.

The day was still young; nobody was ready to go home, everybody wanted to enjoy this blessed afternoon. Suddenly, one of us noticed the Jewish family from the house next to the State Court where my father still posted the *Stürmer*. We didn't live there any longer, but we immediately recognized Sally with his wife and daughter. They were enjoying the day like everybody else, drinking coffee and eating cake. But my father became enraged. He summoned the waiter, pointed to Sally's table, and declared that he would not tolerate the presence of Jews in this garden. A little later we saw the waiter delivering a written note to Sally, whereupon the family hastily finished and hurried toward the exit. As they passed by our table, I saw their pale and distraught faces and suddenly felt an unfamiliar mixture of shame and compassion. The rest of the family must have had similar feelings because everybody fell suddenly silent.

The day was ruined. Nobody spoke a word. Even my father had fallen into a somber mood. Silently, we broke up and went home while all the other guests still enjoyed the beautiful afternoon. I was highly agitated and thought that my father had no right to cause Sally's family such anguish, for I saw no connection between them and the Jewish conspiracy. But I did not say a word because I knew that my father would have considered any criticism from me as a betrayal, and the ensuing bitterness between him and me would have spoiled the last days of my leave. Only my mother murmured so softly that my father could not hear it, "Poor people, what have they done?"

The incident threw me into a turmoil that lasted considerably longer than the anguish I felt when I saw the frightened Jews in Berlin's city transit. I could not forget the bewildered face of the young girl and wished I had not been so rude to her three years earlier, when I met her in the staircase of the house that had seen the worst of my anti-Semitic hatred. In my thoughts I asked her for forgiveness, but I did not tell that to my father. I don't know what I would have said or done if I had known that the murderers of the concentration camps were already planning her and her parents' deaths.

The episode taught me to distinguish between the anonymous Jewish conspiracy and individuals like Sally and his family. Unfortunately, I still believed in the alleged conspiracy; in fact, I was waiting for the full fury of international Jewry to break loose against Germany. In my view, America was the key. Knowing next to nothing about the land across the Atlantic, I still accepted the official party line, according to which this huge country was entirely in the pockets of the Jews. However, as long as it stayed neutral, the Jews were powerless. And as long as that was the case, I felt there was no need for harsh measures against defenseless individuals within our own borders. Indeed, I saw no reason to hate them.

I had no doubt that my view was also the Führer's position. Yet he was busy fighting England these days. Prime Minister Winston Churchill was the statesman he seemed to hate more than any other. The reasons were not entirely clear to me, but I knew that, among all nations, the British were the only ones Hitler admired. I surmised that he secretly wished the British to be our ally instead of the Italians, who were more of a burden than help. His secret aim, I was sure, was a world divided between Germany and England. Actually, this was my own pet idea, which I later revived as a National Socialist Leadership Officer at the Eastern front. An alliance between Germany and England, I believed, would keep the Jews in check and make another world

war unnecessary. Of course, had I read Hitler's book more carefully, I would have known that his eyes were really looking eastward and that his mind was already planning the annihilation of
millions of Jews and other nationals.

The agitation lasted until I returned to my company, where it
quickly abated under the daily pressures of military life. The turmoil had not shaken my confidence in the Führer, but it had instilled in me some doubt about my father's judgment. It seemed
to me that he did not quite understand the nature of Germany's
struggle. This war, I thought, was being fought with real weapons
against real enemies, not with bureaucratic harassment against
harmless people. Sally and his family were not the enemy. Indeed,
not all Jews were as evil as my father and the *Stürmer* magazine
portrayed them. However, the Jewish conspiracy was real. Thus,
I vacillated between faith and doubt. I longed for the truth—the
full truth.

Life at the Neuruppin air base was now a little easier for the
conspirators since we performed corporal's duties. In early 1941
I got an assignment as "commander" of a mock airfield in the
surroundings of Berlin. I supervised about a dozen men whose
job was to operate a system of landing lights that would create,
from the air, the illusion of a military airfield. The purpose was to
attract the British bombs that were meant for Berlin and the Neuruppin air base. However, instead of bombs, the British dropped
a handwritten leaflet saying in German, "You cannot make an ass
out of us." Though I reported this incident to my superiors, the
mock facility was maintained until the war with Russia changed
everything.

In May 1941 I went on my second home leave, this time for
ten days rather than a week. In the meantime, Paul had begun his
studies at the University of Bonn. From there he came for a one-
day visit to my parents' home in Dortmund. This was the last
time we saw each other, and it was another of those wake-up calls

that almost aroused me from my ideological slumbers, only to be drowned in the noise of the war and the incessant propaganda. This time the jolt to my political convictions came from Paul's report about his studies at the university. It stimulated an intense discussion that lasted the whole day, but its effect on my life lasted much longer and was almost as decisive as Theo's influence at high school. The subject was the theory of relativity by Albert Einstein. Paul's professor of physics at the University of Bonn taught the theory to his students even though it was *verboten* because Einstein was a Jew.

I knew nothing about relativity, and Paul knew only the little he had absorbed in two months of studies, but his exposition of the theory was enough to throw me into an intellectual turmoil that lasted until the war with Russia commanded all of my attention and energy. "When a slender object such as a train has a certain velocity relative to an observer standing next to the track," Paul lectured with a slightly professorial tone, "it has a different length; in fact, it is shorter than it is in the state of rest." For a moment I was speechless. After a while I said, probably with a tinge of irritation, "How can that be? Length is an intrinsic quality that has nothing to do with velocity. I can see how an object becomes shorter by compression or longer by stretching, but these are external influences; in fact, they are forces. Velocity is not an external influence or a force, but merely a state of motion of one object relative to another." Paul smiled. "There you hit the right word: *relative*. That's what the theory of relativity is all about."

At that moment I recalled what my father had said about Einstein's theory six years ago, "It's a clever attempt of stultification." With a strange blending of triumph and embarrassment, I echoed my father's dilettantish phrase and topped it off with the cheap retort, "It's rubbish." But Paul was unperturbed. "The same thing happens to clocks," he said. "What," I exclaimed, "when a clock is moving, the pointers are shortened, too?" "No," said Paul, "but they go at a slower rate." Now I was almost angry. "Great!" I mocked. "Now even time is affected by motion." "Bravo," cried Paul, "you hit the nail on the head. Time, indeed, is affected, and so is space." "Oh jeez," I cried, "if this damn wristwatch goes on a journey while I stay at home, it revolves at a slower rate." "Precisely," acceded Paul.

We debated this way until lunch. My father did not say a word, though the name of Einstein must have rung in his ears. He respected Paul's military career and even more so his superior knowledge of a subject he and I knew nothing about. He also did not want to interfere with our friendship, which may have reminded him of the camaraderie he had experienced in the First World War. My mother was fond of Paul because of a photograph that showed the two of us sitting for a studio in Neuruppin. After the war, when she learned about Paul's death in Siberia, she would hold the picture in her hand and shake her head in disbelief.

In the afternoon the family took Paul on a pleasant outing to the water castle where my father had offended Sally. The cake was already a little drier and the coffee a little thinner, but that did not dampen our spirits. Most of the time Paul and I continued our discussion about the theory of relativity while my parents listened with a mixture of awe and amusement. On the way home a train was rolling by. "See the train?" cried Paul. "It's now shorter than it was when you saw it standing in the station." "I don't see that," I retorted with slight irritation. "No, you don't, but that is only because the effect is too small," replied Paul, "and that is so because the velocity is too small. If the train were moving with 90 percent of the speed of light, its length would be reduced to half of its original length."

"Does your professor really believe that?" I asked with exasperation. "Yes." Paul nodded softly, but firmly. After a while he added wistfully, "But not *all* professors believe it." He then told me about a German physicist named Philipp Lenard, who was a Nobel laureate and the author of several renowned physics books. When Einstein still lived in Berlin, Lenard profited intellectually from him, but now he was his fiercest adversary because Einstein was a Jew. "Professor Lenard," said Paul with a disguised voice as if he were a preacher, "has made it his mission to establish a German physics that is free of Jewish pollution." Then he returned to his normal voice. "But what is German physics?" he mused. "And what is Jewish pollution?" I pondered.

After these heretical remarks we fell silent. I wished I knew more about this Jew named Einstein. Where was he now and what was he doing? I thought the idea that space and time were affected by motion was either absolute nonsense or a discovery worthy of a Newton. From Theo's physics class I recalled Newton's postulate: "Immutable space and immutable time exist in and of themselves, without reference to anything external." I always felt that this axiom was one of the deepest thoughts that ever had been conceived by man. To me, space and time were the stage on which the drama of all physical events unfolds, yet they were *not* part of the drama, for they were "immutable." This man whose name was Einstein seemed to treat space and time as if they were physical objects that could be changed and moved around. I was highly agitated. My mind worked feverishly. If this Jew were right, then . . . then . . . then space . . . to hell with space! To hell with time! Here is a Jew, who is either the greatest charlatan of all times or one of the most creative minds that mankind has produced. The Jewish conspiracy is either a satanic lie, or it is much more insidious than I ever thought. But which of these alternatives is true? What should I believe? What does the Führer say? What would Theo say? What should I believe? My God, what should I think!

When we arrived home, I noticed that Paul had started a conversation with my parents. Maybe he felt that my mind needed a rest, or perhaps he needed a respite himself. Now it was time for him to depart. I had regained my mental equilibrium and looked forward to accompanying him to the railway station, hoping to pursue the provocative subject a little further. While we were riding the streetcar, I felt a burning desire to thank him for what he had done, but I could not find the right words. "I don't know what to think," I stammered rather helplessly. Paul gave me a pat on the back. "It's the same with me," he replied, in an almost fatherly fashion. "Believe me, I sometimes don't know myself what to think. Thank God, I have my professor." He sounded quite content; however, after a pause, he added with a bitterness I had never observed in him, "Thinking needs to be learned, but *they* never allow us to learn it. They want us to be docile."

When the train pulled into the station, we embraced each other for the first and last time in our lives. Neither of us was able to say a word. But when Paul boarded the railcar, he had regained his composure and turned around. "Science is science," he said in a tone of voice that sounded like an irrevocable resolution. These were the last words he ever spoke to me. As the train disappeared in the distance, I said wistfully, "And truth is truth."

CHAPTER 9

The Arctic Ocean Front

Germans usually referred to the Soviet Union as Russland (Russia), which may have been a habit from the First World War. Nazi propaganda changed its position with regard to Russia several times. The first more or less official position was taken by Hitler himself in his book, *Mein Kampf.* I had read the book only superficially, but I did recall that the Führer pointed to the European part of the vast Eurasian empire as Germany's future Lebensraum. The word, as simple as it looks, is difficult to translate. Its literal meaning is "living space," but the concept it stands for is "territory to be conquered." I did not have the foggiest idea how he thought to realize the implied expansion, but I did remember that he dwelled on two points.

First, Hitler portrayed the October Revolution in Russia as a triumph of international Jewry. Trotsky was represented as an agent of the Jews who pulled the strings behind Lenin's and Stalin's backs. The second point was that the Bolshevists had ruined

Russia beyond repair. According to Hitler, Russia was a rotten colossus ready to collapse at the slightest push. Strangely, a single sentence, rather vacuous to boot, stuck in my memory. Talking about the decaying empire in the East and Germany's future Lebensraum, Hitler wrote: "Fate seems to give us a hint here." Today I know that he meant conquest; at the time I did not. The scraps of memory from his book led me to believe that Germany merely had to wait until harvest time in the East arrived.

In the *Jungvolk*, under Heino's direction, we sometimes intoned a somber song that began: "Do you see in the East the morning glow?" In spite of its gloomy mood and the minor key, the song always struck me as an imploring admonition. The refrain of "People, to arms!" sounded like a command. True, these ominous words could have been a warning to me, but I was too inexperienced to infer from circumstantial evidence, such as a song, the intentions of the Führer. I did not have the faintest idea that, in his vocabulary, Lebensraum meant conquest and war. Heino had a better nose. He was obsessed with Russia, Cossacks, the vast spaces, the mighty rivers, and the enormous resources. He always referred to the Russian steppe as the cradle and the future Lebensraum of the Aryan race. Once he boasted that he had read only two books in his life, *Mein Kampf* and *Volk ohne Raum* (Nation without Space). I can't recall the author of the second book, but I do remember that it caused quite some stir at the time. Today I am inclined to believe that Heino was one of the few Nazis with whom I came in contact who knew exactly what Hitler had in mind.

Sometime in late 1938 or early 1939, before the campaign against Poland, Nazi propaganda performed a U-turn. Suddenly Stalin was represented as a kind of jovial Uncle Joe, who actually tried to deliver Russia from the Jewish enslavement that was the legacy of Lenin and Trotsky. He already had banished Trotsky from Russian soil and was now conducting a series of courageous anti-Semitic "cleansing actions" to liberate his country from Jewish domination. This new drift seemed to confirm my belief that a war with Russia was neither necessary nor planned.

Thus, the attack on the Soviet Union in June 1941 took me and most other Germans completely by surprise. Only those who were directly involved in it had been prepared. Thus, Nazi propaganda had to perform a second U-turn. Now it turned out that Stalin was the worst of the Communist leaders, who was dreaming of a Pan-Slav empire extending westward to the Vistula and the Danube. In pursuing this goal he tried to blackmail Germany by demanding huge territories on the Baltic, in Poland, and in the Balkan sector. But the Führer had thwarted his megalomania by launching a preventive attack.

I was still managing the little mock airfield in the vicinity of Berlin when I heard the news of the attack on Russia on the radio. At first I could not believe it, but as the news sank in, I became devastated. I always had entertained fond dreams of a cavalier war against the Western powers that would lead to an early peace. Now this dream was shattered. Now we had a war on two fronts, a strategic situation that always had been a German nightmare. Of course, had I known that Hitler would declare war on America about six months later, I would have been even more confounded. But the current situation was bad enough. In spite of the propaganda and reports about the early military successes, there was no doubt in my mind that the war had now escalated to a serious and bloody conflict. I would soon find out how right I was.

In the fall of 1941, Helmut and I received marching orders to an undisclosed destination. We traveled to Hamburg, where we joined a group of about two dozen Luftwaffen foot soldiers. Each carried his rifle and a backpack with all of his belongings. Most were regulars, a few like Helmut were conscripts, and I was the only volunteer. The group leader was an old private, who banded with the other regulars against me because I was a corporal candidate and against Helmut because he stuck to me. In the company of these new comrades I experienced a mild repetition of the disillusionment I had suffered in the first twenty-four hours of my military service, but since I was now hardened and experienced, I was better prepared for the jolt.

We traveled by rail through occupied Denmark and from there by ship to neutral Sweden. Since the Swedes feared the Soviets even more than the Germans, they were persuaded to let us travel through southern Sweden to the Norwegian border, where we were in occupied territory again.

We spent about a week in Oslo, where we freely mingled with a population that was standoffish, but not hostile. The first day I bought a huge bag of broiled shrimp, found a picturesque place by the harbor, and enjoyed the splendid food and scenery. There also was a soldiers' home with German and Norwegian Red Cross nurses. But in the cozy atmosphere of the Norwegian capital, this comfort was hardly needed. In the following days I strolled aimlessly through the streets of the pleasant city, dined in obscure restaurants on whale and ale, and enjoyed the seemingly peaceful atmosphere. Of course, had I known about the Norwegian Underground Resistance, I would have moved around more carefully.

We had no idea what we were doing in Norway nor where we were going. Eventually, we boarded a train and traveled north to Trondheim where, to our astonishment, we were instructed to switch to a Swedish train. We first traveled east to the Swedish border, where we were briefed by a German SD officer (SD stands for *Sicherheits Dienst,* a special branch of the SS, here used for border patrol). This man told us that we were on our way through Sweden to Finland. There was an agreement, he said, between Germany and Sweden that German military units could travel through Swedish territory, provided that the troops were strictly separated from their ammunition. If any one of us still carried any ammunition, he cautioned, this was the time to surrender it.

The days were getting shorter now, and colder. The train was electrified and abundantly illuminated, and so were the train stations. But they were few and far between. At every station, nurses from the Swedish Red Cross offered us food, hot coffee, and Swedish ale. They were surprisingly friendly, but watched carefully that none of us left the train. It was a surreal atmosphere—the dark wintry night, the glaring electric lights, the almost luxurious train, the friendly Swedish women in their white costumes, and the German soldiers dazzled by this island of peace.

As the train rolled ever farther north, I saw an extraordinarily beautiful polar light (aurora borealis). Usually, the polar lights are greenish, and I saw hundreds of them in the cold winter nights at the Arctic Ocean, but this one was brilliantly red and blue. The resplendent spectacle, a comfortable train, and the Swedish hospitality heightened my spirits. For a while I was tempted to succumb to Paul's romantic dreams of a chivalrous soldier in a gallant war. It was the last time I felt this temptation.

The last Swedish town was Haparanda, at the northern end of the Gulf of Bothnia, where we crossed the border to Finland. If my memory serves me right, the Swedish train proceeded to the Finnish border town of Tornio, where we took a Finnish train to Kemi.

By northern standards, Kemi was a large town. Everything seemed to be made of wood—the houses, the churches, the skis, fuel for the locomotives, even the pavements. At a little churchyard a funeral was going on. It was a gloomy visual spectacle and an even gloomier auditory one. I believe northerners like lugubrious music in minor keys; witness Edvard Grieg and Jean Sibelius. Not that I dislike this music—to the contrary, I savor the somber atmosphere, which reflects the earnestness of the northerners without denying their hidden humor. The impression grew as I got better acquainted with Finland. I sometimes had the feeling that the whole country was in a minor key. Much later, in America, when I saw the movie *Doctor Zhivago,* I was reminded of the melancholy Finnish landscape.

Winter was around the corner and had already brought a dusting of snow to Kemi. In a few weeks, the people would no longer be able to dig a grave. As Helmut and I strolled through the town square, I was wondering about the many bicycles leaning against trees and fences, apparently without owners. Pointing them out to Helmut and counting them aloud, I expressed my puzzlement. "Where are the owners?" I cried. At that moment, a Finnish *Lotta* (female conscripts serving as nurses) approached us and asked me in fluent German why I was so perplexed. When I uttered something about thieves, she smiled and said, "There are no thieves in Kemi." She then explained that people in her country routinely left their bicycles at public places to pick them up the next day, or week. "But in Germany—." That's all I could say before she took a bicycle from a tree, smiled, waved, and pedaled off.

I also noticed that people placed silver trays in front of their house doors for bread and rolls to be delivered the next morning. Apparently the *Lotta* was right: there were no thieves in Kemi. Too bad that I could not say this of my own people—and my comrades. The "master race" could learn a lesson here. But, then, the Finnish people had a much easier life; they faced only a fraction of our enemies. No, that was not true. Just a few years ago they were fighting the mighty Soviet empire completely on their own. Their hardships were even greater than ours. So why were they so trustful and serene? And why were there so many thieves among us? I did not know the answers to these questions. I needed time to think them through. But for now, I had better watch out that none of my comrades took advantage of the enviable self-confidence of this small nation.

A few hours later we boarded a Finnish train to continue our journey to the north. This one was quite different from the Swedish trains. Old-fashioned and only sparely illuminated, it was pulled by a surprisingly small steam locomotive fueled by wood. Twenty years later, when I watched Western movies in America, I was reminded of the little Finnish locomotive groaning with exhaustion.

The first snow was falling, and the long winter night was approaching. We were travelling through a vast landscape of lakes and forests that showed almost no sign of habitation. Every hour or so the train stopped at a large woodpile to refuel. We used these opportunities to step out and conduct snowball fights. There was no danger of missing the train because it accelerated so slowly that one could run after it and still catch it. Eventually, we reached Rovaniemi, the capital of Lapland that is situated slightly north of the Arctic Circle. At the time it was the end point of the railroad.

Rovaniemi was smaller than Kemi, and much more of a frontier town. We spent several days there, mainly within the confines of a transition camp of the German army. There was a soldiers' home, but entrance was restricted because it was highly popular with German soldiers. The place of the friendly Swedish Red Cross nurses was now taken by the even friendlier Finnish *Lottas*.

Finland had been in a state of intermittent war since 1918, mostly against Soviet Russia, but sometimes against their own sympathizers with the Soviets. The bloodiest of these fights was the Winter War against Soviet Russia that began in November 1939. In the peace of 1940 Finland lost important territories that held 12 percent of the Finnish population. Thus, Finland was used to war even more than Germany. Everybody had to serve in one capacity or another, and the Finnish *Lottas* had a reputation of exemplary service to their country.

Rovaniemi was also the headquarters of the 20th Mountain Army under the command of Colonel General Eduard Dietl, the conqueror of Narvik. The mountaineers, whom I would join a year later, were the famous Edelweiss troops who had distinguished themselves in the campaigns in Norway and Crete. Now they were defending north Finland against vastly superior Russian forces. General Dietl was one of the most popular war heroes in Germany, but he would soon fall out of favor with the Führer. While reporting to Hitler at his Führer headquarters, General Dietl apparently suggested that Hitler seek peace with the Western Allies. When he left headquarters by air, his plane exploded shortly after take-off. The story is reminiscent of the fate of other German leaders such as Dr. Fritz Todt and Field Marshal Erwin Rommel. Of course, I got this information only *after* the war.

The Finnish front against Russia consisted of two sections, one for the German forces and one for the Finnish forces. The German section from Rovaniemi north to the Arctic Ocean was the responsibility of the 20th Mountain Army, and the section from Rovaniemi south to Leningrad was manned by the Finnish army. The German part was called *Die Eismeer Front* (The Arctic Ocean front). Its backbone was the *Eismeer Strasse* (Arctic Ocean Road). This dirt road, which had been upgraded by the Germans, extended 550 kilometers from Rovaniemi to the Arctic Ocean. Since almost all of the logistics for the divisions of the 20th Army had to travel along the Arctic Ocean Road, this artery was a constant concern of German commanders. The most vigilant of these leaders was General Ferdinand Schörner, conqueror of Crete and now Commanding General of the 19th Mountain Army Corps at the extreme north of the Arctic Ocean front.

Schörner was a legend not only among the German soldiers, but the Russians as well. A brave soldier and a fanatical Nazi, he had a reputation for ruthlessness that showed itself in his methods of protecting the Arctic Ocean Road. The hundreds of trucks that used the road strained it almost beyond capacity. When one truck was following another, their tire tracks had to be offset from each other so that the road would not be hollowed. The penalties for disregarding this order were harsh, and the rumor was that Schörner court-martialed and executed violators on the spot. I saw graves with crosses along the road, but I am not sure whether the men buried there were victims of Schörner's alleged kangaroo courts.

In 1943 Hitler called Schörner to the Baltic section of the Eastern front and soon thereafter promoted him to Field Marshal. As Commander of the Army Group Center, Schörner defended Silesia and the city of Breslau. His attempts to save as many people as possible from the Russians were sincere and laudable. There is no question that he was a brave and able soldier, but there were also some indications that he caused unnecessary losses by blindly following Hitler's irrational orders. He reigned with an iron fist and, in the last months of the war, gave the order that any soldier who was found without written orders behind the front line would be hanged on the spot. Small wonder that he was the Führer's favorite troop commander. One of the few Nazis among the field marshals, he was unpopular with the other generals, but not always with his own troops.

After Hitler had committed suicide and Germany had surrendered, Schörner tried to save his army group and part of the civilian population from the Russians by fighting his way to the west. He surrendered to the Americans, but was returned to the Russians. He then spent several years in Russian captivity, but apparently was treated relatively well because Stalin wanted him to organize the newly created East German army. But Schörner declined and was released several years later. After his return to Germany, he was court-martialed by the West German army for war crimes and found guilty on several counts. A little later he died.

I met Schörner once at the Arctic Ocean front and shook hands with him. He was followed by two *Kettenhunde* ("chain dogs").

This was the nickname for the military police, who were characterized by large badges hanging on chains from their necks. Since they were also quite unpopular, the soldiers referred to them by this unflattering name. I felt intimidated by the stern general and the military police. Though the meeting lasted only a few minutes, I had the uneasy feeling that I would have to fear this man if I saw more of him. Under the circumstances, however, I was awed.

Forty years later, long after I had moved to America, Helmut sent me a biography of Schörner from the library of the neo-Nazis. It presented the late field marshal in glowing terms and attempted to belittle the serious charges against him. Nevertheless, the belated reports from the epic struggle in the cold and dark of the Arctic winter were an emotional experience to me.

The Finnish leader was Field Marshal Baron Carl Gustav Emil Mannerheim, who had served already under the last czar when Finland was part of Russia. Having distinguished himself in the heroic Winter War of 1939, Mannerheim was highly regarded by German soldiers of the Arctic Ocean front. He also was Hitler's favorite ally—until he negotiated the Finnish surrender in September 1944. Since he was of Swedish nobility, the Nazi propaganda was happy to have no problem with his Aryan pedigree.

The Finnish language posed a more difficult problem, since it does not belong to the Indo-Germanic, but to the Finno-Ugrian languages, a fact that the Nazi propaganda played down. The complete integration of Finland's Jewish population into Finnish society was another feature of the Nordic people the Nazi propaganda withheld from us. Today I believe it reflects high credit on this brave nation that the murderers of the concentration camps could never lay their hands on Finnish Jews.

After a week in Rovaniemi we continued our journey by truck on the Arctic Ocean Road. At first there were seemingly endless pine forests; eventually, however, the trees became scarcer as we were approaching the northern tree line. And always snow, and more snow. It also got colder, and we became alarmed that we were ill-equipped for this climate. First we went to Kirkenes in northern Norway, where I saw the Arctic Ocean (Barents Sea) for the first time. The water, though pristine, was green because of light conditions. One year later, when I was on patrol along a cliff high above the ocean, I observed a school of whales travelling in an undulating motion through the icy water, which, to my surprise, had changed its color to a Mediterranean azure.

From Kirkenes we traveled east, always by truck, to the Petsamo air base in northern Finland, which was situated some thirty kilometers behind the front line and about an equal distance from the ocean. The name Petsamo (Pechenga in Russian) denotes a district rather than a town. An area of the size of greater Los Angeles, it counted only a few hundred inhabitants. The harbor, Liinahamari (Linkhamari), was primitive, yet boasted a hotel. Occasionally, a German supply ship would arrive there, but most of the time the sea-lane was interdicted by the British navy.

Petsamo was Finland's only access to the Arctic Ocean. The harbor does not freeze in the winter because it is heated by the Gulf Stream, which brings warm water from the Gulf of Mexico. The Russian harbor of Murmansk benefits from the same natural heating system, whereas the harbor of Archangel, though considerably farther south, is frozen half of the year because of its remoteness from the Gulf Stream.

After Finland's capitulation, Russia annexed the Petsamo area, thus depriving the brave nation of a harbor which, today, would be of even greater value than in the past. Under the Soviets, the whole area was a strategically sensitive air, missile, and submarine base. Today it is still difficult to gain access to the area. Helmut tried it in 1996 and was deterred by the exorbitantly high entrance fee. He traveled all the way through Norway and Finland, enjoyed the hospitality of the two nations, and took part in the festivities of the summer solstice.

I never went back to the old places. I would have liked to revisit the former battlefields and see the Murmansk that we had besieged for so long. I still remember standing high on a cliff, looking down at the green Arctic Ocean, little knowing at the time that, almost half a century later, my youngest son, Julius, would cruise the waters in an American submarine and come closer to Murmansk than I ever did.

The Petsamo air base was a fighter and bomber base. The mission of the bombers was mainly to intercept the convoys that brought supplies from America to Murmansk. The German navy had installed artillery along the short coastline of the Petsamo area, the only heavy artillery the German troops in the north ever had. When a convoy arrived bound for Murmansk, we could infer it from the artillery fire of both sides. The German guns aimed at the ships at sea, and the Russian guns were trained at ours. It was an uneven contest because the Russian artillery, being of larger caliber, was out of reach of the German artillery.

Murmansk played a decisive role in World War II. When the German armies advanced eastward, on a front extending from Leningrad to the Black Sea, they deprived Russia of much of its industry and supplies. However, through its northernmost harbor, Russia received an almost endless supply of weapons and material from America. Preventing these supplies from reaching their destination was one of the missions of the German land, air, and sea forces in northern Finland. But the primary mission was something else.

There was nickel in northern Finland. The mine was in Kolosjoki (now Nikel, Russia). Hitler, whose military instinct sometimes served him well, already had his eyes on the Finnish mineral resources before he invaded Russia. That was one of the reasons why he occupied Norway all the way up to Narvik. It was not a temporary expedient, but an integral step of his grandiose plan to conquer the Lebensraum that would provide, aside from arable land, raw materials such as oil and minerals. The nickel ore would travel from Kolosjoki through Sweden to Narvik, from where it could reach Germany either by land or by sea. The security of the nickel supply was the primary mission of the 20th Mountain Army.

Life at the Petsamo air base was hard, but incomparably easier than the life of the mountaineers at the front. At least we had heated barracks and petroleum lamps. We also had better winter clothes. There was even a limited supply of fur coats and felt boots for those who were momentarily exposed to the extreme cold. The mountaineers had none of this, not even in 1943 when I joined them. But I did not know this at the time and naively enjoyed the preferential treatment, which we owed to Reichsmarshall Göring, commander of the Luftwaffe.

The base commander was a major who had spent several years in Finland and was fluent in the language. After a few weeks, he detailed me to assist the sergeant who ran the air base command. This makeshift office was housed in a shabby barrack that was buried in the snow to keep it warm. It was equipped with a telephone, a stove, a kerosene lamp, a supply of firewood, and a huge dog. I volunteered to spend the night in this haphazard building to man the telephone. My only companion was the dog, who slept on top of me to keep me warm and to ward the lemmings off my face. In the morning he left me to seek food from the *Lottas* who operated the base kitchen, and in the evening he returned to me to seek shelter.

Christmas was approaching. The reports from the front were worrisome, but not nearly as alarming as the situation really was. It was an unusually cold winter, even by Russian standards, and the German army was ill-equipped for this merciless climate, since Hitler had promised his generals at the beginning of the war that it would be over before the onslaught of the Russian winter. Everything was inadequate: food, clothes, ammunition, equipment, fuel, and anti-freeze for the tanks. Even machine guns were inoperable in the extreme cold. Steel was as brittle as glass. A man's eyes, if not protected, would freeze within minutes. The Winter Battle in the East was raging. I believe this term was Hitler's own invention. In the following years, he would brag to his generals that only his iron will had prevented the total collapse of the Eastern front during the winter of 1941–42, and most of them agreed. A medal was awarded to all who partook in the brutal battle.

I had a little radio that was tuned to the *Sender Finmark,* the broadcasting station of the German army in Finland. Finmark is the northern province of Norway. A few days before Christmas, an extra bulletin was aired informing the soldiers of the Arctic Ocean front that Germany was now at war with America. I do not recall any mention of the Japanese attack on Pearl Harbor—I certainly would not have known the place—but I do remember that the name of President Roosevelt rang a bell with me. It reminded me of a speech by Hitler in 1938, in which he ridiculed the American president for asking guarantees for the independence and territorial integrity of countries such as Poland, Czechoslovakia, Denmark, and Norway. Hitler delivered the speech to the *Reichstag,* and we listened to it at school. It was one of his most effective propaganda tricks. He cunningly read each name from the long list of countries the American president had sent him, and the *Reichstag* obligingly acknowledged each name with loud laughter.

Of course, that speech was not mentioned in the extra bulletin, nor was the full name of Franklin Delano Roosevelt. It was not even clear who had declared war on whom. Instead, the "political analysis" that followed stressed the point that the Führer had "forestalled" the sinister plans of American Jews, and that Roosevelt was their agent and front man. Everything was expressed in the jargon of Nazi propaganda and explained in terms of the Jewish conspiracy.

I had neither the leisure nor the mental ability to perform the political analysis myself, but I was fully aware of the military implications. Now my worst fears had come true: Germany was encircled by the three greatest powers on earth. They commanded the resources of huge secondary countries such as China, India, Australia, and Canada. I considered it a masterstroke of the international conspiracy, which now turned out to be as real and infinitely more dangerous than the *Stürmer* had warned us. Why did "they" hate us so much? I had long ceased hating collectively and anonymously. I hated only the war, nothing else. Mercifully, the daily life of the soldier did not grant me much time and leisure to ponder these ominous developments.

Then came Christmas. Some of us had to stand watch at the harbor, where a ship with supplies had arrived; others had to guard the truck convoys that took off from there. I was fortunate enough to spend Christmas night on my solitary telephone post at the base command, where I listened to a radio report on "Christmas on the Eastern Front." The report sampled several army outposts, some buried in snow, some close to enemy lines. At one regiment, the soldiers hosted a party leader whose voice sounded familiar to me. It was Baldur von Schirach, leader of the Hitler Youth, who had composed the bombastic youth hymn we had sung in the *Jungvolk*. He was not the worst of the Nazis by far. At least he had the shadow of a soul that enabled him to hit the magic Christmas mood. This night he sounded like a crafty clergyman comforting a congregation in distress. But he did not comfort me; he only filled me with a burning desire for peace. The emotional effect of the nostalgic speech was amplified by the Christmas carols sung by the rough voices of the soldiers. There were also voices from home. Children were singing, church bells were ringing, and women were sending their love.

When it ended, I was so overcome with emotion that I grabbed my blanket and ran outside into the icy winter night. This was a risky undertaking since a few minutes of exposure at fifty degrees centigrade below freezing can be fatal. I suppose I was looking for some sign, some answer to my solitary quest for peace. Shivering in the merciless cold, I looked up to the stars that were as big as giants' eyes. A polar light ghosted with unearthly speed over the motionless celestial background. It was a dazzling symphony of silence—but no answer to my worried question.

The base commander was fairly well educated and socially skilled. I had the feeling that there was a certain rapport between him and me, and I hoped that he would promote me to corporal, particularly since I was already a corporal candidate. But I was disappointed. The merry major used his skills and fluency in the Finnish language mainly to socialize with the *Lottas*. On my telephone post I had to connect him with the ladies, who seemed to pursue him with as much ardor as he chased them. Though I did not understand a word of the conversation, I understood enough to envy the Bon Vivant of Petsamo. Meanwhile, the expansion of the air base, as ordered by the German air command in Oslo, was neglected.

Soon the all-too-sociable major was replaced by another major who was almost the exact opposite. A native of Hungary and fluent in the language, he was rough and unmannered, but quite effective. Under his leadership the air base grew quickly and produced ever more bomber and fighter sorties. His pet project was the replacement of the shabby barrack, which housed the command headquarters, by a new barrack that was extravagantly spacious in comparison. He brought with him a woman from Austria—I presume she was his mistress—who had a certain predilection for intrigues and presumption of authority. Conflict between me and the power-hungry lady was inevitable. But, in spite of the disputes I had with her, the major soon promoted me to corporal and put me in command of the new headquarters.

There was another woman who played quite a mysterious role at the air base. A stunning blonde from Sweden, she was assigned to the base command as an interpreter. Though she had no security clearance, she liked to look over my shoulder, showing a conspicuous interest in the secret telegrams from higher headquarters. She also frequented the officers' barracks, an activity that got her in trouble with the Austrian mistress. I was anxious to see the outcome of the burgeoning struggle between the two valkyries, but I missed it because of my upcoming leave. When I returned, the Swedish woman was gone. The rumor was that she had been executed for espionage.

My long-awaited leave occurred in the summer of 1942. I was fortunate to find a seat on a Junkers Ju 52 cargo plane, which flew first from Petsamo to Pori in southern Finland. From there it was scheduled to fly to Königsberg, East Prussia, now Kaliningrad, Russia. But over the Gulf of Finland, only a few miles from Leningrad, the aircraft was attacked by Russian fighter planes and hit in one fuel tank, which caused it to lose fuel. The next airfield was Reval (Tallinin), the capital of Estonia, and that's where we then headed for an emergency landing. In the meantime, the fumes from the damaged fuel tank came into the cabin and made all of us violently sick. There was no other remedy than holding one's head out of the window, hoping that altitude, air speed, and temperature would cooperate, which they did. A few minutes later we landed safely.

In Reval I boarded another Ju 52 that took me to Königsberg, which was a pleasant city with a rich historical past. I thought of Immanuel Kant, who had spent his entire life there without ever setting foot in any other larger city. I then took an express train to Posen (Polish Poznan), the capital of the western province of Poland the Nazis had annexed in 1939. There I boarded a commuter train to a nearby village, where the farm of Helmut's parents was located. Helmut wanted me to visit his parents, and I obliged, not entirely without selfish interest, for I was hoping to get some food for my parents, who were starving.

The commuter train was used by Polish farm workers who were on their way to the various farms that were all in German hands. In this train I had another encounter with Nazi arrogance. Though Germans and Poles were strictly segregated, I couldn't help noticing that I was surrounded by Poles. But I didn't mind. Their demeanor had an almost Mediterranean flavor, merry and noisy. And while they laughed and chatted, they lured ever more kinsmen into the cabin so that it became quite crowded. Some carried produce, others small animals. It was a carnival atmosphere, and I was quite animated, even though I could not take my thoughts off my parents, who already suffered from food shortages and Allied bombing raids. I was just happy to see happy faces. When the cheerful people noticed that I enjoyed their hustle and bustle, they even smiled at me.

Alas, the fun would not last long. At one train stop, a government functionary in uniform entered the cabin, and the laughing and babbling ended abruptly. In the typical manner of the master race, the fatuous hireling chased the harmless people from the cabin as if they were animals. He then tried to reproach me for having tolerated a transgression by his subjects. But I cut him short and told him that I had better things to do than enforcing rules in which I did not believe. The answer left him speechless. Silently we sat facing one another in the empty cabin, until the train arrived at Helmut's village, where his father picked me up in a horse-drawn carriage.

The parents were warm and decent people, who treated me like a king. Only when I mentioned the story of the commuter train did they become temporarily uncommunicative. When I departed the next day, they loaded me with so much food that I could hardly carry it, particularly the freshly slaughtered duck, which I had to hide from hungry onlookers, Poles as well as Germans. I would never see the old man again, but the mother I met once more after the war, together with Helmut, in West Germany. While Helmut had become an incorrigible neo-Nazi, his mother had turned into an unbearably sanctimonious religious sectarian.

The train ride was relatively uneventful. In Berlin I had to switch trains, but I was in no mood to see the imposing buildings that were still being erected on Hitler's orders. So I went to the Zoological Garden next to the railway station. It was a pleasant summer Sunday, enjoyed by a large crowd. Two years later, the whole area would be rubble. As I was watching the lions, I noticed a procession of women dressed in rustic garments and wearing scarves, who were chatting in a foreign language. It was clear to me that they were alien laborers in the armament industry, but not that they were forced laborers. Since my eyes were not trained for such things, I noticed neither signs of starvation nor any other distress.

An hour later I boarded a military express train to the west, which was so crowded that I hardly could get in. The closer the train approached the industrial Ruhr district, the more damage from the bombing raids became noticeable. The railroad station of Dortmund was quite damaged, but still functioning, and so was the city. This was the last time I was able to ride the streetcar. On my next leave, I would climb over smoldering rubble.

My parents were so touched that neither was able to say a word. I was shocked at how emaciated they looked. But, when I spread out all the food from Helmut's parents, our spirits lifted. The next day I picked up my ration cards and the Führer Package, which was Hitler's gift to the front soldiers on home leave. It contained a canister of sunflower oil, some flour, sugar, and other delicacies he had pilfered from occupied Ukraine.

German morale was still high. Most people stuck to their belief that Germany would win the war, my father and I included. The

Goebbels propaganda encouraged that belief by leaking rumors of miracle weapons, which the Führer was holding in reserve to be used at the right moment. I fervently hoped so, because my faith had been shaken ever since Hitler had declared war on America. I could not help seeing a disturbing element of emotional rashness in that decision, and I was desperately looking for some explanation that would make it appear more rational. In this predicament, the tales of the miracle weapons came in handy. When the last battle was fought, I persuaded myself, it would turn out that the Führer knew all along what he was doing.

The only casualty was the doctrine of the Jewish conspiracy. To me, though not to my father, this bogeyman had gradually lost some of its terror. If the American Jews really wanted this war, they could have started it much earlier; they certainly didn't have to wait until Hitler did it for them. No, this was an old-fashioned power struggle. Stalin had tried to expand his empire to the west, and the Führer was now using the opportunity to conquer the Lebensraum he wrote about in his book. My father did not deny the Lebensraum theory, but he still thought that the primary force behind this war was the Jewish conspiracy. He still traveled once a week to the other end of town to post the latest issue of the *Stürmer* at the fence of the State Court, an activity that I now considered a tilt at windmills. But I did not tell him that. In fact, we no longer talked as much about the Jews as we did before the war, because our minds were now occupied with more pressing problems such as food, the bombing raids, and the huge numbers of men killed in action.

My mother told me that she would stand by the window every morning and watch the local party leader visiting families in the neighborhood to bring them the sad news that their son had been killed in action, and every morning she prayed that he would not come to her. Once he did come to our house, but he skipped the lower story where we lived and went up the stairs. Minutes later there was inconsolable crying. Freddie, whom we knew well, had been killed.

By sheer coincidence, my older brother also came home on leave at this time, so we had a few days together. He was with an army division that, at one time during the Russian campaign, reached the Caspian Sea almost 500 kilometers east of Stalingrad. Fortunately, he did not belong to the Sixth Army that was annihilated in the battle of Stalingrad. My younger brother, who still attended high school, served as an anti-aircraft gunner. Instruction took place at the outskirts of the city next to the cannons. The teachers, mostly older men, traveled on bicycle from one cannon site to the next. My sister, who was the youngest, had been evacuated with her school to a resort hotel in the Carpathian Mountains of Czechoslovakia.

Almost every night, the sirens sounded, and we had to descend into the cellar, which had been converted into an air raid shelter. There we heard gruesome tales about the raids, some so graphic that they made us sick. Today I wonder why, in this macabre environment, the even more horrible events of the concentration camps were never mentioned. I ask myself whether anybody knew about them at the time. I am virtually certain that my mother did not know because she would have told me so after the war, when we discussed the ever-growing evidence of the events that were later called the Holocaust. My father had more opportunity to know because of his professional activities, but, even after the war, he denied the atrocities of the concentration camps.

Since my father had a talent for drawing and painting, he had decorated the shelter with caricatures, which were supposed to boost morale. Interestingly, his ridicule was directed almost exclusively against Churchill. I believe this was a reflection of the well-known fact that nobody aroused Hitler's ire more than the British leader. On the radio the Goebbels propaganda flooded us with tales about Churchill's lies and crimes, accompanied by mock songs about the "Lord of lies from the sea piracy." Even before the war, Hitler referred to Churchill as "the notorious drinker." Now the dogged warrior with the cigar graced the walls of our air raid shelter. To my great relief, there were none of the ugly anti-Semitic caricatures from the *Stürmer*.

In spite of his war injuries, my father was house warden for air raid protection, which gave him police power and made him responsible for the whole house from top to bottom. When the bombs were falling, he climbed the stairs to watch under the roof for incendiary bombs. At the same time, he was responsible for the blackout, the water reserves under the roof and in the shelter, medical equipment, gas masks, and emergency equipment. Though these duties were almost beyond his physical capacity, I think they helped him psychologically by diverting his attention from his anti-Semitic hatred to the needs of the moment.

My mother was in more dire straits. The worry about her three sons, the acute food shortages, the blackout, the nights in the bomb shelter, and the grisly tales of people burnt or buried alive had taken their toll. As the day of my farewell was approaching, she put all her love in a cake she wanted me to take along. I knew that it depleted her last food reserves, and when I later un-wrapped it somewhere in Finland, I was so choked with emotion that I could hardly swallow it.

Farewell was sad. On our way to the railway station my father carried my rifle. The last minutes of waiting for the train were the worst. I still recall the announcer's voice, *Achtung, Achtung.* Pull-ing in is express train for front soldiers. *Maastricht, Köln, Berlin, Königsberg, Bialystok.* It was a military express train for front sol-diers that traversed half of Europe. Pulled by two huge locomo-tives and pushed by two more, it was so long that it did not fit into the station. When it finally came to a stop, the first two loco-motives had disappeared in the distance, and the last two were not yet in sight. It was so crowded that there was no chance of finding even standing room somewhere in the middle section. Thus, we rushed toward the front end, I in front, followed by my mother and then my father, who carried the rifle and watched my half-blind mother. We climbed over tracks and ties, desperately trying to find a door I could enter. I had to get in at all cost. If I missed that train, the penalty would be harsh.

My mother fell and my father had to help her up. Then he hobbled after me because he was still carrying the rifle. My mother could no longer follow and stood under the window of a first-class car, which was reserved for officers. From there I heard her imploring voice, "My God! Gentlemen, please make room for my son. He is fighting for the Führer as well as you do." Now the stationmaster arrived and tried to open a door for me, but the passengers inside desperately kept it shut.

The military station commander was called, who arrived on crutches. A highly decorated officer with only one leg, he appealed to the passengers' sense of camaraderie. That helped. To my relief the stationmaster was able to open a door. Half laughing, half swearing, the two men pushed me in and closed the door behind me before my father could hand me the rifle. In the last minute, as the train already started to pull out, he handed the weapon through a window from where it found its way to me four hours later when the train stopped in Berlin. Squeezed, but relieved to have found a place on the train, I could put only one foot on the floor, which prevented me from turning around to get a last glimpse of my parents. Instead of seeing their dear faces, I stared through the opposite window at a huge poster: *"Führer befiel, wir folgen:* Führer, give the order; we follow."

The author's paternal grandfather, Karl Manz, around 1890. Director of a coal mine in the town of Schaffhausen near the French border, he is wearing his director's uniform with medals from his military service earned during the Franco-Prussian War. He was a stern man who handed down to his son his contempt for the French and the Jews.

The author's father, Albrecht Manz, as a German soldier in 1914. He was seriously wounded by a grenade in the early months of World War I. Like many who joined the Nazi Party, he blamed an "international Jewish conspiracy" for Germany's problems during the interwar years.

The author's mother, Erna Manz, in 1917. Mrs. Manz was a quiet and proper woman who did not share her husband's bitter hatred for the Jews.

The author (in his mother's lap) with his parents and older brother, Gunther, in 1926.

The author (second from the right) and his older brother (fourth from the right) playing cowboys and Indians with neighborhood friends, 1928.

The author's father in 1930.

The author (left) and his friend Paul (right) as soldiers, 1940. After failing to pass the Luftwaffe's pilot examination, the author remained in the Luftwaffe as an air base guard until he joined the army in early 1943.

The author (second from right) and his friend Karl (right) with fellow soldiers at Neuruppin Air Base, north of Berlin, 1940.

The author on the Baltic coast of Germany in 1940. This photo was taken near the camp where he attended a training course for corporals.

Bruno Manz in his corporal's uniform, 1942.

The author (right) and his older brother (left) on military leave with their father and sister, Jutta, in Dortmund, 1942.

The author and his bride, Renate, in Darmstadt, 1953.

Renate and their first son, Matthias, 1955.

The author as an assistant professor at Technical University in Aachen, 1955. Two years later, he immigrated to the United States as part of Project Paperclip.

The Manz children in White Sands, New Mexico, in 1966 near where the author worked for the Air Force Missile Development Center at Holloman Air Force Base.

Bruno Manz in 1988.

CHAPTER 10

"Do You Want Total War?"

In January 1943 a top secret telegram from Reichsmarshall Göring arrived at the Petsamo air base. I was the first to read it: "The Führer has ordered the establishment of ninety air force field brigades." That was serious; that meant me!

It was a fallout from Stalingrad. The savage battle at the Volga was just drawing to its bitter end, leading inexorably to the annihilation of the Sixth Army. Close to a quarter of a million men were either dead, wounded and lucky to be evacuated, or on their way to Siberia.

The fiasco at Stalingrad was my greatest shock during the Nazi era, except for the total defeat of 1945 and the devastating truth about the concentration camps. Of course, the official bulletin from Führer headquarters put the best face on the defeat. In a desperate attempt to boost morale, it closed with the pathetic phrase, "However, at this very hour the divisions of the Sixth Army are already in the process of being reestablished." Though

I could not help noticing the uneasiness of the High Command hiding behind that stupid phrase, I was relieved that the military leaders—as I understood it—had finally awakened from their slumbers. Ill-informed as I was, I laid the blame for the disaster of Stalingrad at the generals' feet, rather than Hitler's. I fervently hoped that the defeat would whip them into shape and prompt them to support the Führer wholeheartedly in his titanic struggle against the "heirs of Genghis Khan." It still escaped me that this was not Stalin's war, but Hitler's. Indeed, the fact that the fiasco at Stalingrad was his fault alone was carefully hidden from the German people.

But this was no time for fault-finding; this was time for action and sacrifice. I was ready. Though I hated the military with all my heart, I was willing to do my share to fill the army's depleted ranks. I knew I would be called very soon, but in my heart I had already volunteered at this crucial hour. It was the second and last time that I did this.

On my radio I listened to a rally in Berlin's renowned sports arena, where Goebbels delivered a powerful speech to an assorted crowd of wounded soldiers, nurses, Hitler Youths, women, and some older factory workers who could be spared for a few hours. This was the speech of his life that earned him even the Führer's praise. Screaming at the top of his voice, he closed each sentence with the devious question, "Do you want total war?," which his war-weary listeners always answered with a desperate "yes." It was a masterstroke of propaganda that mobilized the last reserves of a nation on the verge of exhaustion. From everywhere within the German war machinery, from the armaments industry and agriculture to universities and the Luftwaffe, the last able-bodied men flocked to the army to fill the ranks of the divisions that were slowly bleeding to death.

Göring's telegram was followed by a flood of special instructions. Fifty men immediately had to be sent to Kirkenes for training by battle-hardened instructors from the mountaineers. A week later another fifty were to go, then another, until the last able-bodied foot soldier of the Petsamo air base had joined the mountaineers. Helmut was among the first to go because he had aroused the commander's ire by putting a bunk bed in the underground command center. I was among the last.

The commander, a lieutenant colonel, did not want to let me go, but I knew that my time had come. I certainly did not want to spend this critical phase of the war in relative safety and comfort. I was ready to lay my life on the line. With the commander's concurrence, I was already training my replacement, a sixty-year-old man from the *Organisation Todt,* the equivalent of the American Corps of Engineers, who was hard of hearing and short of military skills. Wherever I looked I saw personnel shortages. There were not enough men for loading bombs, standing watch, defending against air attacks, and guarding against Russian commandos operating behind the lines. The commander sent urgent telegrams to higher headquarters in Oslo, pleading for an exemption from the relentless requisition of his last able-bodied soldiers, but to no avail.

At the end of February 1943 I received my marching orders. The commander decorated me with the Cross for Distinguished War Service Second Class. Then it was time for me to go. In total darkness I climbed on a truck that took me to the Kirkenes air base. The newly established Luftwaffen field brigade for the Arctic Ocean front had a training camp there for one of its companies. I met a few friends from Petsamo, though not Helmut. He had joined another company somewhere else.

Now I was a Landser, as the German infantrymen called themselves. I suppose the expression stems from *Landsknecht,* which was the German name for mercenaries in the Middle Ages. The conventional translation is "lansquenet," and the literal interpretation is "land serf." For the German soldier, the word "Landser" had a nostalgic ring, which reverberated through many songs such as "What in the world can the Landser dream of? He dreams of his sweetheart." As much as I hated to be a soldier, at this moment I was not proud but content to be a Landser, fully aware that the hardest time of the war had begun.

Immediately upon arrival I was ordered to report to the first lieutenant from the mountain troops who was in charge of training. From the very beginning there was a mutual, instinctive mistrust between us that reminded me of my strained relation with Heino, the former *Jungvolk* leader. I also felt a similar fear, a kind of unspecific angst, though on a minor scale. Since I was now more mature and experienced, I could cope with such fear better than in my childhood.

Good-looking, arrogant, decorated, and vain, the lieutenant was a fanatic soldier and an exacting superior. As had been Heino's aspiration, his ambition was to forge us into competent fighters. Ironically, that was exactly what I had in mind; indeed, both of us were there for the same reason. The only difference was that I considered fighting and bravery a means to an end, whereas he saw them as values in themselves. He resented my pensiveness and slightly unsoldierly composure, and I his arrogance and insensitivity.

Training was extremely hard and sometimes brought us close to the breaking point. In stark contrast to the useless parade drill we had received at the beginning of the war, this training was strictly no-nonsense, designed exclusively to teach us fighting skills. Part of it was on foot, part on skis. A classic infantry attack cannot be carried out on skis but must be performed on foot, since it alternates between lying on the ground or in the snow and jumping ahead. On the other hand, activities such as reconnaissance and hauling supplies were performed on skis.

We wore hooded white winter suits over our ordinary army uniform. In almost any climate this outfit would have kept us warm, but in this murderously cold weather nothing was warm enough. We always carried our backpacks with all our belongings plus ammunition. This made us so heavy that sometimes we sank up to our arms in the snow.

The most severe test was a five-day maneuver carried out on foot. It alternated between long marches and special exercises, such as reconnaissance, attacking, escaping an ambush, and—most dreadful—setting up camp. We did not have the splendid tents of today, but triangular tarpaulins that had to be buttoned together to form a tent. In the extreme cold and darkness of the Arctic winter, handling the aluminum buttons was an almost impossible task that everybody tried to avoid. I saw men crying while doing this job. Digging holes in the snow and filling them with brushwood was a picnic in comparison. When a tent was finished, it was a covered hole in the snow, in which one could freeze to death, but not sleep.

Fire and lights were not allowed during the entire exercise. The whole situation had to be as realistic as possible, which meant, among other things, complete darkness and merciless exposure to the environment. The instructors from the mountain troops had gone through similar tribulations while facing the enemy, so they saw no reason to save us from any hardship they had endured. Huddled together in our tents, we anxiously waited for the morning, which brought neither light nor warmth, but at least some relief from the extra freezing caused by immobility.

On the march back to barracks it became obvious that the lieutenant, who conducted the affair on skis, had overestimated our endurance and underestimated the elements. Already close to exhaustion, we were caught in a snowstorm that almost buried us. The company broke up into ever smaller groups that desperately fought their way back to the camp. Fortunately, they all made it, but some only after long delays and with severe frostbite. The lieutenant, who could have been court-martialed if there had been fatalities, anxiously awaited the arrival of each group. My group was one of the first to arrive. Yet, when I reported the men under my command safe and sound, he dismissed me with his usual disdain.

Fortunately, we soon got rid of this unpleasant specimen of an officer. It happened when the whole battalion was assembled for its first assignment, at which time ordinary commanders were installed on all levels. The new battalion commander, a captain, would play an important role in my future life, until the very end of the war. At our first encounter he scolded me for a lax salute. A mountaineer and a native of Bavaria, he tried to be as severe and demanding as the lieutenant who had just departed, but he was not as convincing. Though he later earned himself the Knight's Cross and a promotion to major, I had the impression that he felt insecure and that his lack of self-assurance was the prime reason why he barked so much. After Germany had surrendered, he made the telling remark, "Now I have to sell shoe laces again."

As corporal, I was the leader of a group of fifteen men. Twelve of them carried rifles, three operated a machine gun, and I carried a submachine gun. Our main duty was to guard a huge power station near Kolosjoki, which provided the electricity for processing the nickel ore. The corps of engineers was encasing the vital parts of the plant in concrete to protect it from air attacks. Since they were working day and night, the construction site was brilliantly illuminated, in spite of potential air attacks.

Our second duty was performing reconnaissance runs along the power line that was subject to sabotage by Russian commandos. Since the front was not a continuous line, but a chain of strongpoints separated by long stretches of tundra, it was frequently penetrated by commandos from both sides. They sometimes operated up to thirty kilometers behind enemy lines.

Because there was snow on the ground most of the time, the

reconnaissance runs were mostly performed on skis. There was always the danger of running into an ambush, a contingency for which we were especially trained. At the command "Richard" a reconnaissance column would swing out in a row to the right and try to fall into the back of the attacker. At the command "Ludwig" the same move would be carried out to the left. There were other maneuvers for all sorts of situations that sometimes saved us casualties. At one such occasion I gave the "Richard" command, but only with limited success. We avoided casualties but were unable to inflict any on the enemy.

There were also mines. The Russians knew our paths and mined them, as we did theirs. In spite of all warnings and precautions, we soon had our first casualties. We were looking for mines under the snow, but the Russians had just invented a new booby trap that hung in the brush. One such contraption maimed the faces of three of my men beyond recognition. One did not survive his cruel evacuation on makeshift sleds.

In the summer of 1943 my group of fifteen was assigned to Fort Romanoff, a promontory at the Arctic coast between Petsamo and the Fischer peninsula. Our mission was to provide infantry protection to the naval artillery stationed there. The fort, a Gibraltar-like rock protruding into the Arctic Ocean, was subject to almost continuous bombardment from the superior Russian artillery on the Fischer peninsula. When a convoy with war material from America was approaching Murmansk, the artillery barrage rose to a hurricane. Each shell generated a hail of iron and stone on the naked rock. Some of the navy gunners opined that the mounted guns of the Russians, which took a heavy toll among us, could only have come from America, but others pointed out that the Russians had been excellent artillerymen ever since Peter the Great. At any rate, the navy cannoneers took the brunt of the barrages because they had to return fire, while the infantrymen at least could seek cover in caves and crevices.

There were two exceptions, however. One was carrying the wounded to a little boat that took them to a military hospital in Kirkenes. I hated this task ever since a severely burned artilleryman had begged me to kill him. The other exception happened at one of our reconnaissance runs.

These runs took place along the cliffs above the ocean. On one such trip, while we were descending, we came under heavy artillery fire that drove us into an almost hopeless situation. Since I was ahead of my group, I was at the lowest point. Hanging on the cliff, unable to go either up or down, and being responsible for twelve men, I was in desperate need of mountaineering skills, which I did not possess, of physical bravery which I am not abundantly endowed with, and of leadership qualities which, I suppose, I gained on that special occasion.

Momentarily paralyzed by fear and acrophobia, I told myself that I had to hide this spell of weakness from my men at all cost. That helped. At the first pause in the shelling I directed the topmost man to climb back up the same way he had come down. At the next pause, the second man ascended, and so on. When it was my turn to scale the cliff, I had the benefit of having been shown the way by my unsuspecting men. Nevertheless, the two hours I was hanging there seemed like an eternity to me.

In the fall of 1943 our entire battalion was assigned to the Litsa Front about fifty kilometers west of Murmansk. This part of the Arctic Ocean front along the Litsa River consisted of a chain of strongholds that were separated by vast stretches of no-man's-land. Generally, a stronghold was occupied by one platoon, about forty-five men. In 1941 the mountaineers had suffered huge losses there, as was testified by the large army cemetery at Parkkina (part of the Petsamo area). When we retreated from Finland in 1944, losses were even greater, but only the lucky comrades were buried; most had to be left where they died. Now, in 1943, casualties were more moderate, and the Parkkina cemetery had no trouble accommodating them.

Military operations consisted mainly of sniper fire, reconnaissance, and local surprise attacks that sometimes resulted in hand-to-hand fighting. The Russians also shelled us with heavy artillery, which we did not have.

The Landser's life at these strongholds was so primitive that it almost defies description. One third of the platoon, about fifteen men, were always on their way to haul supplies of food, water, coal, ammunition, and so forth. Another fifteen men were standing guard. The remainder were either sleeping or doing chores such as cleaning weapons or cracking lice. All forty-five men lived in a hand-made bunker with a floor space of about fifty square meters, but only one third of them could sleep there at any one time. There was only one wash bowl in which everything was cleaned, from feet to clothes to dishes. Since detergents were non-existent and soap was scarce, the bowl had a thick black rim of indeterminate composition.

Light was provided by a hand-made carbide lamp that consisted of an open can, a wine bottle, a wick, a cork, and a rifle bullet. The bottle, which contained the carbide, stood in the water bath of the can. It had a hole in the bottom for the wick to draw water from the can and the carbide to generate gas. The slender rifle bullet penetrated the cork with its tip pointing upwards. By drilling a hole along its length axis, the bullet was converted into a nozzle for the gas to escape. I don't know who invented this contraption, but when I saw it for the first time I was quite impressed by this kind of Landser ingenuity.

There was no room in the bunker for even the most modest personal belongings, except for paper and pencil to write letters. No books, no musical instruments, no pictures, certainly no radio, nothing but weapons, ammunition, and the bare essentials of existence. The only picture that graced the entrance door was a huge poster depicting the anatomy of a louse, courtesy of the German army. Underneath was the official form on which everybody had to report every day how many lice he had cracked. A pencil was provided. Today I wish I had at least one photograph of the bunker idyll, but there were no cameras.

One of the scarcest commodities was the truth. There were essentially three sources of information: the monthly *Das Reich*, the soldier's radio station at Finmark, and comrades returning from home leave. The monthly was controlled by the ministry for propaganda and regularly brought the latest pep talk by Goebbels. The battalion received one copy, which was passed on to officers and occasionally reached our bunker. The radio sender was the official mouthpiece of the 20th Mountain Army. Yet there were no radios in the bunkers, and only one at the battalion command post. I do recall having heard there the announcement "We now read to you the article that Reichsminister Dr. Goebbels has just published in the magazine *Das Reich*."

Thus, as far as real information was concerned, we were essentially left with the news the men on leave brought from home. Yet even this information was tainted by the Goebbels propaganda machine. Nevertheless, occasionally the truth leaked through. To me, this happened a year later when a comrade brought me the only news I ever received about the concentration camps.

Our pay resembled the information we received. Both were false. We were paid with three sorts of "money": Russian rubles, German *Kreditkassenscheine* (certificates of credit equivalent to ordinary Reichsmark), and Finnish markkas. The rubles, huge notes bearing the portrait of Lenin and the emblem of hammer and sickle, were entirely worthless and all ended in the latrine. The German *Kreditkassenscheine* were a classic example of "funny money." The only thing we could buy with them was tobacco and alcohol which, however, were strictly rationed. Since we received more "funny money" than we could spend, we accumulated it in our mandatory chest money pouches. Eventually, these leather purses became so bulging that the Landsers referred to them as "brassieres." The markkas had a limited buying power, since Finland had been bled white by several wars. Of course, we were far away from even the smallest Finnish town where we could have bought something with the "Finmark," as we called it, except on our way to and from home leave. But even this limited shopping opportunity was too much of a burden for the Finnish economy, which is why we received ever fewer markkas and eventually none.

The mood in the bunker was a blend of all sorts of emotions, some buried in the depth of the Landsers' souls, others lying closer to the surface. At the bottom of the collective psyche subsisted a stoic resignation to the inevitable. Next came a sense of duty that was tempered with fear of injury, death, and Russian captivity. This sentiment, I suppose, was not much different from the feelings of the men in the trenches of World War I, regardless of which side they fought on. But the faith in the Führer, which lay a little closer to the surface, was totally new. Instilled by education, propaganda, indoctrination, even the oath of personal loyalty, it differed greatly from one man to the next, unshakable in some, riddled with doubt in others. It goes without saying that the believers were more vocal than the doubters. The most openly admitted sentiment of the men in the bunker was an endemic homesickness that led to endless talks, reminiscences, fantasies, lamentations, even poetry. But the most palpable temper in the bunker was an all-pervading mutual irritation that flared up at the slightest provocation.

One comrade, who was from Berlin, often sang a nostalgic ditty that ended on the refrain "When the church bells are ringing again, yes, then will be peace in Berlin!" Another offered a more humorous rhyme that depicted the homecoming of the last soldiers from the Arctic Ocean front years after the war had ended in victory. The Führer had long retired to his comfortable residence in Linz, Austria, and everybody was enjoying peace and prosperity. In that cozy situation, nobody recognized the ragged, toothless homecomers who were pulling mules behind them. When the bearded warriors were asked whence they came, they always gave the same, lethargic answer: "From the ass of the world."

Life in the bunker was so stressful that the inhabitants had difficulties keeping their irritation in check, and elders had their hands full maintaining peace. For me the greatest hardship was the physical closeness of men—and their smell! To this day, I have to turn my nose away when soldiers are marching by. Strangely, most inhabitants of the bunker did not complain about the smell, but all suffered from the lack of privacy. The result was tensions that could erupt at any moment into open hostility. When one man felt annoyed by another, he yelled at him, "You stink to me!" In spite of my own suffering, I noticed the expression with muted amusement and wondered to what extent human relations are subconsciously affected by smell. It seemed to me that the graphic expression was less of a metaphor than the Landsers suspected. At any rate, as far as my nose was concerned, my discomfort was real, not metaphorical.

My pastime in the bunker was writing letters to my parents and to Paul, my friend from the Neuruppin air base. Unfortunately, the letters to my parents got lost in the bombing raids, and those to Paul disappeared with him in Siberia. As far as I know, only one of my letters survived the war. I had written it to an aunt of mine, who presented it to me after the war in her defense against my criticism of her continued adherence to Nazi ideology. It was a typical political hold-out letter in which I rambled on about victory and praised Hitler for having appointed Himmler, of all people, to a high position on the Eastern front.

At the time I did not know anything about the genocide that Hitler had ordered and Himmler had organized. I simply thought that the old party champion and SS leader would make a good fighter against Communism. Of course, I was wrong on that account, for Himmler proved militarily incompetent. But that was not why the letter embarrassed me when my aunt showed it to me. I was ashamed because it revealed the blind faith I once had placed in precisely the two men who had conceived and unleashed the Holocaust.

At the time I thought the Russians were better off than we were. For one thing, they were supported by a more developed hinterland of roads and railways. They also had the ingenuity to put railroad tracks over frozen lakes, which enabled them to employ heavy artillery and even tanks. Most important, however, was their numerical superiority, which allowed them to concentrate manpower at strategic places and launch surprise attacks. The unit opposite us was a Siberian Reindeer Ski Brigade that enjoyed several advantages over us. Apart from being more familiar with the climate, they were also better equipped for it. We envied them the padded uniforms they wore under their white winter suits, which not only kept them warm but also made them look more massive than they probably were. The Siberians were also masters at using the knife as a weapon. I don't know if they had learned this savage art from the Finns during the Winter War of 1939, or vice versa, but both excelled in it. It reminded me of the German author Karl May, who wrote popular stories about the American Wild West and the Indians.

The Siberians were able to spend hours in the snow while sneaking up on our guards. While this alone was sufficient to make standing watch a nerve-racking experience, it was exacerbated by the climate, the darkness, and the landscape. There were no trees, but only brush, moss, and huge boulders. If one stared long enough at a large rock, it started to move as if it were a man. The worst part of it was that one never knew whether or not to alert sleeping comrades. Sounding a false alarm always had unpleasant consequences, but failing to sound an alarm in the presence of a real threat was an invitation to disaster. We always slept in our uniforms, minus winter suits, covered with one blanket that was standard equipment, loaded rifles at our sides, and winter suits and shoes as pillows under our heads.

My political views had changed in the last two years. Since I was no longer subjected to anti-Semitic propaganda and had not seen the *Stürmer* magazine for three years, I had almost forgotten the horror story of the Jewish conspiracy. My thoughts and feelings were focused almost exclusively on the Russians. The thought that they might defeat us and occupy our homeland terrified me. Even more horrifying was the possibility of falling into Russian captivity. Like many of my comrades, I was determined to end my life rather than march to Siberia.

Such thoughts and the daily struggle for survival convinced me that this war was not against Jews, but against Russia, notwithstanding the fact that America, which had many Jews, had joined our enemies. At the time why and how America got into a war against us was a mystery to me. That the British were still fighting us was bad enough, but at least I could rationalize this calamity as a kind of private bout between Hitler and Churchill. But why America? About President Roosevelt I knew next to nothing. Could it be that he was another Churchill? If so, what a coincidence!

Pearl Harbor was long forgotten, and so was Hitler's irrational declaration of war on America. Had the memory of this rash reaction endured in my mind, it might have planted some doubts about Hitler's judgment and leadership qualities. On the other hand, I must admit that I probably would have suppressed such doubts with the expedient justification that I lacked the information to understand the fine points of world politics. Since I had grown up with the slanted worldview of the Nazis, I was not aware of America's industrial might and even less so of its spiritual power, which I comprehended only many years later when I became an American. Had I known these fundamental facts, I might have come to the conclusion that we could not win this war even with the best of luck. But my mind was fixated on the Russians, and my hope was that we could still beat them.

Apart from the Russians, only the British occupied my thoughts to such a significant extent. If Churchill had never been born, or if he suddenly died, would peace with England be possible? Would it be desirable or even prudent? Wasn't that what Rudolf Hess had in mind when he flew to England? Of course he was in disgrace now, but, according to the Bible, a prophet has little credibility in his own land. The thought frightened me because it implied that Hitler might not be as wise as I wanted to believe he was. Since I was not ready for such heresy, I quelled any further brooding about the subject with the cheap excuse that I lacked the necessary information for independent thinking.

There was one more problem, however. In spite of the news blackout, it had not escaped me that Hitler had not spoken to the nation or the *Reichstag* for quite some time. For a speaker of his caliber, the present quietude was conspicuous, not to say ominous. In his stead, Goebbels spoke to us through the periodical *Das Reich*. But Goebbels' carefully crafted articles were a poor substitute for Hitler's invigorating speeches. Indeed, from the propaganda minister's recent article I got the impression that the skillful wordsmith had trouble hiding his own anxiety. One sentence, in particular, worried me: *"Wie weit wollen wir uns denn noch absetzen?"* (How far do we still want to distance ourselves?). The verb *absetzen* has several meanings. In the present context it means to put some distance between us and the enemy. Thus, it was a euphemism for retreat, which the army High Command had invented to rationalize the backward movements on all fronts. It troubled me that the Führer's closest paladin saw fit to borrow this dubious expression from the generals.

But there were also positive signs. The periodical, which brought us Goebbels' pep talks, if we were so lucky to receive it, was also sprinkled with vague hints about new miracle weapons, such as jet fighters, rockets, guided missiles, and superior tanks. Undoubtedly these secret weapons under development were the explanation for the Führer's persistent silence. Maybe he was busy preparing the decisive blow. He had always used the element of surprise; no doubt he would use it again. At any rate, at this fateful hour he needed our trust, and he certainly had mine.

At about the same time I started to let my comrades in on my thinking, which so far I had kept mostly to myself. My foremost objective was to strengthen fighting spirit. We had to win this war at all cost. Our enemies were Russia, Russia, Russia. To mention the Jews in this context was absurd. To my surprise, most of my comrades agreed. Indeed, the few critics I encountered went even a step further; they did not want to hear about the Jews at all.

One of my comrades, who had just returned from home leave, seemed to have some information about the Gestapo. He was careful not to attack Hitler, but he told me to my face that Himmler had converted Europe into a giant jail. This man was the most outspoken critic of the Nazi regime in our company. He was a sergeant, and I was a corporal. Thus, we were both non-commissioned officers, and he was one rank higher than I. About five years older than I, he was a student of law from Vienna. His name, ironically, was Walter Führer, which he regretted and tried to defuse with the earthy doggerel "Führer Walter, when he farts he thunders," which, in German, rhymes quite convincingly. We had numerous discussions, mostly in hushed voices because, inside the bunker, the comrades wanted to sleep, and outside the enemy was too close.

Once we were fortunate enough to attend a movie theater for

soldiers just a few kilometers behind the front. The price of admission was one log of firewood. When technical difficulties delayed the movie, we finally had the opportunity to conduct our discussion in relative comfort. Walter denounced the race ideology as hocus-pocus, a characterization to which I no longer objected. But our opinions deviated when it came to more concrete issues such as the war and the fate of his homeland, Austria. He thought that the war was already lost and that Austria should be free and independent, whereas I took the position that the war was winnable and Austria was an integral part of Germany.

Finally the movie started. Though it was a German production, it was unadulterated Hollywood. Against the moonlit background of a beautiful beach on the Mediterranean, under palm trees and overhanging bougainvilleas, a lady-killer in a white suit sang, "If only I knew whom I had kissed one midnight at the Lido." Did we really need this? My stomach was empty, my eyes were burning from the smoke of the wood fire, my feet were cold in spite of the fire, and my mind was still upset by the unresolved issues I had just discussed with Walter. In about two hours we would return to a life of death and misery. And now this! Who were the idiots who had sent us this schmaltz?

When we reported back to the company commander, Walter claimed—probably with some exaggeration—that I had lifted his spirit. The company commander, a second lieutenant, was not a Nazi but a reasonable man who simply did his duty as a reserve officer. He was not much interested in ideology but appreciated it if somebody did something to lift the fighting spirit. Walter and I sometimes poked fun at him behind his back because he had the peculiar habit of closing each sentence with the rhetorical question, "Can you follow?" Nevertheless, he seemed to feel that I was able to follow his high-flying thoughts, for he advanced my modest military career more than any other superior.

The company commander was a native of Dortmund, which

was another factor in the rapidly developing rapport between us. Most of the officers of the battalion were south Germans, either Austrians or Bavarians, and the popular bias among north Germans was that the Austrians had too much and the Bavarians too little of manners and civility. While the two southern clans were not exactly fond of each other, they agreed that the Prussians were faceless yes-men who had neither humor nor culture. I do not subscribe to these clichés, but it still intrigues me that Hitler was an Austrian by birth and a Bavarian by choice. He hated Vienna as much as he loved Munich, and yet he was incapable of grasping the spirit of either city.

The company commander, being a "Preuss," suffered from isolation among his fellow officers. "Preuss" is southern lingo for *Preusse* (Prussian) and has a slightly derogatory connotation. Since I tried to dampen regional animosities wherever I noticed them, he called me a pan-Germanic wizard and even a wise man, though he was at least ten years my senior. It was a strange relation: strictly formal, with lots of "Can you follow?" and spiced with occasional lecturing and left-handed compliments. Nevertheless, this man was the most pleasant military superior I ever had, and I was eager to reciprocate. Soon I would have two opportunities to do so, but each time special circumstances hid my acts of gratitude from him. First, I saved his daily fried potatoes from a repulsive kind of pollution, and a year later I saved his life.

This officer would soon give me two assignments that caused quite a change of my military career. But first he surprised me with a reward of an entirely non-military nature. He had nominated me to attend a concert for front soldiers in Kirkenes. Each company could send only one man there, and each nomination had to be approved by the battalion commander.

The battalion commander, a captain whom I mentioned earlier, was a Bavarian by birth and a *Kommiskopp* by choice. This is

a slightly derogatory name for a person who is nothing but a soldier. Like *Kommisbrot* (army bread), the name is based on the
word *Kommis*, which the Landsers used for the Wehrmacht as
long as their feelings toward it were neutral. In a more aggravated
mood, they used the harsher term *Barras*, the origin of which I
don't know. Being a *Kommiskopp* par excellence, the captain considered music a decadent pursuit and even forbade the singing of
Christmas carols on the grounds that they "weakened the fighting spirit." He was not our friend, neither the lieutenant's nor
mine. The more surprising was it that he had granted permission
for me to attend the concert. A little later I should learn what was
behind this unexpected favor.

It was a long trip to the concert in Kirkenes, first on skis, then
by truck, and finally on foot. The pianist played the A-Major
Sonata by Mozart. The first movement, the *andante grazioso,* in
spite of its soothing mood—or because of it—struck me with
such force that I had trouble hiding my emotion. When one suddenly emerges from a life of utter insensitivity into an environment of sheer beauty, the effect can be dramatic. A whirlwind of
sentiments and questions raced through my mind and almost
spoiled my pleasure. But when the pianist played Beethoven, I
regained my composure.

Shortly thereafter the company commander gave me the first
of the two assignments I alluded to earlier. It was a position
within the company, which was called *Kompanie Trupp Führer.* As
such I was the commander's deputy and the leader of an elite
group of five men who served as messengers to platoons and battalion headquarters. Hitler had been such a messenger during
World War I. As *Kompanie Trupp Führer,* I took part in tactical
planning concerning reconnaissance, forecasting enemy attacks,
allocating manpower, and so on. I liked the new assignment
because it offered me at least some relief from the bunker routine

by allowing me to visit the platoons on their strongholds. It also offered me the first of the two opportunities to pay my debt to the commander.

Messengers and I were stationed at the same bunker as the company commander. One of my men had to prepare the lieutenant's fried potatoes every morning. The dish was not at all as appetizing as the name may suggest. For one thing, the little grease the lieutenant could spare from his daily ration had to be augmented by coffee grounds, which was not coffee at all, but a barley brew. The worst ingredient, however, was the potatoes, which were almost black from frost and rot.

One morning, when the familiar stink of the commander's fried potatoes drifted through the bunker, I absentmindedly watched the man who was preparing them. Obviously, he was mad at the lieutenant, for he referred to him repeatedly as a swine dog. That caught my attention. To my dismay I noticed that the angry cook spit into the potatoes each time he pronounced the unflattering sobriquet. For a moment I didn't know what to do, for I did not want to get between the lieutenant and my men. Eventually I ordered the disloyal chef to discard the dish and prepare a new one from his and my ration, which was quite a sacrifice for both of us. I later learned that the untrustworthy cook had used the revolting recipe for quite some time, but the lieutenant had never heard of it. I pledged to myself never to offend a cook!

I enjoyed my solitary trips to the strongholds, though they brought additional danger because both sides tried to capture messengers. Soon I would have even more opportunity to move around. General Ferdinand Schörner, Commanding General of the 19th Mountain Army Corps, had ordered the installation of National Socialist leadership officers at all levels. With this enactment Schörner anticipated Hitler's order of July 1944 to appoint such officers in all of the armed services, which was a reaction to the attempt on his life. The new institution was not much different from the Soviet commissars, but the Wehrmacht, by emphasizing the purely ideological nature of this function, took great pains to convince the Landsers that there was a world of difference.

For the installation of the NS leadership officers, each company had to send two men to battalion command post. To my surprise, I was ordered to attend this ceremony. The delegates from the four companies reported to a second lieutenant, whom I later called Joseph because he rivaled Joseph Goebbels in the art of twisting words. A few months later I would have a bout with him, but, at the moment, we were on friendly terms.

Joseph vigorously shook my hand, which was quite unusual between commissioned and non-commissioned officers. Then he said that my company commander had praised me as an exemplary National Socialist and that the battalion commander had approved my nomination as the company's NS leadership officer. The permission to attend the concert in Kirkenes, he said, was a reward for my "ideological reliability." I had the impression that Joseph liked me, while I was still struggling with the old problem that, ideologically, I was mostly on the side of the Nazis, but, personally, I had a hard time getting along with them. In this regard Joseph was no exception.

It turned out that Joseph was the battalion NS leadership officer. In this capacity he now presented us to the battalion commander, a captain who reminded me of Old Grouch, the Hitler Youth leader of olden days. His specialty was *den Landser anzuscheissen* (literally: to shit sideways at the Landser) for being improperly dressed or giving a lax salute or whatever. *Anscheissen* was one of the great words from the Landser's vocabulary. No other expression could relate more graphically the feeling of being scolded by some simpleton for some trifle, while standing at attention.

As the captain inspected us, he wasted no time demonstrating his mastery of the art of *Anscheissen*. First he admonished the group for its non-uniform appearance—four of us appeared in white, and four in gray—then he rebuked me for not standing correctly at attention. After this inspiring introduction he gave a little speech that apparently was meant to be a pep talk, but turned out to be a demonstration of spiritual poverty. Long on bombast and short on meaning, the pathetic address caused only a mixture of amusement and embarrassment. After a while the dull speaker felt his own inadequacy and murmured, "Bah! Why do I talk so much? Words are not my cup of tea." With that he turned around and left us more confused than enlightened.

Now it was Joseph's turn. He was a history teacher, and it showed. His talk was relatively well designed, full of quotes and historical facts—or distortions—but not convincing, at least not to me. He began his sermon with the tired race ideology. Opening a field edition of Hitler's *Mein Kampf,* he thundered, "The Aryan has always been mankind's Prometheus." The mindless claim rang a bell with me, for it was the same phrase I had absorbed in my school days when I was most gullible. Now it sounded less convincing, particularly when Joseph contrasted it with the thousand-year-old dictum *ex oriente lux* (from the East [comes the] light), which sounded rather elegant by comparison. Curiously, it was this cryptic phrase that aroused his ire, for he repeated it several times during the course of his lecture, while making a face as if it were the dirtiest of lies. Not satisfied that his facial artistry had brought home the message, he topped the facile phrase off with the awkward remark, "However, light does not come from the East, but from the North." I thought this sweeping statement sounded even more artless than the Führer's. Though he was smart enough not to point north, I couldn't help turning my eyes in that direction—and saw only barbed wire, snow, and a black sky.

The long-winded lecture on the origin of "Aryan light" was only an overture to the long-forgotten fairy tale of the Jewish world conspiracy. My God, did this man hate the Jews! I suddenly felt transported back to my school days when I had heard the director cracking dirty jokes about lecherous old men in caftans. I even saw him plucking his goatee while sounding his obnoxious laugh. But that was long ago. Now we were facing a real enemy, not a bogeyman that existed only in hysterical minds. Nobody around here, save this idiot, had any taste for the old *Stürmer* canards. I was disgusted. I was desperate! It took all my self-control to repress the outcry, "God save us from this National Socialist leadership officer."

Early in 1944 our battalion was reassigned to the Fischer Hals front, which ran across the isthmus of the Fischer peninsula west of Murmansk. The peninsula itself was in Russian hands, but we controlled the mainland south of it including the isthmus. The artillery fire was most intense there. Thanks to the Americans, the Russians seemed to have an inexhaustible supply of ammunition, which enticed them to fire even at one-man targets.

By now I had acquired some fame within the battalion as ideological-hold-out-apostle, which brought me speaking engagements from companies other than my own. They all wanted to hear my pep talks; I unabashedly preached my conviction that our enemy was Russia and Russia alone. I even went so far as to declare that we urgently needed peace with Britain and America, but stopped short of saying that entering the war in North Africa had been a strategic mistake, because that would have been a reflection on Hitler's leadership qualities.

It was clear to me that half of the German forces were deployed in Italy and the Balkans, and the Atlantic coast. If they were freed to fight the Russians, we would still have a chance to beat them. I even dreamt of an alliance between Germany and the Western powers. Little did I know that the unconditional surrender of

Germany had long been their declared war goal, and even less did I realize that Germany's enormous war crimes had poisoned the political atmosphere to such an extent that a settlement with the West was impossible.

In general, my heretical preaching was well received. Eventually, however, somebody must have complained about me, for I was suddenly summoned to the battalion command post. To my relief, the commander was not present and Joseph received me in his stead. He seemed to be well informed about my ideas and even quoted some of them verbally. "There is some truth in what you say about England and America," he lectured me, "but we must leave thinking about these problems to the Führer. He knows best." With that I was graciously dismissed, happy in the belief that my unorthodox preaching would have no further consequences.

I was grievously mistaken. Soon after my audience with Joseph I learned that my political escapades had an entirely unexpected effect on one of my comrades whose name was Röper. His life eventually ended in tragedy, while mine was never the same.

The Great Retreat

It was Röper who brought me the first and only news I heard about Nazi atrocities. During a tense encounter, while facing the enemy, this luckless comrade confronted me with the truth, but I turned him down. The fateful meeting occurred in the spring of 1944. The tundra was still covered with a thick blanket of snow when I visited the stronghold of one of our platoons. Corporal Röper, who was stationed there, had sent me a message that he was "fascinated" by my political ideas and wanted to tell me his own. Since he did not wish to speak in the presence of the other men, he asked me to join him while standing watch. That was quite unusual because talking on watch was generally not allowed. However, his solemn face and secretive manner persuaded me to follow him to the rampart.

Since we had the same rank, we were on a first-name basis, but today I recall only his last name, not his first. With the benefit of hindsight I am inclined to believe that this gap in my memory has some deep-seated, psychological reason. At any rate, the fact is that I remember only his family name, Röper, which lives in my memory as a painful reminder of that somber morning in 1944 when I failed to respond to a call of destiny. I believe that everybody, once or twice in his life, is called upon to stand up for truth and decency. Of course, had I done so, I would not be alive today, for it is a distinctly German tragedy that it does not always speak well of a man's past if he has survived his nation's darkest hour.

Röper and a few other men had joined our company a few weeks earlier as reinforcements. Thus, I was only superficially acquainted with him, but somehow I had learned that he was half-Jewish. That was unusual in the German army. Even more extraordinary was the fact that his brother was serving in the SA Standarte Feldherren Halle, an elite division of the SA, equivalent to the Waffen SS. Such things happened only toward the end of the war, when Hitler needed ever more lives to be sacrificed on the battlefield. There is also the possibility that Röper was not half but "only" one quarter Jewish. Anyway, as I learned later, his father was a renowned neurosurgeon in Hamburg, and his mother was the Jewish part of the family.

It was a cold morning. The Russians were only a few hundred meters away. Röper, who had come directly from Germany, wanted to tell me a few things he had learned there. We were standing behind a rampart of beams and rocks. In the east a pale stripe of daylight was rising in the gloomy sky. I was nervous because, only a few days before, the Russians had tried to overrun one of our strongholds. I also suffered from the old weakness of seeing movement where there was none. Röper was uneasy because of the things he wanted to tell me.

He began not with the Jews but with the German Resistance fighters and the fate of their families. "When these men are trying to hide from the Gestapo," he said, "their wives or parents are thrown into prison." I was thunderstruck. Taking hostages went against every fiber of my being, against my instincts, my sense of decency, and my concept of justice, everything I had learned in my parents' home. But I wasn't sure whether Röper spoke the truth. Why was he telling me these things? What was his motive? I didn't want to ask him because I didn't wish to hear more of this. Vacillating between belief and disbelief, I busied myself staring at the boulders in the distance that a vivid imagination could persuade to move. There was a long silence.

I dared not look at Röper, but I could feel that he observed me intently. I think he was struggling with himself, trying to decide whether to trust me or to let this brief encounter empty into a sea of silence. Finally, his burning desire for empathy won the upper hand. With a hushed but imploring voice, in a few terse sentences, he told me that Jews were being systematically murdered in the concentration camps. I do not recall him mentioning the crematoria, but I distinctly recollect the name Theresienstadt. "That's where they kill the Jews," he said. I also remember him saying that this particular extermination camp lay in Silesia, Germany.

Searching for the place of horror after the war, I learned that the arrogantly germanized name Theresienstadt stood for Terezin in Czechoslovakia, and that the Nazis used the camp as a demonstration model for International Red Cross inspectors. This meant that the victims were treated relatively well—before they were murdered. As I am writing these lines, I receive from the U.S. Holocaust Memorial Museum a calendar entitled "Children's Drawings from Terezin, 1998." The accompanying letter says that the children were allowed to paint only flowers, blue skies, and happy faces. I am afraid they went to their death at the time Röper tried to alert me.

Now I turned around. I shall never forget his face! Glowing with emotion, it reflected a bewildering blend of age-old grief, intense questioning, and anxious hope. This was the truth that stared me in the face, and it demanded an answer. But I could not utter a word. I felt pushed with my back to the wall. I knew that this was the trial of my life. But if I believed his allegations, then . . . then . . . then everything would change. My whole life would be affected. The consequences would be enormous.

I trembled. I looked for an escape, for I could not muster the courage to face the truth. It is said that, in a moment of mortal danger, a person's whole life unwinds before his inner eye within an instant. I had a similar experience, but with regard to the future rather than the past. I saw the frightening implications of answering—in whatever form—Röper's appeal to my conscience. I imagined myself standing before a military tribunal; I saw my own death by firing squad. I envisaged my helpless parents and bewildered brothers. I even read the official bulletin that another enemy of the people had been exterminated. Paralyzed by fear, I suddenly heard myself murmuring, "Well, if thousands of our people are dying every day, we must see to it that an equal number of our enemies also die."

It was a cop-out and a double lie. Germany was not the only nation that was losing thousands of people every day. Our enemies were also dying. But we were not talking about dying in battle—we were talking about genocide. This was as clear to me then as it is now, but I lacked the fortitude to bear the consequences. That's why I chose to distort the issue. And that's how that gloomy morning hour at the Arctic Ocean became the moment in my life I now am most ashamed of. At the time I desperately wished it away, but today I feel otherwise. Shame is a God-given catharsis to cleanse the soul. I welcome it. It keeps the episode of 1944 alive in my consciousness as long as I live. It tells me who I was—and who I am now.

Discouraged by my lame reaction, Röper fell silent. He must have been deeply disappointed. Today I know that he was seeking a confidant, as he was already planning the desertion that cost him his life. He needed an ally and interpreted my criticism of Hitler's strategic conduct of the war as a veiled signal that I opposed the whole regime. He knew about my friendship with Walter and his criticism of the Nazis, and he suspected the same anti-Nazi sentiment in me under the guise of my patriotic demeanor. It was my reaction, or lack of it, that dissuaded him from taking me any deeper into his confidence.

The second part of the tragedy happened in late summer of 1944, but first I went on home leave, my last leave of the war. It was June, the month of the Allied invasion of Normandy. Shortly before leaving my company I participated in a search and destroy operation against Russian commandos, during which we inflicted some casualties and took a few prisoners. Each of the Russians carried a small can made of white metal that obviously contained an emergency ration. Hoping that the cans contained some meat, we lost no time taking them as spoils of war, especially since we suspected them to have come from America. Happy with my little prize, I decided to save it for my starving parents.

Finally my long-awaited day of departure came. The journey was a combination of all sorts of transportation. The first leg was a ride on a one-axle cart pulled by a mule. It took me to the delousing facility through which all soldiers bound for Germany had to pass. Then came a 500-kilometer truck ride on the Arctic Ocean Road to Rovaniemi. There I boarded a boxcar of the Finnish railway for a twenty-four-hour ride to Turku in south Finland. Next came an even longer journey on the Baltic Sea in the bowels of a ship bound for Danzig (now Gdansk, Poland). The following trip on the military train to Berlin was the least uncomfortable part of the journey.

The capital was already heavily damaged by air attacks, but functioning remarkably well. A short ride on the city transit took me from Berlin's Stettiner station to the city's Potsdamer station, where I boarded a military train to the west. Since trains in western Germany were attacked with increasing frequency by low-flying American fighter aircraft, the passenger soldiers were instructed to fire at the attackers in the event the train was forced to stop. This was one of the reasons why all of them carried their weapons and ammunition. Fortunately, they didn't need them this time.

The other reason was the Allied invasion of June 1944. Many soldiers arriving for a hard-earned vacation from the Eastern front were sent immediately into combat at the Western front. In the eastern part of the country it was the other way around. The situation at both fronts was so precarious that the hard-pressed Army Command, in moments of crisis, had no other recourse than sending vacationing soldiers into battle.

The Landsers had coined a fitting name for the officers who had the hated job of sending vacationers into combat. They called them *Heldenklaus* (hero thieves), following the proverbial *Kohlenklau* (coal thief), whose black face lurked everywhere from posters with the inscription *Kohlenklau geht um* (Coal thief is going around). The verb *klauen,* an etymological relative of "to claw," is a German colloquialism for "to steal." The hard-pressed ministry for armament and war materials had invented the villain *Kohlenklau* in an attempt to motivate the population to save coal and energy.

It was midnight when I arrived in Dortmund. The sky was still red from the fires of an air raid the night before. The railway station was heavily damaged but functioning, while vast stretches of the city lay in ashes, with no telephones, no streetcars, no communication or transportation of any kind.

It was a walk of about an hour from the station to the house of my parents, but it took twice as long because, at a site where rescue operations were under way, I was asked to help. The rescuers were freeing corpses from a shelter in which they had been scalded by boiling water. The seething fluid had come from an industrial plant in the vicinity and flooded the shelter. We had to wade through a jelly of human flesh. As one rescuer pulled on a leg sticking out from the horrible morass, he had the bare bone in his hand.

An hour later I passed the ruins of the synagogue the Nazis had burned during Kristallnacht of 1938. Now trees were growing on the rubble, while grass was already sprouting from the more recent ruins of some German houses. I thought of Theo, who had the courage and the decency to condemn the barbarity of persecuting innocent people.

It was dawn when I arrived at the ruin of my parents' house. There was a sign with the address of their emergency quarters on the outskirts of the city. While streetcars to the outlying districts were still functioning, it was too early for the first vehicle to arrive. Thus, I sat down on the wreckage of the house I had left four and a half years before. Across the street was the car stop where my father had waved goodbye. The very bricks I was sitting on were the remains of my childhood bedroom that had been located high under the roof. Maybe I could find some of my belongings here. No luck! The looters had already taken care of that. Germans, after all, were not as companionable and brotherly as ultra-nationalist propaganda wanted us to believe.

The war went on. A rescue crew was marching by. Sirens were sounding. American fighter aircraft were overhead. A book from the First World War came to my mind: *All Quiet on the Western Front,* by Erich Maria Remarque. It had always been the paradigm of treason to me. Now it was the truth.

I was mentally so exhausted that I felt tempted to open the little can of meat I had taken from a dead Russian. Almost without thinking I pulled it from my backpack and weighed it in my hands. Only then did I remember that it was to be a present for my parents. Overcome with sudden emotion, I put it back and wept.

When my parents saw me, they also cried, while I was shocked at how emaciated they looked. The continuous air raids and the constant hunger had taken their toll. I was glad to have the small can with me; it turned out to contain corned beef, a cherished delicacy. My father pronounced the name "cornette biff" and said it could only have come from America. My mother didn't touch it, pretending a spell of nausea. Food rations were already below the minimum requirement for maintaining body weight. The Führer Package for front soldiers was a thing of the past because Ukraine, where the food had come from, had been lost.

Every second day I had to report to a registration center for front soldiers, which was operated by invalid officers who were no longer fit for combat and often had only one leg or arm. Sometimes entirely new military units were established at the registration places and rushed to the fronts in east, south, or west. I had to do my first two reportings in person because telephones were still down. After that I could do it by phone. Miraculously the *Heldenklaus* never snatched me, maybe because they couldn't make up their minds at which front the crisis was the worst.

My father was depressed by the Allied invasion, and so was I. It worried us that there did not seem to be a decisive counteroffensive. Of course we didn't know that Hitler had predicted the landing of the Allied forces at the Pas de Calais rather than the coast of Normandy, and that this was the reason why he forbade Field Marshal Rommel to deploy his tanks at the actual landing site, where they were urgently needed. "How long do we want to wait before we drive them out?" my father asked. I was reminded of Goebbels' rhetorical question of almost the same wording a year earlier.

On one occasion my father's mood was lifted, though not mine. It happened when we listened to a radio report about the attacks on England by the revenge weapons, V-1 and V-2 rockets. In an effort to boost morale, the report exaggerated the effect of the raids on the British population. I still remember the overly dramatic words of the radio reporter, "The Island trembles, and England is ablaze." My father was so impressed that he thought the war had reached a turning point. But I questioned both the wisdom and the effectiveness of the raids. If we wanted to win Britain over as an ally, this was not the way to go. Moreover, the logical targets for the rockets would have been the Allied forces in Normandy, not British civilians.

This was the first time I had serious doubts about the Führer's leadership qualities. I felt reminded of the relatively mild uneasiness I experienced in 1942 after Hitler attacked Sevastopol in Russia and Tobruk in North Africa within the same week. However, in those early days I was not ready to admit that two simultaneous offensives against different enemies on separate continents were a strategic blunder. Now it was different. With the Allied invasion in full swing, I could no longer escape the conclusion that using the powerful rockets for cheap revenge rather than purposeful combat was a grievous mistake.

Though I had made some progress in liberating myself from the mental prison of my childhood, I had still a long way to go. My weakness was that I saw only Hitler's strategic blunders, not his crimes. Part of this imbalance was undoubtedly the result of the fact that his military misfortunes were all too obvious, while his crimes were relatively well hidden, at least to my eyes. But part of it was also psychological. Hitler had been my hero since childhood. He was still the rock on which my world was founded. In this regard, not much had changed since the days I had marched with the HitlerYouth. My life was still dominated by the evil sorcerer, and I was not yet ready to take him down from his pedestal.

When my mother heard the exaggerated report of the destruction the rockets had caused in England, she was sad. "My God," she murmured, "the poor people." Constant worrying about her three sons, the neural injury from the air raids, and the pain of starvation had heightened, rather than dulled, her sensitivity to the suffering of others. The only occasion on which she used harsh words was when she referred to the Allied bombers. She called them beasts, but that was more an outcry of pain than an expression of hatred. She hated nobody, only the war.

My parents told me that they had evacuated our former house only a few weeks before it was destroyed. All of their belongings, except the few clothes they carried with them, were lost. After the First World War, my father's Swiss life insurance had been confiscated by the Allies as part of the war reparations. "I had paid for it in gold mark," he lamented. "And now it's the same thing all over again. Everything we have accumulated in the last twenty years is reduced to rubble." He did not mention the Jews, which I noticed with relief. Apparently he had forgotten the senseless hatred I had come to hate.

We enjoyed the few days of my vacation as much as possible. Had it not been for the constant threat that the *Heldenklaus* might snatch me, we would have enjoyed the beautiful summer days even more. Once, while we were walking through the village, American fighter aircraft strafed it with machine-gun fire. "Too bad we left your rifle at home," my father said wistfully.

On the day of my departure I insisted that my parents stay at home. The military trains were now greatly improved. They were shorter and more frequent. While some of the cars were damaged, there was plenty of room. I was amazed at how well everything was functioning. Trains were rolling east and west, laden with soldiers and material. It was a marvel of organization, but it was also the last time I felt anything akin to national pride.

The Americans, who had unwittingly provided me with the welcome gift of corned beef, also gave me a farewell present. Shortly after the train had pulled out of the station, it was attacked by fighter aircraft. Having hardly gained any speed, the train came to a quick stop. We rushed out to return fire, but the aircraft had already disappeared. Just as I got up from the ground, I discovered a bullet the aircraft had left behind. Though I didn't treasure the bullet as much as the can of corned beef, I picked it up as a souvenir for my comrades at the Arctic Ocean front.

As I was reentering my railcar, I overheard the conversation of two officers. They used an expression I had never heard before, but would hear with increasing frequency in the months ahead, particularly after the war. It was *Gröfaz*, a sardonic acronym for *Grösster Feldherr aller Zeiten* (greatest military genius of all times). At the time I did not understand its meaning, much less its ridicule, but I had the uneasy feeling that it was an unflattering nickname for Hitler. After the war I learned that it was used mainly by disillusioned officers and other people who, as far as information was concerned, were more privileged than I was.

In Danzig I entered a Front Sammel Stelle (Front Soldiers Assembly Facility). The Nazis had Stellen (offices, places, facilities) for everything. There were Stellen for delousing, receiving ration cards, registering losses from air raids, declaring possession of foreign currencies, reporting for duties such as clearing away rubble, rescuing the living and the dead, extinguishing fires, collecting paper and metal, receiving training and indoctrination, and so on. There were even Stellen for Jews to assemble for transportation to the concentration camps.

Waiting for a ship to take me to Finland, I spent about a week at the front assembly facility in Danzig. The place was so dirty that I used every opportunity to escape. One beautiful summer evening I went to town to admire the Gothic brickwork of the old patrician houses and churches. This was the town in which the first shot of the war had been fired. It was still unscathed, but six months later most of it would be rubble.

As I was standing in front of a picturesque church, I overheard two elderly men in civilian clothes. *"Gröfaz,"* said one of them. "Yes," replied the other, "he thinks he is another Alexander." Now I got the message. Ironically, it made me angry. "Watch your tongue," I yelled at the two elders, whereupon they quickly disappeared.

When I arrived in Rovaniemi, the capital of Lapland, I entered another front assembly facility, waiting for a truck to take me to the north. During the day the waiting soldiers had to work, but in the evening they were granted a few hours to enjoy the last days of the Nordic summer. That's when the second part of Röper's tragedy occurred.

It was a pleasant summer evening. We were about a hundred soldiers, loitering in front of the camp gate. Most were smoking the atrocious stuff that passed for tobacco, but I did not because I always exchanged my cigarettes for something edible. I was talking to some new acquaintances when I heard a voice behind me saying, "Unteroffizier Manz" (Unteroffizier meant corporal). Turning around, I saw Röper. Though it was unusual for him to address me by rank and last name, I unsuspectingly extended my hand to greet him. With a sad smile he raised his arms to show me that he was handcuffed. Then I saw the two military policemen behind him. Before I could ask any questions, they ordered me to avoid any contact with the prisoner and then pulled him away. It was the last I saw of Röper, but not the last I heard of him.

When I arrived at my company, I learned that Röper had tried to desert to Sweden. He was already on Swedish soil when the military police caught him with the help of their bloodhounds. That evening, when I had seen him in Rovaniemi, he had just arrived as a prisoner in the custody of the military police. His fate was sealed. A military tribunal quickly sentenced him to death by firing squad. However, for reasons unknown to me, he was not executed in Finland, but loaded on a ship headed for Germany.

Today I don't remember the name of the ship, but a few months later I heard it again aboard a ship from Hammerfest to Narvik.

In the meantime there were two developments of overriding importance. One was the attempt on Hitler's life on July 20, 1944. I was shocked and outraged. The official bulletin spoke of "a small clique of ambitious officers." That was for me the key-word. I had never trusted officers, and now I felt contempt for them. They were still remnants from Imperial times, *Herren,* feudal lords, not Landsers, even less National Socialists. I was so angry that I behaved disrespectfully to the company commander. Fortunately, he didn't mind, for he was as outraged as I was.

In the next few days, to my own amazement, I calmed down considerably and felt as if I had been drugged. Ironically, the sedative effect came from the mysterious expression *Gröfaz* that had baffled me ever since I had heard it on my journey back from home leave. The officers who used this pejorative term for Hitler must have had a reason. Perhaps they felt that things could no longer go on the way they did. Maybe the conspirators had come to the conclusion that peace with the West was imperative. Obviously, that would have brought them into conflict with *Gröfaz,* who was fanatically determined to continue the two-front war at all costs.

Thoughts of this nature appeased my anger at the plotting officers. After all, I had pondered equally heretical ideas and even aired them to my comrades. Moreover, these high-ranking officers had information I was not privy to. "If I knew all the things they know," I persuaded myself, "I might . . ." I dared not finish the thought. It was too seductive and potentially destructive. Where would it end? I could not afford such daydreams. I had to do my duty. Over there was the enemy! Sad and sobered, I picked up my submachine gun and went to inspect one of our strongholds. No, I did not give a pep talk there; I had grown out of that.

The other development was the capitulation of Finland in

September 1944. Field Marshal Mannerheim, whom I held in high esteem, had secretly negotiated the terms of surrender. Now the Nazis took him down from his pedestal and branded him a half-Jewish sub-human. The concern was understandable, though not the ire. The 20th Mountain Army operating at the Arctic Ocean front was now cut off from the homeland. Quick and forceful action was needed to prevent another Stalingrad.

I took Mannerheim's decision as another bad omen. He was a competent general and statesman, and he certainly was no friend of the Soviets. If he was ready to put his nation at the mercy of their archenemy, then he must have come to the conclusion that Germany could no longer win the war. Adding to my suspicion was Hitler's continued silence and absence from sight. Only Goebbels and Speer allowed themselves to be seen in the bombed cities. Where was *Gröfaz?*

I was still brooding over these problems when word arrived that the 19th Mountain Army Corps would retreat to Norway. The plans and directives for the retreat were so sensitive that they could not be discussed over the field telephones. Mentioning them on the wire by only a single word was a major offense to be dealt with by military tribunal. It was a busy time for the messengers who went back and forth with messages in their heads, never on paper.

In planning the retreat of our company, the commander assigned me the task of leading the support group. My column consisted of two field kitchens, food, ammunition, medical equipment, and horses. On the day of withdrawal, the group was to leave as soon as it was completely dark, and the company was to follow a few hours later. Hiding the retreat from the Russians as long as possible was of the utmost importance.

I had six men and seven horses. We marched in total darkness along a trail I knew fairly well. The first hour or so passed without incident. Suddenly, however, the Russian artillery opened up. They fired from all barrels and almost without pause. It was the heaviest artillery barrage I have ever encountered. At times the whole landscape was illuminated from the flashes of the exploding shells. Somehow, the Russians had discovered our retreat.

We had to take cover while holding on to the horses, but the animals panicked and dragged us over the rocky terrain. Shell fragments ricocheted from boulders and banged against the field kitchens. Suddenly my horse collapsed over me. As I tried to free myself, I felt warm horse blood running down my face and over my uniform. The stains would remain there for more than a month, and the horse blood would mix with human blood. Another horse was wounded. Both had to be killed, and their load redistributed. Thus we spent more time taking cover and reloading equipment than marching.

It was long past the time when the company was supposed to follow. Eventually they caught up with us—and so did the Russians. There was some hand-to-hand fighting amidst renewed artillery barrages. Apparently the Russian artillerymen didn't mind killing a few of their own people. Confusion reigned. The lingering darkness made it difficult to distinguish friend from foe. Shells exploded, ducking figures darted from cover to cover, scraps of words from two languages intermingled, wounded men moaned, horses panicked, while the wavering dawn cast an eerie light over the ghastly scene.

As I was crawling toward a big boulder, I suddenly recognized the company commander. He said the company could hold its position long enough for me to move on with the support group. He wanted me to deliver it to the battalion as fast as possible. Which I did—with one dead man hanging over a horse like an outlaw in a Western movie.

Our battalion served as rear guard for the division. The Russians were trying to encircle our troops, and we had the mission of holding them up as long as possible. There was only one way from east to west, a German-built supply road that met the Arctic Ocean Road at Petsamo. Everything on wheels moved along that artery. The Russians had landed tanks at Liinahamari, Petsamo's harbor, trying to interdict the traffic on the supply road. To make it impassable for them, our sappers mined the road as soon as the bulk of our troops had passed through. They didn't wait for us, however.

We were marching and fighting almost day and night. After a few days we had used up the food and drink we carried with us. New food was not coming, and the emergency ration could only be touched on express orders. Worst, however, was the lack of sleep. I was almost delirious from sleep deprivation. Then there were the casualties. Time permitting, the dead were buried on the spot, and the wounded who were unable to walk were loaded on one-axle carts and pulled by one of us on the dirt road, in spite of the mines. Since these were anti-tank mines, it was hoped that they would not detonate if a man stepped on them.

After about a week our company was taken out of the front line and held as battalion reserve. We were directed to some abandoned barracks down the road, where we also found some food. We had just started cooking, washing, and sleeping when a messenger arrived. The poor man was in total shock and unable to speak. With foam in his mouth, he emitted only animal-like sounds and gesticulated wildly toward the front line. The company commander interpreted this as an alert and gave the order to break camp. A few minutes later we were again on the march, this time in an eastern direction, toward the Russians.

After a forced march of about twenty minutes, we reached the battalion command center where the captain was waiting for us behind a huge boulder. I still remember his exact words: "Men, who wants to earn himself the Iron Cross First Class?" I immediately raised my hand, whereupon I was appointed leader of an assault troop of about ten men.

The Russians had just overrun one of the battalion's companies, and our company had to perform a maneuver called *Gegenstoss* (counter-thrust, as distinct from a well-prepared counterattack). My group was to spearhead the assault.

My men exchanged their rifles for submachine guns, and each tucked two hand-grenades under his belt. Then we took off. As I stormed ahead of my group, I lost the fear that normally was my steady companion. I think the others felt the same. We were in a rage; otherwise, we could not have maintained the accelerated pace. After two or three minutes of ducked running, we reached the makeshift defense position where the Russians had broken through. Since we did not immediately realize that hand-to-hand fighting was still going on, we first threw our hand-grenades and then jumped in.

I stumbled on two men lying on the ground who were wrestling face to face. The upper man, a Russian with a knife in one hand, tried to stab the lower man, a German, who had grasped the attacker's wrist with both hands, trying to deflect the knife. The Russian in his padded suit and spiked headgear looked huge to me. Today I am not sure whether his enormous size was real or merely the result of my agitation. At any rate, I stepped next to the frightful giant, put the muzzle of my submachine gun tightly to his head, and pulled the trigger. So enraged was I that I didn't let go until I had emptied the entire magazine, sixteen bullets in all, into his head. It was a grave mistake, as I should learn minutes later.

The German cried for help in freeing himself from the colossus who had collapsed over him. He was covered all over with blood. As I pulled him out from under the dead enemy, I also covered myself with blood. Now I recognized the comrade. He was a corporal from one of our sister companies, a barber in civilian life, who had cut my hair a few times. Neither of us spoke a word because there was no time, but six months later we met again in Narvik.

Now the company commander arrived with the rest of the company. Seconds later the Russians waged a counterattack. As we had done before, they first threw their hand-grenades and then leaped forward. One Russian who emerged from a make-shift foxhole jumped at me. I pointed my submachine gun at him and pulled the trigger, but the magazine was empty. Luckily, the man stopped and maintained his position for a split second, just enough time for me to turn my weapon around and slam it into his head. The blow put him out of action, but it also broke my weapon into two parts. To my horror I noticed that I held only the barrel in my hands.

Now I was without a weapon except for the bayonet I had always considered a useless appendage. Nevertheless, I drew it. At that moment somebody cried that the company commander was wounded. I put my bayonet back in its sheath and crawled over to the lieutenant. He had a gushing wound over one brow, probably from a hand-grenade fragment, but was still conscious. As I tried to bandage him, he ordered me to stop and organize one more counter-thrust.

The Russians were about thirty meters away. Some of us had one hand-grenade left. On my command, we sprayed the enemy with submachine-gun fire, threw the remaining hand-grenades, and jumped forward. To my surprise we did not receive much fire in return. The Russians seemed to retreat, awaiting reinforcements. At any rate, we were in control of the situation, at least for the time being. Thus I ordered my men to take defensive positions. Then I crawled back to the wounded company commander.

Now the lieutenant was barely conscious. That should have been reason enough for me to take command of the company on the spot. Instead I tended to his wounds. Today, I can't tell whether I was looking for an escape from combat or acting out of real concern for the only officer to whom I felt a strong personal allegiance. The human heart sometimes likes to hide its feelings, even from its owner. Today the whole scene appears unreal to me, as if I was in a trance. At any rate, the following thirty minutes or so were the low point of my military career. Today I am neither proud nor ashamed of them.

After applying a bandage, a messenger and I laid the lieutenant on a tarpaulin and dragged him down to the road, which was about a hundred meters away. He cried out with pain and then lost consciousness. At the road we loaded him onto a cart and then raced off in a westward direction, hoping to meet a medic or somebody to whom we could consign the wounded officer. But the road was mined. That alone wouldn't have bothered us so much, had it not been for the continuing rain of artillery shells that detonated the mines.

Eventually we reached the sappers who were laying the mines, and knew that the road ahead of us was not yet mined. A little later we met a column of reinforcements, headed by an officer in a Jeep-like motorcar. It was a risky situation, as I was without a weapon and running away from the enemy. But the officer simply threw me a loaded rifle and pointed east, whereupon we surrendered the wounded lieutenant to him and turned around. A little later I was back at my company and took command.

It was just in time because a messenger from the battalion commander arrived with special instructions addressed to me as company commander. We had to take defensive positions until nightfall, then withdraw under cover of darkness. Our retreat went undiscovered for about twenty minutes before Russian infantry attacked. There was renewed fighting, and there were again casualties. The dead were left on the spot, and the wounded were carried down to the road where a few carts still could be found, yet not as many as were needed. Walter was one of the wounded lucky enough to be evacuated. I never saw him again.

The company was now reduced to about sixty men. When we were not in immediate contact with the enemy, I marched ahead of a long, stretched column. As we were snaking around a little hill to our right, we unexpectedly received fire from ahead. I thought we were encircled and gave the Ludwig command, whereupon the column performed a large sweep to the left. It was the right thing to do, though not exactly for the right reason. Nevertheless, it took the Russians by surprise. Instead of pursuing us, they only fired after us, which we acknowledged with some fire in return. Eventually we broke contact.

It was then that I gave the fateful command to throw our gas masks away, an action that later brought me an indictment for sabotage before a military tribunal. When I gave the rash order, I had persuaded myself that discarding the relatively bulky piece of equipment would accelerate our retreat, and possibly save us from Russian captivity. I also thought that nobody would wage chemical warfare at the shore of the Arctic Ocean. However, as I would learn a few months later, the military bureaucracy thought otherwise.

The following days were an alternate succession of marching and fighting. Little food, not much drink, and hardly any sleep. Eventually, we reached the Petsamo River that emptied into the Arctic Ocean at Liinahamari. The Arctic Ocean Road ran parallel to the river, on its west bank. A steel bridge over the river connected the supply road with the Arctic Ocean Road. On our side of the river, the east side, stretched a narrow meadow that would be the scene of an unsung tragedy the following day. Apparently the meadow once had been the main support of a farm that was now abandoned.

The battalion was forming a bridgehead around the east end

of the bridge. Since it was already dark when I arrived with the rest of my company, we were ordered to take positions before dawn the next day. That gave us a few hours of rest. Yearning for a place to sleep, my messengers and I entered a barn that was crowded with mountaineers. It was pitch-dark. As we tumbled over sleeping bodies, we generated a chorus of Bavarian swearing. Eventually I found a tiny spot to lie down. Before I sank into a hypnotic sleep, I had two sensations I still remember. One was the spicy smell of the moss I used as a pillow. The other was the beginning of a little speech offered by an officer who apparently found the situation quite interesting: "Now I shall tell you where the Russians will attack tomorrow." I couldn't care less.

It was still dark when we assumed defensive positions on an elevated plateau from which we could control the bridge. At daybreak we could see our troops crossing the bridge and the Russian tanks rolling in from the north. Then the Russian infantry attacked. According to orders, we fought back and withdrew at a pace that had been planned in advance. We had to surrender so much terrain in such and such time. All company commanders and most platoon leaders had official wristwatches for such occasions. Now the much-coveted pieces of equipment helped us to draw the semi-circle around the bridge ever tighter at a preset pace.

In the last hours before crossing the bridge, I had one of those experiences that mold one's character. It concerned a corporal of one of our sister companies, whom I had always considered a wretched yes-man. At one of the pep talks I had given almost a year ago, he told me that my ideas about America and Britain were "heretic" and that he preferred, as he put it, "to follow the Führer blindly wherever he would lead him." I had ridiculed the man for the qualifier "blindly," though not for following the Führer. "What do you have eyes for if you don't want to use them?" I had argued. "We all follow the Führer, but with our eyes open."

With that inconsistent polemic I had hoped to silence the poor fellow, but he had the temerity to rebut, "If the Führer leads me, I don't need eyes." Since that time I had always referred to him as "The Blind Man."

Now The Blind Man was holding a defensive position which, according to orders, should not be surrendered for another thirty minutes or so. I was afraid of being captured by the Russians and wanted to retreat faster. But he refused and coolly stayed behind a boulder, firing shot after shot at the advancing enemy. Without knowing it, this blind follower of *Gröfaz* was teaching me a lesson worthwhile to remember: A man who unknowingly serves evil does not lose his dignity as long as he is absolutely true to himself. Under a hail of gunfire, I silently begged this paragon of loyalty for forgiveness and stayed with him until it was time for a legitimate retreat.

About two hours later the two of us approached the bridge. There was only a handful of men left who still had to cross it. The sappers, who were ready to blow it up, were waiting on the other side, yelling for us to hurry. The trouble was that we first had to cross the narrow meadow along the river. Now it was under fire from a Russian heavy machine gun. We were all lying behind a shallow earth wall, from where we could hear the persistent "sist, sist" of the bullets. As my new friend, The Blind Man, leaped forward to run across the meadow, he was hit. With his hands pressed against his chest, he returned in panic. As his heart's blood was gushing out, he collapsed over me. "Put a bandage on" were his last words. I still hear him saying that in his southern dialect. It was too late. Before I could even reach for my set of bandages, he convulsed and died. All I could do was to rip open the blood-drenched tunic over his chest to retrieve his identity badge. As we were trained to do, I broke off the lower half and later turned it in to identify him as killed in action.

There was no time to bury him. The sappers shouted that the

bridge would blow up very soon. I don't know how I crossed the meadow; I only recall that I wanted to look back at the good comrade I had left at the other side, as one of the engineers wrestled me to the ground. "Don't do anything stupid, my boy," he said in a fatherly tone of voice as he pinned me down. He was an elderly man with a kind face. When he saw that I was covered with blood, both fresh and stale, he patted me on the shoulder: "You shouldn't be here, neither should I."

Seconds later the bridge blew up and collapsed into three pieces. We were just raising our heads from the ground when the Russians on the east bank sounded a frenetic hurrah, as if to applaud us for a job well done. We knew we had to retreat quickly before they were able to train their heavy machine guns on us. There was only one road to the west, a dirt road from Petsamo to Kirkenes. It was the same road on which my company had been broken up by a snowstorm in February 1943. Now the company was broken up again, this time by the Russians.

Night was falling. I marched with someone whose identity I never found out. Sometimes we rested by the roadside with a tarpaulin over both of our heads, to protect us against the cold. I believe if I met the unknown comrade again I would recognize him by his bad smell. Once, when we were resting, a messenger arrived on a motorcycle, tore the tarpaulin from our heads, and told us that we were supposed to march as fast as possible.

After several days, I had reassembled my company, only some forty men in all. Now the greatest hardship was the long marches day after day. There was some danger that the Russians would land ahead of us and cut us off, but it never happened. Apparently, they didn't have the naval power.

One day we found an abandoned German food supply camp. Unfortunately, it stored only butter and sugar. The storage barrack had been flattened by heavy vehicles, and the ground was covered with a thick layer of butter, sugar, and mud. Worse still, there were a few decomposed corpses of Russian soldiers lying around. Apparently they had been prisoners of war who worked at the supply camp. I don't know who had killed them, and I had neither the time nor the stomach to investigate. There was also a cistern with water that was covered with a green mold.

Minding neither corpses nor mold, each of us broke off a piece of the sugared butter and gulped it down. Carefully pushing the green mold aside, we filled our pots with water from the cistern and drank it. Under normal circumstances, such eating habits would have been harmful, to say the least. But I don't recall any incidence of sickness among my men. One of the worst things that could happen to a man during the great retreat was diarrhea, particularly at night when we were sleeping in tents. It seems that nature provides its strongest protection when immunity is most urgently needed.

However, one problem bothered me greatly, a bleeding blister on the small toe of my right foot. The infected wound had turned marching into torture for me. I often looked longingly after the Jeep-like motorcar in which the battalion commander rode back and forth to supervise his troops on the march. Now I was so desperate that I wanted to cut a hole in the shoe to relieve the pressure. But that would have been "sabotage of a piece of defense property." To circumvent the problem, I was looking for an ownerless shoe that I could "sabotage" to my heart's content. Luckily, I stumbled on the grave of a German soldier that was marked by a pair of shoes dangling from a makeshift cross. Never in my life had I thought of becoming a grave robber, but on this relentless march I had dreamt incessantly of a shoe with a hole in it. Now the dream came true. My own shoe was in my backpack, and the sabotaged shoe with the hole was on my foot.

One cold morning, when we were just crawling out of our tents by the roadside, the battalion commander arrived in his motor car. The driver, a sergeant, jumped out and instructed me to present the company to the commander. When my men were lined up, the sergeant announced that the commander had just been promoted to major and should be addressed accordingly.

Then the major stepped out, wearing a coat over his tunic. As he sounded his accustomed *Guten Morgen, Männer!*, he was smiling for a change. Our unaccustomed *Guten Morgen, Herr Major!* was not quite as cheerful, causing me to expect his habitual rebuke. But the freshly baked major was in an unusually good mood: "Men, the Führer has just awarded a soldier of the battalion the Knight Cross."

That was more than I expected. Of course, I had not forgotten that the commander had promised me the E.K. I (Iron Cross First Class, the higher one of the two iron crosses) on the battlefield. But the Knight Cross? Truly, my deeds were not that great. Well, as it turned out, the commander seemed to share my opinion. With a theatrical gesture, like a magician on the stage, he opened his coat to reveal the Knight Cross dangling from his neck. I still expected to receive the E.K. I, but it never came. Several weeks later, I was awarded the Iron Cross Second Class, the lower of the two.

I was deeply disappointed. I didn't dispute that the commander deserved the Knight Cross; I simply thought that I deserved the E.K. I. True, I had panicked in the middle of the battle for about thirty minutes, but virtually nobody had noticed, certainly not the battalion commander.

Today I feel differently. The commander's Knight Cross is none of my business. Moreover, whether or not I deserved the E.K. I no longer interests me. All that counts is whether or not I am the kind of person who wants to be decorated with insignias from Germany's most shameful period of history. The answer to this question, I believe, is these memoirs.

Before the war, I had been denied several insignias from the Hitler Youth, among them the shoulder strap, the Munich ID card, and the Golden Hitler Youth Emblem. And now, at the war's end, I added the E.K. I to the list. At the times when these decorations were denied to me, I coveted them. Today, I consider it conspicuously meaningful that I never received any of them.

It was snowing when we arrived at Hammerfest, the northernmost town of Norway. There were only two hours of light left in the day. A ship was waiting to take us to an undisclosed destination. Before we left, our men forced a Norwegian farmer to dig out the carcass of a pig he was trying to hide from us. In spite of the hunger that pained me, I was unable to eat any of the smelly roast. The next day, as we sailed out of the mountain-lined fjord, the sun climbed over the horizon and immersed the snow-covered mountains in glimmers of red and gold.

A few days later we passed through the Tromsö fjord north of Narvik. In dim daylight we witnessed one of the less heralded naval tragedies of the war. A German battleship—the *Tirpitz*, sister ship of the *Bismarck*—had keeled over in November 1944. The British bombers had learned to place their bombs not on the ship, but next to it, causing the water pressure to turn it over. Several rescue boats were swarming around the helpless giant, trying to cut holes through the armored hull for the 1,800 sailors trapped inside to escape. But only eighty-five were rescued.

Forty-eight years later, when I visited the watery grave of the battleship *Arizona* at Pearl Harbor, I remembered the *Tirpitz*. For a moment I felt a certain bitterness about the supposed injustice of life, but soon regained the treasured equanimity that I owe partly to old age and partly to America, my chosen country. With a sense of wholeness I had never felt as a German, I experienced a truth, which, to me, not only is a lesson of history, but a revelation of the meaningfulness of human affairs, both personal and national.

Standing above the tomb of the *Arizona*, I thought that all brave and decent soldiers deserve to be honored, no matter on which side they fought. But the sailors of the *Arizona* died in the defense of freedom, while the sailors of the *Tirpitz*, knowingly or not, died in the service of evil. Thus the iron tomb of the *Arizona* turned into a monument to freedom, while the watery grave of the *Tirpitz* became a tragic reminder that valor alone is not a sufficient guard against the onslaught of evil. Therein lies the meaning that history eventually confers to all the tragedies of war, no matter how meaningless they may appear at the moment.

CHAPTER 12

Total Defeat, Total Disillusionment

Our ship was headed for Narvik, the seaport from which the Finnish nickel ore was shipped to Germany. Hidden behind the Lofoten Islands about 200 kilometers north of the Arctic Circle, Narvik saw bloody fighting in 1940. Now the British, who had finally gained the upper hand in the North Sea, threatened us with surface ships, submarines, and aircraft. Our ship, a former freighter now commissioned by the German navy, was defended by only a few small cannons and machine guns. We were on constant alert and had to wear life jackets all the time. Our quarters were like a tomb deep in the bowels of the ship. It was there that I learned the third part of Röper's tragedy.

Since it was cold and almost always dark, we did not spend much time on deck. I wondered aloud how quickly we could climb out of our "tomb" in the event of a torpedo hit. "Don't worry," a sailor quipped, "the water is so icy, it will kill you in an instant, whether you stay in the ship or jump from the deck." As if that outlook was not gloomy enough, he grimly added: "A month ago, a freighter was hit by a torpedo just off the coast of Narvik." He mentioned the name, which I forgot, but it sounded familiar. "It went so quickly," the sailor continued, "that most of the men probably drowned under deck, while the few who jumped ship enjoyed the privilege of dying a little quicker. What's your choice?" I did not answer because I suddenly realized that the vessel he mentioned was Röper's ship.

In the following days, Röper was closer to me than he had ever been while being alive. When we passed the capsized *Tirpitz* in the Tromsö fjord, he was as much my comrade as were the sailors who were dying there before our eyes. He was my companion in adversity, as were Paul, Walter, the company commander, and The Blind Man. These men had not much in common, except for one thing: They had been caught in the same cataclysm, and each dealt with it according to his own inner law, as we all must do when lawlessness reigns.

In the following fifty years I thought of Röper perhaps a thousand times. He was a victim of Nazism, as was Theo, my cherished teacher from high school. Today I consider Röper a victim of the Holocaust, though he did not die in a concentration camp, but in the icy waters of the North Sea. The same hatred that sent millions to the gas chambers sent Röper to his watery tomb. Today, I wish I had understood this on that fateful morning in 1944, when we were standing watch and he told me about the ongoing genocide. My God, I wish I had understood this even earlier when I was a child and insulted a Jewish girl, who also became a victim of the satanic hatred.

In spite of the British naval vessels that were lying in wait for us, our ship took us safely to Narvik. Before receiving a new assignment, my company was billeted in a requisitioned school building, where it was replenished with new personnel and material. However comfortable these words may sound, the process itself turned into a minor nightmare for me. The source of my troubles was the lieutenant who had become our new company commander. The officer, who was decorated with the Iron Cross First Class, was a Bavarian from the mountaineers and a school-teacher by profession.

When I presented the company to the new commander, he immediately noticed that the gas masks were missing. "Where are the gas masks?"—"We threw them away."—"What?"—"We threw them away."—"On whose order?"—"On my order."

This brief exchange was followed by a tirade of recriminations and reproaches. I attempted to defend myself, but the lieutenant forbade me to speak. When the flood of accusations did not stop, I made a second attempt, but got only as far as "Herr Leutnant..." before he cut me short. In extreme anger he shouted, "Quiet, quiet, you *Scheisskerl* [shit guy]!" This outburst was followed by another diatribe of denunciations and profanities.

In the German language, the swearword *Scheisskerl* expresses contempt and can even imply cowardice. Hence it was an assault on my honor as a soldier. Even in Hitler's army that was behavior unbecoming an officer. After I had collected my thoughts and grasped the implications of this fact, I relaxed and made no further attempt to defend myself. The lieutenant's improper conduct was a weakness I was determined to use to my advantage should that be necessary. At the moment, however, he had the upper hand, announcing with unmistakable gusto that *Tatbericht* (criminal charges) for "sabotage on armed forces' property" would be filed against me.

I was worried. A military tribunal could sentence me to clearing mines, a penalty that meant almost certain death. I was also concerned that I had an unequal fight on my hands, feeling much like David facing Goliath. Hence I had to be cunning. To avert the threat of a court martial, I had to stage a counter-threat. However, in the Wehrmacht, that was a dangerous course to take.

Whatever threat I came up with, it was imperative that it did not contain the slightest reference to the criminal charges I was threatened with. So I decided to submit a formal complaint for having been insulted with invectives such as *Scheisskerl*. The complaint posed a threat to the lieutenant insofar as it could potentially delay or even prevent his promotion.

I had to act quickly before the criminal charges could be sent to the military tribunal in Oslo. My first step was a formal action called *Sich zum Rapport melden* (literally, to report for *Rapport*, meaning to appear before a superior, either to be reprimanded or to submit a grievance). In full military dress, including steel helmet—but without gas mask—I asked for permission to enter the lieutenant's room, where I extended a studiously correct salute and then waited deferentially until allowed to speak. "What do you want?" "I respectfully ask Herrn Leutnant to please withdraw the insult *Scheisskerl.*" His answer consisted of a single word: "Out!"

A few minutes later I reported again for *Rapport,* not on my volition, however, but on the lieutenant's order. He came right to the point: "I punish you with five days' *Geschärftem Arrest* because, on day so and so, you disobeyed my order to be silent." *Geschärfter Arrest* meant confinement on dry bread and water. That was an unusually harsh penalty for the trifling misdemeanor of which I was guilty. Moreover, it was revenge. Clearly, the exaggerated penalty was the lieutenant's answer to my motion that he withdraw the insult. It was another weakness I quickly used to my advantage by filing a complaint about an assault on my honor followed by unreasonable punishment.

The tenor of the complaint was that "I had volunteered for service in the Führer's army to defend the Fatherland, not to suffer insults by anybody." The Führer was the strong point of my defense. The strategy was to suggest that he was on my side, and I on his. After this attempt to call the Führer to my rescue, I added the line: "If the Führer knew of this assault on my soldier's honor, I am sure he would not tolerate it." This was a veiled threat that I would take my grievance up as high as gravity would allow.

Now followed a lengthy tug of war between the battalion commander and me. Since he wanted to promote the lieutenant, who was his buddy, his aim was to persuade me to withdraw the complaint. The lieutenant himself was no longer in the action because he was the subject of the complaint. The criminal charges concerning the gas masks were also removed from negotiation because they were already on their way to Oslo.

The major, in his regal manner, did not negotiate with me in person, but let one of his lieutenants do it for him. The job went to Joseph, the battalion's National Socialist leadership officer. I had two or three meetings with Joseph during which he bombarded me with phrases such as "the Führer needs disciplined soldiers" and "we are involved in a struggle of life and death against international Jewry." I replied that I knew this but insisted that all soldiers had to be disciplined, both subordinates and superiors.

Since neither side yielded an inch, we got nowhere. Eventually Joseph grew impatient and called me names such as "spoiled kid" and "touch-me-not." I thought these expressions were rather harmless; in fact, I welcomed them because I interpreted them as a sign of weakness. Apparently my opponents no longer hoped to persuade me to accept the penalty imposed by the company commander. With a bittersweet taste of irony I observed that, finally, I had gained some respect. My suspicion was confirmed when Joseph terminated the negotiations with the feeble remark, "As a National Socialist leadership officer you ought to know better. But now I see that you haven't learned anything, not even in the Hitler Youth."

Now it was the major's turn. Obviously he could not afford to issue a complete annulment of the penalty imposed by the company commander. On the other hand, my reference to the Führer left no doubt that I was determined to take my complaint up to the highest authority. Hence the major had to seek a compromise. Careful not to create the appearance of a formal *Rapport,* he "invited" me for a "chat." "You are a brave soldier and a good National Socialist," he said with a mildness I had never observed in him. "I am sure the Führer would be proud of you. But you disobeyed the lieutenant's order. That's a misdemeanor I cannot let go unpunished. Thus I have decided to commute your penalty into a simple reprimand. How is that?" When I did not immediately answer, he assumed the harsh tone of voice I was used to: "My decision is final. Take it or leave it. Dismissed."

I was surprised. A simple reprimand was the lowest disciplinary penalty in the Wehrmacht. Since the criminal charges were already out of the major's hands, I had no further motive to keep up the fight. Besides, the threatened court martial was months away. In fact, before the military bureaucracy was able to act, *Gröfaz* blew his brains out, and his generals signed instruments of surrender in east and west. Of course, I did not foresee these events at the time, nor did I desire them. But change was in the air, and there were more serious things to worry about than the silly court martial.

Shortly before Christmas the battalion was reassigned to Björnfjel, a tiny spot on the railway from Narvik to Sweden, directly at the border. Our mission was to guard the border and the railroad that once had carried nickel ore from Finland to Narvik. Of course, the nickel mines had been lost in the meantime, and the Swedes probably would no longer have allowed us to ship the ore through their country. Hence there was no real purpose for us to be there. I guess if *Gröfaz* had been able to move us to beleaguered Germany, he would have loved to send us to the collapsing fronts in east or west.

I never saw any Norwegian civilians in Björnfjel. Our company occupied a splendid three-story building in the middle of nowhere. We treated the wooden structure, which once had served as a home for retired Norwegian railroad workers, reasonably well, though I cannot guarantee that it was as well preserved as it should have been when we left. In a letter from the Reich's Commissioner for Norway, we were advised to treat the Norwegian civilians "correctly but firmly," whatever that meant. We were also told that a German soldier who had raped a Norwegian girl in Kirkenes had been sentenced to death and executed.

Morale and discipline were sagging. In January 1945 I was summoned to Joseph. He was still sulking, but also seeking help to restore discipline. "We need your assistance," he admitted. "The major has decided to send you to a National Socialist training course." I do not recall the name of the place, but I do remember that it was a beautiful spot by the sea not far from Narvik. I welcomed the change and looked forward to the undoubtedly better living conditions there. Besides, I felt slightly guilty for having contributed to the declining discipline by having waged— and won!—a battle against the military establishment.

A few days later I was on my way to the NS training course. It was a splendid boat ride through icy fjords lined by snow-covered mountains. There were two German nurses on board dressed in gray capes and white cornets. Having just escaped from an environment of coarseness and vulgarity, I noticed their poise and womanly dignity with a mixture of sadness and gratitude. It turned out that they were heading to the same place I was. After the German surrender I would meet them again under decidedly less pleasant circumstances in a British prisoner of war camp.

The NS school was housed in an exquisite building that once had served as a resort hotel. Living conditions were even better than I expected: semi-private rooms, real beds, white linen, central heating, though sparsely used, and the pleasant women who were running the hotel. Even the food was better than usual, if not more caloric then at least more carefully prepared. After dinner, everybody got an apple. For me it was the first since 1939.

The instructors were assorted officers, mostly elderly gentlemen who, for a change, also behaved as such. It was a relaxed atmosphere, but with a taint of unreality. We only had to think of the unfathomable suffering of the people at home, both soldiers and civilians, to appreciate the exaggerated, luxurious living conditions we enjoyed. At home raged a *Nibelungen Kampf* (Battle of the Nibelungs, a heroic dynasty from German sagas and Wagnerian operas), while we were sitting at laid tables and pontificating about the superiority of the Aryan race. When I sensed that others shared my uneasiness, I made a few remarks to that effect, which were received with sincere, though subdued, applause. One comrade told me with tears in his eyes that his entire family had been wiped out in a bombing raid.

The political teaching was orthodox, but relatively free of the anti-Semitism I had absorbed in my childhood and now resented. The instructors took pains to emphasize the "positive" rather than the negative side of race ideology. The Scandinavians were praised as the purest Aryans of Europe, and the Norwegians, in particular, were spoken of as potential allies. One of the instructors had an amazingly positive attitude toward England. He talked in glowing terms of Admiral Nelson and General Wellington. That emboldened me to pursue a similar line when it was my turn to talk. As a natural scientist, I added Isaac Newton and Charles Darwin to the list of Anglo-Saxon heroes.

I suppose my and my predecessor's presentations of Anglo-Saxon creativity were so persuasive that even the more orthodox Nazis couldn't help seeing the point. Encouraged by the resonance from my listeners, I proceeded to project the picture of a Germanic–Anglo-Saxon family of nations around the Atlantic. Sorry to say that I tainted the shiny picture with some remnants from the indoctrination I had received in the Hitler Youth and in school, for I thought it advisable to include some bait for the more orthodox members of my audience. Not having freed myself completely from the mental imprisonment of my youth, I added a few idiotic phrases from Nazi ideology such as Lebensraum and "hordes of Genghis Khan." While that concession may have made the ideological dish more palatable to the Nazis among my listeners, it contaminated it with the toxin I had not yet purged completely from my bloodstream. Nevertheless, I received sincere but cautious applause. One of the instructors even shook my hand and said, "Well done."

A few days after returning to my company, I was again summoned by Joseph. Apparently he had received a report about my talk at the NS school and now wanted to express some reservations. "You should speak less about England and more about the Jews," he cautioned me. "The major orders you to deliver a real fighting hold-out talk to your company. He wants you to speak about 'fighting to the death.'"

I still considered it my duty to do everything in my power to strengthen the fighting spirit. Thus, I gave a patriotic sermon. Today, I wish I had never delivered it. As far as effectiveness is concerned, it was my best; as far as timing is concerned, it was the worst. As I had learned in school, in the Hitler Youth, and recently at the NS education course, I peppered my talk with quotes from Frederick the Great, Bismarck, and, of course, Hitler. I even went afar and quoted the inscription from the monument commemorating the heroic stand of the Spartans under Leonidas against the Persians: "Wanderer, should you come to Sparta, let it be known there that you have seen us lying here as the law provides."

I had learned the epigraph from Paul, who had cited it in a letter I had carried with me until I lost it during the retreat. Now I used it in conjunction with the battle of Thermopylae. From school I remembered a quote of Frederick the Great, who, at the morning of the battle of Leuthen, told his generals, "Gentlemen! I either shall beat the enemy, or I shall be buried in front of his batteries." Only with regard to the battle of Stalingrad was I at a loss for a suitable quote. In fact, I felt a little uneasy because Hitler had not exactly covered himself with glory during that disastrous battle. Thus I had to perform a little diversion by indulging in "creative history." Against my better knowledge, I told my listeners that the entire Sixth Army, a quarter of a million men, had fought to the death, "as the Führer had ordered." Nobody seemed to notice the deception. Thus, for the last time in my life, I preached the steely moral of fighting to the death, though with slightly shaky conviction.

Our lieutenant was deeply impressed, and so were most of the others. I, however, had mixed feelings. If my talk could turn this man from a despiser into an admirer of mine, then surely something must have been wrong with it! And so it was. A day after the sermon, the lieutenant informed me that he had recommended me for promotion to sergeant. The proposed advancement was approved before the Third Reich collapsed, but reached me only thereafter when I was in a British prisoner of war camp. At that time I bitterly resented the promotion and tried to persuade the British officer who interrogated me to ignore it. But the man stoically entered me into his register as sergeant.

That wasn't all. On one of the last days of the Third Reich, the lieutenant placed himself squarely in front of me and begged me to punch him in the nose. "Bruno, sock me in the mouth!" Discipline had suddenly lost its appeal to him, and dignity had never been his mettle. His values were turned upside down. Instead of the urge to insult me, he now felt a desire to be smitten by me. Rather than being a *Scheisskerl* to him, I now was a kind of pastor. "Give us another pep talk," he pleaded. "When I hear you talking, I think I am in church." The man had turned from a sadist into a masochist. I was disgusted. Disregarding all military etiquette, I abruptly turned around and left him standing there.

Then came the extra bulletin over the radio that I shall never forget: *Aus dem Führer Hauptquartier erreicht uns die Nachricht, dass unser Führer, Adolf Hitler, bis zum letzten Atemzug für Deutschland kämpfend, gefallen ist* (From the Führer headquarters we receive the message that our Führer, Adolf Hitler, fighting to his last breath for Germany, has been killed in action). The terse announcement was followed by the dark and haunting sounds of the funeral music from *Götterdämmerung* (Night falls on the gods, the last of Wagner's four operas of *The Ring of the Nibelung*.)

I was devastated. My mental pain was so severe that it became physical. Since I am entirely at a loss to describe it, I will not attempt to do so. The plain fact is that the day of Hitler's death was the low point of my life. For the next twelve months or so I stayed in the valley of despair until I recognized very slowly and reluctantly that I was mourning the death of a monster. This growing awareness was the antidote that eventually broke down the poison Hitler had injected into my blood more than a decade ago. "The truth will make you free," the Bible says. It did.

During the days immediately following Hitler's death, I desperately sought comfort from a congenial mind, either in person or in spirit. With the exception of one comrade, there was no living soul around capable of feeling what I felt. The officers, who once had been arrogant and now were undignified, were the least helpful of all. The heretofore almost omnipotent propaganda machine now suffered from the same impotence. However, in one of its last broadcasts, the German radio offered some respite by quoting a world-renowned voice that had a certain ring of dignity, though it came from a man who had been led astray as thoroughly as I had been.

The misguided dignitary, of all people, was Sven Hedin, the

famous explorer from Sweden who had the reputation of being a Germanophile during World War I. As a boy, I had read his book *Through Asia's Deserts*. Now I read his eulogy of Adolf Hitler. Tragedy seems to be as capable of irony as is comedy. In his tribute to the Führer, Sven Hedin spoke of "Europe's Genius," and I drew passing comfort from the injudicious words.

The congenial comrade I mentioned was a corporal who had joined us recently. His name was Willy and his home was in eastern Germany, where he expected to return. He was not the kind of person one can move to tears with a Schubert song, but he was unassuming and honest, both to others and himself. He shared my love of country, my socialist inclination, and my mistrust of officers. Most important, however, were the bitterness and the loss of faith that united us. "I no longer believe anything," Willy cried out in anguish. "I detest this world." As painful as the situation was, I had to smile and think of my school days when we performed *Hamlet* and I acted the part of the prince: "How weary, stale, flat and unprofitable seem to me all the uses of this world."

After the war I worried that Willy might have fallen victim to the siren songs of the Communist regime in East Germany. On the other hand, I could not imagine him entering a second mental prison at the very moment he had escaped from the first one. Today I would consider it a grace of fate to meet this upright man again.

When the news of the unconditional surrender arrived, it turned out that we had a few anti-Nazis among us. Understandably, they had been silent all that time, but now they showed their relief and gratification in various ways. One of them even endangered his life by celebrating Germany's defeat all too triumphantly. Since he had just arrived from another company, I was not personally acquainted with him, but had heard by the grapevine that criminal charges for corruption of the fighting spirit had been filed against him. Not knowing his name, I shall call him "The Celebrator."

Upon hearing the news of the capitulation, the Celebrator jubilantly ran around and shouted incessantly, "Unconditional surrender!" I was irritated, and so were Willy and a few others. Today I realize that I have done injustice to the man who was almost delirious with joy. After all, he was a fellow sufferer and most likely would have been a victim of more serious persecution, as I might have been, had the Third Reich lasted a little longer. Nevertheless, I was hurting, and the Celebrator was rubbing salt into my wounds.

A few days later it was announced that a commando unit of the British Royal Army was at sea on its way to Narvik. The officer in charge sent advance orders over the radio to separate ourselves from our weapons and surround both men and weapons with barbed wire. So we did. When I threw my rifle on the heap of war material, I felt an almost religious deliverance. Never again in my life have I touched a weapon.

When the Celebrator heard the announcement that the British were coming, he boarded a Swedish train to Narvik that was still operating once a day. That did not go unnoticed by the two SD men from the Security Service, a branch of the SS, who were detailed to our company and responsible for searching the trains to and from Sweden. They suspected that the Celebrator might seek special treatment from the British in exchange for information.

A few days later the Celebrator was expected to return from Narvik. Thereupon the SD men gathered a small group, including Willy and me, to intercept the man when he deboarded the train. I am not certain what our specific intentions were, but I am afraid that at least some of us had violence in mind. As for myself, I can say truthfully that I would not have actively partaken in such acts, but I am not sure what I would have done if the others had resorted to violence. All I can say is that I was terribly afraid of some kind of unlawful action on the part of my comrades.

We were standing in the dark and chilly snow tunnel of the railroad, waiting for the train. One of the men accidentally hit the power line with a wet stick and was electrocuted. I wished I were in Finland or on the moon. Eventually, the train arrived. To my great relief, the Celebrator was not in it. The next day, the SD men wanted to look again for the hated man, but I persuaded them to let him go. Thus, I was saved from becoming an accomplice to what might have been one of the last crimes committed in the name of the Third Reich.

The British were still nowhere to be found, and we still guarded our weapons and ourselves. Eventually we learned that the announced commando unit had gone, not to Narvik, but to a former German supply base nearby, which they had selected as a transition camp for the shipment of prisoners of war to Germany. Since I had learned some English in school, I was detailed as an interpreter.

The farewell to Willy was one of the saddest of my life. I had known him for only a few months, but he had become my friend in the best sense of the word. Now he was standing at the gate to say goodbye. When he sensed my emotion, he patted me on the shoulder, unable to say a word. Then I jumped onto the truck that took me to the transition camp. I never saw Willy again.

There was only a handful of British soldiers at the transition camp, not nearly enough to guard the hundreds of German prisoners. Thus, we guarded ourselves. A German colonel who was responsible for the internment reported to the British colonel who was in charge of the whole operation. The English soldiers were all elderly gentlemen, correct, almost cozy, but not fraternizing. As an interpreter, I was in daily contact with them. Sometimes they would eat a sandwich in my presence. That was hard to endure because of the hunger that now was and would be my steady companion for the next three years.

Every once in a while, a contingent of German soldiers left the camp and marched to a nearby harbor, where a ship took them to Germany. Or so we thought. One day a Russian general appeared, and we learned that the soldiers from eastern Germany were to be handed over to the Soviet army. That caused heart-rending tragedies. At first, the men beseeched the British to send them to western Germany, but the British refused because they were treaty bound to extradite them to the Soviets. Having been denied escape, some of the men committed suicide, while others tried to falsify their soldier's ID. As an interpreter, I witnessed these tragic developments firsthand. Seldom have I seen men in so much terror and despair.

Meanwhile, I watched the Russian general with his scarlet red insignia and stripes along his trousers. It was a strange feeling to gaze at the former enemy without having to shoot at him. I thought he looked merciless, but that may have been a product of my imagination. Nevertheless, the British looked downright human in comparison. Hence I was glad that my home was in western Germany, but I was worried about Willy. Today I am afraid that he might not have survived Soviet captivity.

It was summer now. As an interpreter I was relatively free to move around in my spare time. Occasionally, I walked to a nearby alpine lake where I tried to find solace in the beauty of nature. As is still my habit today, I whistled classical music. This time, of course, there were no happy tunes, only heroic ones. Sitting by the lakeside, I brooded over Germany's defeat and sought comfort from the "glory" of days long past.

From one of my parents' last letters I knew that they had been evacuated to the Teutoburger Wald, a hilly forest in northwestern Germany. In A.D. 9, this rugged landscape had been the scene of a historic battle between the Romans under Varus and the Germanic tribe of the Cherusci under Arminius. A popular statue of Arminius, also known as Hermann the Cherusker, thrusting his sword into the sky, is now standing at the place where three Roman legions had been annihilated. When I was about twelve years old, I visited the memorial with the Hitler Youth from a nearby youth hostel. The warden, who narrated the battle, told us that the voice of the Roman Emperor Augustus could still be heard resounding through the forest at night: "Varus, Varus, give me back my legions!" He did not say in which language the emperor was lamenting, but my childish mind was so impressed that I went out at night to hear the imperial voice. As the wind was rustling in the trees and the owls were calling through the darkness, I fancied I heard the emperor's desperate call.

Now, dazed and desperate at a lonely lake in northern Norway, I remembered this national shrine in the Teutoburg forest. To my amazement, I noticed that Arminius rather than Hitler was now my hero, and the heroic music I whistled was Beethoven's "Eroica" rather than Wagner's *Götterdämmerung*. Reluctantly, almost fearfully, I blamed Hitler for having lost the war. Had I known his crimes, my feelings would have been incomparably stronger. Nevertheless, I was making the first serious effort to free myself from the chains of mental imprisonment, though this was not clear to me at the time. While I did not find much relief from my pain, I was collected enough to start distrusting Hitler and Nazism. Today I comprehend that I had suffered the fever of detoxification that must precede the onset of healing.

On my way back from the lake, I met the two nurses from the NS training course. They had not yet gone home, but had volunteered to serve in a makeshift hospital for the soldiers of the transition camp. "We are on a pilgrimage to seek peace and comfort," said the older one with an engaging smile. Her words struck me in an ineffable way. "Oh," I called almost joyfully, "you are on your way to that lake!" "Yes," she replied, "how did you find out?" "Because," I stammered, "because . . . you see . . . I know you . . . you must go there, you of all people . . . it will do you some good." Now it was the nurse's turn to be at a loss for words. "Amazing," she murmured, "amazing." After a while, she added, "Come and see us tonight, we shall have a concert. By all means, come. It will do *you* some good."

The concert was a remarkable performance by a string quartet of German soldiers. Before they played the last piece, a mild-mannered colonel announced, "Now we shall play something that, I am sure, is close to your heart." It was the slow movement of the Emperor Quartet by Joseph Haydn, which still serves as the German national anthem. Never in my life have I sensed the nobility and beauty of this melody as deeply as on that summer evening in northern Norway. Technically, the performance was probably not perfect, but it breathed the spirit of the music. In the previous twelve years, I had heard the melody a thousand times played by bands of Storm Troopers at a tempo more suitable for a march than a hymn. Now I realized the uncomfortable truth that it is possible for something noble and graceful to be usurped by ignoble and graceless minds.

There was another episode of wandering around in liberated Norway. A comrade and I were strolling along a scenic dirt road when we met a group of young Norwegian soldiers. They seemed to be happy, and I envied them for their innocence. Apparently they had recently arrived from England and now enjoyed the new freedom of their beautiful country. One of them asked us in English what we were doing here, and I replied that we were taking a walk. "You are not supposed to do that," cautioned the young man with a tone of voice that betrayed more embarrassment than conviction. "You are prisoners of war." Though the lad had reason to be angry, he sounded almost apologetic, as if he regretted to have run into us. The others must have felt the same, since they betrayed the same engaging embarrassment. I had the uneasy feeling that we were spoiling their fun. As they deliberated on what to do with us, I watched their decent faces and thanked fate that I no longer had to shoot at human beings. Finally they decided to let us go. As they walked away, I asked myself what we would have done had the situation been reversed.

In September 1945, it was my turn to board a ship bound for the home country. It was a former troop transport manned by a German crew. Because of the mines that had been laid by both parties during the war, the journey was tricky and dangerous. For reasons unknown to me, the ship took us only to Trondheim, where we spent a few days in a makeshift camp. As we marched through the pleasant town under a guard of Norwegian soldiers, some civilians watched us from the sidewalks. I was amazed that there was virtually no demonstration of hatred. Six years later, my older brother would tell me about his experiences as a prisoner of war in France that were decidedly less pleasant.

The next ship, also a former troop transport with a German crew, finally took us to Neustadt, a little seaport on the Baltic. To get there, we had to pass through the Emperor Wilhelm Channel that connects the North Sea to the Baltic. When the homeland came in sight, all soldiers were on deck. Generally, the view was decidedly unpleasant. Destroyed houses, blown-up bridges, and demolished vessels marred the landscape. But when some civilians on the embankment waved and clapped their hands, it was like a ray of sunlight breaking through a gloomy sky. All we soldiers rushed over to bask in the warmth of the welcome, causing the ship to tilt dangerously to one side. The captain implored us from the bridge to move to the other side, but that was not easy because the vessel was now tilted so heavily that we could only crawl on hands and knees across the iron deck. Slowly, slowly, the ship returned to its upright position. Some of us cheered;

others laughed timidly, for laughter was rationed in 1945. I thought it would have been cruel, indeed, to have died so close to home and so late in the history of the Third Reich. And for what?

In Neustadt the British marched us to another camp, where we were separated into groups depending on where we lived. My group travelled by railroad to Münster in Westfalen for final discharge. The town and its beautiful churches were cruelly ruined. Half a century later, when I revisited the town as an American, it was fully restored and more beautiful than ever. Now, on my last day as a German soldier, I stood with a group of a few thousand others at an open space in Münster for the official discharge procedure by the victors. A British officer on a rostrum conducted the affair in German over a loudspeaker. He repeatedly asked for order, but I did not notice any particular disorder.

Everybody wanted to go home; nobody was interested in any more military circuses, except the British officer who seemed to have a strange predilection for Prussian drill. He let us stand at attention and theatrically descended from his rostrum to see that it was done according to the German military code. Apparently he was not satisfied, for he repeated the discipline several times. The farce lasted for about two hours that were enjoyed by nobody save this strange specimen of a British officer. "Well," said the man next to me, "apparently the British have some of the same stinkers among them as we had, though hopefully not in the same profusion."

I was burning to see my parents. Most of all, I was anxious to get away from the military. For almost six years, I had tolerated the unnatural state of affairs in which one mental dwarf can run a whole group of men like a herd of cattle. Now I had to suffer the perversion one more time. Ironically, it was a British officer who conducted the final episode of my military life. "A German officer got lost in you," I murmured, while the pompous ass still sounded his commands over the loudspeaker. Eventually, however, the fool grew tired of the silly game and turned it over to some subordinate who seemed to have more sense in his head. Without much ado, the circus came to an end. Everyone received his certificate of discharge and a railroad ticket to his final destination.

Free at last! No more war, no army, no weapons, no officers, nobody to tell me what to do. The Nazi Party had disappeared without a trace. With it had vanished the little propaganda minister and his spokesmen who told me what to think. The lies of Aryan superiority and Jewish inferiority had fallen silent. What a relief to shed the last vestiges of national hubris and racial conceit! The Third Reich had left no legacy, except corpses and ruins. Its place was taken by a never-experienced, unwonted freedom! Painful and uninvited though it was, it was freedom nevertheless. Even though my mind was still filled with despair and humiliation, it suddenly was suffused with a miraculous sense of wonder and gratitude, as I felt the mental chains loosening and the injection of ideological poison ending.

CHAPTER 13

The Truth Sinks In

My destination was the little town of Örlinghausen in the Teutoburg forest, an elongated crest that runs from north to south through the plain of northwestern Germany. The train ride was as dismal as everything else. Even though this part of northwest Germany had not seen much fighting, the devastation was substantial. The railroad cars were full of bullet holes and mostly without window glass. Even the little train station of Örlinghausen was severely damaged. It was a miracle that the trains were still running.

It was a long march from the train station at the foot of the crest to the town at the top. While the station was virtually destroyed, the town was unscathed. At the city hall I wanted to inquire about my parents' whereabouts, but the two young secretaries did not let me finish my sentence. Scarcely had I pronounced the family name, when the first of them cried, "Manz—*Badeanstalt*" (swimming pool). "Look, how happy he is!" shouted the other before I could finish my question. And happy I was. The unexpected welcome was heartwarming, and my thanks were equally heartfelt. After receipt of my ration cards, I was on my way to the community swimming pool at the edge of town where my parents now lived.

Only my father was "at home" at the *Badeanstalt*. When he saw me, he hobbled toward me with his walking stick and embraced me with his usual warmth. I was shocked at how emaciated he looked. His head was only skin and bones, which gave it the appearance of a death's head. I had some dry bread with me. He gulped it down within an instant.

My father had always been a passionate eater, which made him particularly vulnerable to the near-starvation of the postwar years. Some thirty years later, long after his death, when I was enjoying a plentiful meal in America, I often wished my father were with me sharing the feast. Strangely, whenever I felt this desire, I also wanted him to receive his meal out of Jewish hands. Today it is clear to me that this fantasy was a Freudian dream rooted in the desire that the sobering experience would cure him of his anti-Semitic mania.

On the day of my return, my mother happened to be on a "hoarding trip" in search of food, and my younger brother and sister were with her. The eighteen-year-old boy had recently returned from American captivity. He had been drafted in 1945 into the elite division *Grossdeutschland* and happened to be in Czechoslovakia at the war's end. To avoid Russian captivity, he marched under cover of darkness until he reached the Americans, to whom he surrendered. My sister had also returned from Czechoslovakia, where she had spent the last war years with her school. There was no word from my older brother, who, at the war's end, had served on the Western front. About a year later we got a message from the International Red Cross that he was working as a prisoner of war in a French coal mine. He returned a broken man in 1948.

Eventually, my mother and two younger siblings returned from the hoarding trip. Unfortunately, they had not met with much success. The little food they carried came from my mother's sister, who was married to an executive in the steel industry. Apparently the uncle had ways to get some food on the side. A few years later, when I was a student, the same aunt and uncle supported me with food and clothes.

In the fall of 1945, millions of starving people were on the road, trying to get something to eat from the farmers. The railroads were so overloaded that passengers were standing on the running boards or sitting on the roofs. The farms were overrun by hungry people. The situation was so desperate that the farmers sometimes used dogs to ward off the onslaught of starving masses. Everything of value, such as jewelry, silverware, or fur coats, was offered in exchange for food. People remarked with grim humor that a farm without a Persian rug in the pigpen was substandard. A loaf of bread on the black market went for a thousand Reichsmark, and a pound of lard for ten thousand. As always in such situations, a few people got filthy rich while many starved to death. The death toll during the winter of 1945–46 in western Germany is estimated variously at a few hundred thousand to one million people.

The most desperate among the starving people banded together to raid farms, and the harried farmers joined forces to defend themselves. When it came to a confrontation, "right" was always on the side of the numerically superior party. Firearms and knives were strictly prohibited by the occupation forces, so bats became the chief weapon of the food hunters.

Gathering food was also on my father's mind when, a day after my homecoming, he took me on a walk to a small farm in the plain at the foot of the Teutoburg crest. There he pointed wist-fully to a goose that was roaming around freely. Apparently, he had been watching the potential roast for quite some time, but a big dog had always foiled his design. To our dismay the guardian was still around, and the expedition ended in failure.

My family was in particularly dire straits. As evacuees and strangers in a little town, we had even less to eat than the locals. The little food available on ration cards provided about half the calories needed for maintaining body weight. All members of my family showed various symptoms of malnourishment, rang-ing from edema to a dull pain in the back of the head. Once my mother showed me, with tears in her eyes, how my younger brother had carved little notches in his bread so that he knew the next morning how much he could eat that day.

Once my father procured a sack of sugar beets in exchange for some tools. My mother added some flour she had obtained by giving away her last jewelry. She prepared a tasty soup from these two ingredients that enticed my father to ask the naive question, "Why didn't you make that dish more often in the good old days?" "Because you wouldn't have eaten it then," she replied.

At the time, my sister had a job as a mess hall attendant with the local British occupation forces. We were hoping that she would bring us something to eat when she came home at night. But we were grievously disappointed, since she was strictly for-bidden to take any food from the premises. We took this for sheer cruelty; in fact, we believed that the extremely low food rations were a calculated act of revenge that reminded us all too vividly of the continued blockade after World War I. Today, I am not so sure about this, for it is a fact that, at the end of World War II, there were food shortages all over the world. And since the Amer-icans virtually had to feed the world, one cannot hold it against them that they fed their friends first.

One must also take into account that a nation is never so

homogeneous as to act with one single will. Nor is the predominant will unalterable. Thus, the degree of influence on a nation's policy and the resultant responsibility for its actions differ greatly from one individual to the next. In this regard, I feel that the Morgenthau Plan and the Marshall Plan offer some instructive insight into the American psyche. I think the Morgenthau Plan, a project to convert Germany from an industrial into an agrarian society, was mainly the result of a rather short-lived hatred. Serving a ubiquitous instinct for revenge, the plan originally met with Roosevelt's (also Churchill's) approval, but was discarded when the American people regained their innate magnanimity, which even the crimes of the Nazis could not numb forever. The Marshall Plan to rebuild Germany, on the other hand, seems to be a more authentic expression of the American mentality.

Clothes were as scarce as was food. Since my civilian garments had been lost in the bombing raids, I continued to wear my army uniform for the next three years. But I had to dye it—cap, tunic, and pants—on orders of the military government that was eager to erase any trace of German militarism. The color was optional. I chose blue.

I was all too happy to comply with the "demilitarization" order, though I was dismayed when I pulled the garments out of the dye. They were neither gray nor blue, but checkered like the costume of a clown; worse, they were one size too small. The cap was so tiny that I had to wear it sideways, as if I had imbibed too much. To make matters worse, my army shoes had changed in the opposite direction. Since the soles had long worn out, I had replaced them with pieces of rubber from a truck tire. Naturally, the rubber stubbornly insisted on its original curvature, causing the tips of the shoes to point ostentatiously toward the sky. This apparent extravagance made the shoes look like the boots of a giant. The total effect of the well-intentioned demilitarization effort was a gross mismatch of body and garment sizes that would have guaranteed laughter on any circus stage. But I didn't mind. In fact, I soon began to like the costume, for I considered its ostensible lack of fit a telling allegory of my misuse as a soldier. A year later, the odd attire earned me the nickname "Billy the Kid" from an American journalist. With that, I renewed my childhood excursion into the American Wild West.

I received my first decent suit about three years later from an aunt who visited us from America. She was the wife of one of my father's brothers. All five of his elder brothers had emigrated to the United States before World War I. Only the girls and the two younger boys had stayed at home. When my wife and I immigrated to America, we visited the aunt and several descendants of my father's brothers. Some of them had fought against Germany in World War II, and one recalled having bombed my hometown, Dortmund. But none hated Germans, except one who refused to talk to us. He was the son of my father's oldest brother, who had been known for harboring strong anti-German feelings ever since he had left his despotic father's home.

My war decorations, the only legacy from the army, were now dispensable. Eager to part with the dubious mementos, but not wanting my father to witness the symbolic act, I took a solitary walk to the farm that he had circled so often in search of a roast. I wanted the throw-away to be a little ceremony, but the farm's watchdog had other things in mind, forcing me to part with the medals rather unceremoniously. Nevertheless, it was with a delicious sense of satisfaction that I threw the decorations onto the dung heap in front of the paltry farmhouse. As I walked away, I knew that I had broken another chain of my mental imprisonment.

During this time, my father told me a little story that happened in Örlinghausen shortly before my homecoming. A British colonel whom my father described as "a Jew, but a gentleman, nevertheless," visited the *Badeanstalt* to take a swim. When the visitor offered my father a cigarette, the two men got into a conversation. The gentleman told my father in fluent German that he had lived in Berlin before the war. When my father gloomily remarked that he hated the war, the colonel replied, "Well, if one doesn't like war, one shouldn't make war." The answer took my father completely by surprise. "Do you believe, then, that we started the war?" he asked in total disbelief, without intent of being argumentative. "Yes," replied the colonel with an earnestness that deeply impressed my father. "Yes, you did."

When my father told me the story, he used even stronger language than I used above: "The gentleman's solemnity," he murmured with a mixture of admiration and bewilderment, "sent a shiver down my spine." Being intimately familiar with my father's political mindset, I understood how he felt. To me the encounter with the British colonel would have been a grace of God; to him it was an event with which he could not cope. The frankness of the answer and the conviction with which it was given were already disturbing enough for my father, but the fact that it came from a living human being, rather than a printed text, gave it additional weight and immediacy for which he was entirely unprepared. In the Third Reich he had read or heard only prefabricated opinions in the press or on the radio. Now, for the first time in a decade, a person of flesh and blood stood before him and frankly stated his personal opinion that Germany had started the war.

Unfortunately, the experience did not change my father's mind. In spite of the colonel's obvious sincerity, the old man did not believe him then or later. While he was humbled by the unanticipated display of humanity from a member of "the inferior race," he lulled himself into believing that the gentleman's behavior was the exception rather than the rule. In the last years of his life, my father's obstinacy filled me with bitterness, but also with pity, because I empathized with the suffering it caused him. Since

I did not want to rub salt into his wounds, and also because I was convinced that any attempt to change his mind was futile, I avoided discussing Nazi crimes with my father. Today I sometimes wish I had done otherwise. Perhaps, in anticipation of death, he might have been amenable to the truth. When he died—I was already in America at the time—it pained me not to be at his side; it pained me even more that I had not freed him from the mental chains of his racial mania. Today, it hurts me to write this book. But to do so, I believe, is my sacred duty to the victims of anti-Semitism. In a deeper sense, it is the highest form of loyalty to all that was good and lovable in my father.

Since we had neither newspapers nor radio in 1945, we were virtually without information about the atrocities that the Allied forces discovered when they penetrated into Nazi territory. Nor was it clear to us that Hitler had started the war. In that state of ignorance, my brother and I took a day's hike to the national monument in the Teutoburg forest dedicated to Hermann the Cherusker.

It was a bitter trip. Uninformed and mentally helpless, we blamed the whole world for our misfortune. "All people are liars," I told my brother, being well aware that the sweeping statement included Goebbels, the former minister for "people's enlightenment," who was the master liar. I had no longer any heroes. Hitler and his cronies were deposed, but nobody had taken their place. Had somebody shown me the Declaration of Independence or the Gettysburg Address, I believe I would have found my way out of the darkness. But I had no inkling of the spiritual lift that liberators like Jefferson or Lincoln had to offer. This discovery was yet a year away.

My brother was barely eighteen years old at the time and mentally even more vulnerable than I was. A year later I deeply regretted what I had told him during that unhappy walk through the Teutoburg forest. He trusted me and relied on my judgment, but I misled him as I had misled my comrades during the war when I encouraged them to fight to the bitter end. Today, these remembrances fill me with remorse, but also with a deep sense of gratitude for the mental liberation I owe to America. It was still a long way until I was admitted to the land of Jefferson and Lincoln, but it was then and there that the second and happier part of my life began.

The British military government decreed that all able-bodied men had to work. The ordinance was practically compulsory since those who did not show up for labor service did not receive ration cards. But it was also largely illusory because not much work could be expected from the emaciated bodies that gathered every morning at the British motor pool to be transported to the various working places.

Once we were taken to the little town of Detmold, which was, and still is, famous for its coziness and beauty. The place was virtually unscathed, but a few of the most luxurious mansions had been ransacked. Windows were smashed, broken furniture and household effects littered the ground, and all valuables had been removed by looters. The wanton destruction reminded me of Kristallnacht, though I was not sure against whom it was directed. Since the raid was fairly recent, it could hardly have been an outburst of anti-Semitism. The most plausible explanation was that it was directed against the Nazi bigwigs, for it was well known that the party fat cats had a tendency to gravitate to the most beautiful places of the country. Thus, it seemed to me that the raid in Detmold was Kristallnacht in reverse. The villains of 1938 had become the victims of 1945.

The labor service was mostly woodcutting for the coming winter. Everybody had to produce a certain pile of firewood before being released. This would have been hard work under normal conditions, but for our undernourished bodies it amounted to a mild form of slavery that robbed us of the few calories provided by the inadequate food ration. Nevertheless, we were hoping that some of the wood would make it into our stoves and ovens in the coming winter. No such luck; it all went to the British occupation forces. Thus, the winter of 1945–46 was for me almost as cruel as the war winters in Finland.

Sometimes a young man in the town who was mentally retarded offered us an ironic break from misery. Known in town as "The Culture Pioneer," he wrote poems that always ended on the refrain:

> Three times Heil Hitler, forever and ever!
> Your Karl Bobe, Culture Pioneer

Apparently, the poor devil was not aware that the Thousand Year Reich had ended. Luckily, in the mirror of his enfeebled mind, Nazism lost its terror, and only its grotesquerie remained. The following doggerel, which the Culture Pioneer recited to me while pacing through our little kitchen, sounds like a parody of Nazism. But it isn't. It accurately reflects the poverty of ideas and the intellectual shallowness of Nazi "ideology."

> Hard work at fair compensation:
> Obvious clarity of German religion.

Compared to the intellectual wasteland of Nazism, reflected here unwittingly by an enfeebled mind, Marxism appears like a fertile ground of social analysis and historical insight.

Late in 1945, my family relocated to what is now the tiny state of Saarland of the Federal Republic of Germany. Located directly at the border with France, Saarland had been the target of French expansionary policy for centuries. Now our neighbors to the west thought the time had come to claim the prize. They did not use brute force, because that would have been an ostensible betrayal of the principles proclaimed by the Allied powers. Nor did they have to, since an empty stomach can be as persuasive as a gun. By offering slightly higher food rations to the people of Saarland, the French government hoped to persuade them to opt for union with France in an upcoming referendum. While this policy was certainly not a model of democracy, it is well to remember that Imperial Germany treated France much worse after the war of 1870–71, not to mention the more recent terrorist regime of the Nazis.

Since my father was a native of Saarland, he and his family were entitled to relocate there, and since we expected to find slightly better living conditions in that area, we exercised our right of repatriation. The railroad journey was a nightmare. Rubble and human despair everywhere. In Cologne the train crossed the Rhine on a makeshift bridge next to the remains of the old one, which were lying in the water. But the equestrian statue of the first emperor, Wilhelm I, was still standing, and so was the magnificent Gothic cathedral.

The worst part of the trip was the train ride along the Rhine. The traffic on this route was particularly heavy, because of the freight trains that transported coal as war reparations from the Ruhr district to France. After my brother and I had secured places in a cabin for my parents and sister, we could find a place for ourselves only on the running board at the side where trains in the opposite direction rushed by. Clinging with freezing hands to a door handle, I told myself that, having survived the war, I would also endure this ordeal. Once a young girl with the face of an angel handed us a sandwich through the window. Unable to thank her, I was glad to see through the window that my mother did it for us.

The French occupation forces in Saarland were not nearly as oppressive as they had been during the invasion of the Ruhr district in 1923. Most of them were polite, some even friendly. But they seemed to have a knack for bureaucratic rigmarole. People needed permits for everything. If one wanted to travel from Saarland to the American or British occupation zones, or even the French zone, one needed a visa. When I was a student at the University of Mainz and wanted to visit my parents in Saarland, I had to apply for this permit each time I travelled, even though Mainz lay in the French occupation zone.

Now I had to submit to another form of red tape for which the French, curiously, used the German word *Erfassung* (registration). Every member of the former German army had to be registered by the French administration. When I reported to the local office of the military government, I was told that I would have to submit to interrogation by a French officer. The prospect irritated me because I had been interrogated already by the British. Little did I know that the master interrogators were the Americans, as I was to learn about ten years later when I applied for immigration to the United States. But now it was the turn of the French.

I was escorted to the comfortable office of a French officer, who had the courtesy to offer me a chair. The unexpected politeness assuaged my irritation, and when I noticed a friendly smile on the gentleman's face, I was willing to play whatever game he wanted to play. And a game it was. "Who was your company commander?" the officer began. His tone of voice was rather business-like, but the embarrassed smile on his face gave me the impression that he was not fully convinced of what he was doing. It must have been this impression that sent the devil into me. Without much thinking, and even less hesitation, I invented a fictitious name. "Lieutenant Nyselman," I replied. Then spelling the silly name, I placed particular emphasis on the letter *y*. Unperturbed, the officer entered the bogus name into his register. Now I knew that the next question would concern my battalion commander, and I had already the answer: "Captain Klysencamp, with a *y*." This time, the gentleman looked up, but when he saw the serious expression on my face, he continued the interrogation. As I expected, the third question was about my regiment's commander, and as the interrogator should have expected by now, my answer was "Colonel Klysterbrink, with a *y*." Now the good-natured officer had enough. Half cursing and half laughing, he threw me out, and that was the end of it.

Of course, the prank could have cost me the precious right to live in privileged Saarland, but the congenial Frenchman apparently had enough sense of humor not to make an affair of state out of it. In fact he even had the caprice to enter the three bogus names into my personal papers, as I found out six months later when I applied for a visa to travel to Mainz.

One advantage of the better living conditions in Saarland was the availability of newspapers and radio. At first, I avoided the political news, for I had come to hate politics. But when I heard the first authentic reports about Nazi atrocities, I paid attention. That was the beginning of the end of my mental imprisonment.

My immediate reaction to the reports, however, was disbelief. I found the allegation of systematic genocide so preposterous that I refused to take it seriously. The accusation seemed to me an invention of Allied propaganda, designed to whip us into total submission. Since my childhood, I had been acquainted with many Nazis, from home to school to Hitler Youth and the military; however, with the exception of one or two, I could not imagine any of these persons as a brutal mass-murderer.

Thus, the documentaries from the concentration camps did not convince me. The pictures of the ovens, I thought, could have been made in Hollywood, and the photographs of piles of corpses could well have been taken after the bombing raids on Dresden or Hamburg. With desperate but fading conviction I argued that the so-called documents of the hideous crimes were fabrications by the same people who had concocted the Morgenthau Plan. To paraphrase Clausewitz, the policy of the Allies seemed to me a continuation of war by other means. First starvation, then humiliation, and now defamation!

I hungered for the truth. It was a spiritual hunger that rivaled even the physical craving for food. At the same time I felt in my bones that I would see the truth soon. Yes, *see* it, as one sees a tree or a mountain. I had been fooled so often that I could believe only what I saw. Words meant nothing to me, whether spoken or printed. They had been misused so many times, first by the Nazis and then by the Allies, that I grew angry whenever I read or heard a statement of any significance, no matter in which language. I trusted neither the vanquished nor the vanquishers. I needed visible, irrefutable proof.

It came to me in the form of physiognomies! In a desperate quest for truth and justice, I searched hundreds of photographs from the war crime trials, looking for nothing but faces. Whenever I found one, I studied it with the obsession of a monomaniac. There were physiognomies from all races and nationalities, belonging to the victims as well as the accused. To me, these faces spoke the truth, no matter which words their owners used. Whether mirrors of horror or telltales of guilt, the faces articulated the unspeakable truth with an almost unearthly eloquence. That is how I *saw* the truth. It was as harrowing as Judgment Day, but it was the truth, the sacred truth.

The photographs came from three kinds of sources: the Nuremberg trials, the other war crime trials that ran parallel to them, and a series of documentaries from the ghettos and the concentration camps, particularly from the liberation of Dachau in the American zone and Bergen-Belsen in the British zone. I had an insatiable hunger for these pictures. Whenever I got my hands on a newspaper or magazine, I looked for reports from the war crime trials and the concentration camps. And when I found one, I wasted no time reading the words but turned immediately

to the photographs. Every face that was at least halfway recogniz-
able, I searched with inquisitorial relentlessness. Every picture
with a face on it was a priceless acquisition. Whenever I found
photographs of witnesses or, for that matter, of the defendants, I
cut them out and collected them in a shoebox. Every night before
going to bed, I looked at them, often past midnight.

There were all kinds of faces: Jewish, German, Polish, American; men and women; old and young; innocent and guilty. They
formed a collective face of humankind that now gave visual testimony to crimes unparalleled in history. No matter what their
owners said to me, these faces did not lie. Whether horror-
stricken, accepting guilt, or trying to deny it, they spoke the
unassailable truth. Night after night they haunted me with over-
whelming cogency, convincing me that the unfathomable atrocities had really happened.

This was the breakthrough. Now I followed, in the newspapers
and on the radio, the Nuremberg trials, where the top Nazis were
sitting in the dock. Strange as it may sound, in my eyes these men
were witnesses rather than defendants. Their stony visages spoke
the truth with an eerie eloquence, whether they were repentant
as Frank (Nazi administrator of occupied Poland) or defiant
as Göring, whether silent as Hess or talkative as Speer. Solely
through the expressions on their faces, Hitler's former paladins
convinced me that they were every bit as guilty as charged. Truly,
if the charges had been untrue, the defendants would have
invoked God and the stars, and the tribunal would have burnt in
the fire of their protest. Indeed, if I had been accused of such
atrocities, I doubt whether the military police could have restrained me. But the big-shots of the Third Reich didn't know
any better than to protest meekly that they just happened to look
the other way when the henchman seized his next victim. For the
first time in their oratorical careers, Hitler's cronies were speechless. *Sic transit gloria mundi.*

By sheer coincidence I got my hands on a six-month-old newspaper that reported the beginning of the Nuremberg trials. Without expecting a revelation, I read the opening statement of the chief prosecutor, Justice Robert H. Jackson. It was a German translation, but it must have been a good one, for I still remember how deeply it touched me. Particularly, the following words— which I present here in their original text—I shall never forget:

> That four great nations, flushed with victory and stung with injury, stay the hands of vengeance and voluntarily submit their captive enemies to the judgment of the law—is one of the most significant tributes that Power has ever paid to Reason.

I was thunderstruck! Never in my life had I heard such words spoken in public. I had read Shakespeare in school, even the Funeral Oration of Pericles, but that was literature or history; this was shocking, painful actuality. The nobility of the statement touched me as deeply as the beauty of the language. Most stirring, however, was its undeniable truth. The defendants had not been shot or hanged on the spot, as they had done so often to their enemies—and as their captors surely must have been tempted to do to them—but were awaiting the "judgment of the law." When had the Nazis ever shown such loftiness?

A year later I was stopped in the street by an American journalist. "You look like Billy the Kid," he said laughingly in fluent German, alluding to my grotesque attire. "Who is Billizekit?" I asked, and he explained. We then had a little conversation. When I told him how impressed I was by the opening statement at Nuremberg, he offered to give me the whole speech in exchange for an interview. For reasons unknown to me, the interview never happened, but the speech was in the mail a few days later.

I was not that fluent in English at the time, but twenty-four hours later I had translated the complete text into German. Now the enormity of the charges and the dignity of the process of law impressed me even more. Particularly the following sentence lives on in my memory:

> The wrongs which we seek to condemn and punish have been so calculated, so malignant and so devastating, that civilization cannot tolerate their being ignored, because it cannot survive their being repeated.

As a curious aside, I mention how I suddenly understood why I was so disappointed when, as a young boy, I tried to read Hitler's book and failed to finish it. At that time I did not feel the evil of the author, but I certainly sensed the dullness of his language. It is not an overstatement to say that the poverty of Hitler's language, both in speaking and in writing, was a reflection of the barrenness of his soul. At the time when he soaked up anti-Semitic hatred from the gutter of Imperial Vienna, his soul was void of any gentle feeling, with the possible exception of love for his mother. Now I understood what bothered me when I tried to read his book: It was the complete absence of any constructive idea or tender emotion.

Listening to the Nuremberg trials, I burned with shame. I had trusted the monsters that were now sitting in the dock. I had put my life on the line, while they cowardly watched women and children being led to the gas chambers. Oh, did I hate them! When the verdict came in—I was already a student at the University of Mainz—I felt that urgently needed justice had been done. Much later, in America, I softened my judgment somewhat. I then believed that the two generals, Keitel and Jodel, did not deserve to be hanged, but I always regretted that Göring had escaped the hangman, for he was one of the most brutal Nazis. Streicher, who certainly was the most repulsive and probably the most stupid of Hitler's cronies, fully deserved his shameful death on the gallows. With regard to Speer, I still believe that he knew more than he admitted. If word of the concentration camps had reached me at the Arctic Ocean front, then surely it must have reached Speer in Berlin. As engaging a personality as he was, I believe he deserved his long prison term in Spandau.

Convinced, but still craving more of the terrible truth, I intensely followed the other war crime trials in the newspapers and, when possible, on the radio. I clipped every photograph, particularly those of witnesses, and tried to comprehend the enormity of the crimes, if that is at all possible. To me the portrayals of the living were sometimes more shocking than the testimony of the dead.

I had acquired several photographs from the liberation of the three main concentration camps in the west. One picture from Dachau showed General Eisenhower and other American soldiers viewing corpses the fleeing Nazis had left behind. I did not need to see the dead, because the horror on the faces of the living struck horror in my own heart. A photograph from Buchenwald, which I always carried with me, showed an American soldier comforting a prisoner who had just been liberated. Here it was the personal drama, reflected in the faces of the liberator and the liberated, that made me comprehend the otherwise incomprehensible truth. The longer I looked at the picture, the more bewildering became the hurricane of emotions: horror, shame, rage, incomprehension, spells of disbelief, self-recrimination, and a burning envy of the Americans for the blessing of being innocent.

There is a corollary to the Buchenwald picture. About twenty years later, when I had become an American, I mentioned the photograph in a letter to my wartime comrade Helmut in Germany. At the time we were engaged in a heated discussion by letter about the Holocaust. He claimed that it was a gigantic lie, whereas I wanted to convince him that it really happened. Thus, I offered to send him the photograph of the liberated prisoner and his American comforter, but he refused it on the grounds that it was "staged." Instead, he put my name on the mailing lists of two publishers of neo-Nazi propaganda material, one in Germany and one in Canada. The result was a flood of anti-Semitic smut that lasted for more than a year. To end it, I had to threaten the publishers with legal action.

I also had photos from Bergen-Belsen that showed German civilians being marched through the camp by the British occupation forces. Since these men and women had lived in the vicinity of the camp, they must have smelled the stench of death. But that was conjecture. Hence, I was not sure whether I saw guilt on their faces, but I did see the horror that lay before their eyes. The truth was burning on their foreheads. Maybe they had evaded the truth while the atrocities were still going on, but now they could no longer do so. Twenty years later, when I received another letter from Helmut in which he denied the Holocaust, I wished he had been *forced* to face the truth.

Collecting pictures from the Holocaust became a habit of mine. Today, of course, there are whole books of these pictures. Many of them have been engraved into my mind. One shows the evacuation of the Warsaw ghetto by the SS. A group of women and children, holding up their hands, marches past a soldier who is pointing his rifle at them from the hip. A little boy, wearing a cap and also sticking up his hands, looks at the brute with an expression of horror and incomprehension. Another picture that went around the globe shows a German soldier aiming his rifle at a mother who cradles a child in her arms. Still another picture is a rear view of an elderly woman carrying an infant on her arm and leading two other children by the hand. They are treading unknowingly, almost trustingly, to the gas chamber. I cannot forget this picture. The brute who took it probably felt no emotion; but whenever I take a child's little hand in mine, the heartrending scene he unintentionally passed on to posterity appears before my inner eyes, filling me with ever-renewed sadness.

And then there are the faces behind barbed wire, faces I had seen with my own eyes while riding a military train through Poland. The wartime picture had been buried in my soul, but now it arose to new life to solicit the pain I had not yet paid. There are hundreds of pictures from the satanic death machine that I shall never forget. Each time I view them, they are more horrible than before, and each time I must force myself to believe what I see.

By the end of 1946 my mental liberation was complete. What once I considered the crown jewel of humankind, the Third Reich, I now recognized as the abyss of human deprivation. The man to whom I had looked up as humankind's genius, Adolf Hitler, was unmasked as the personification of evil. If ever there was hell on earth, it was the satanic chain of death camps with which he raped the earth of Europe. Humankind has at all times seen frightening barbarities by all races and nations, but never crimes as massive, calculated, and unnatural as the systematic genocide that is now known as the Holocaust. It has been my fate to serve the creator of this horror system, and I shall bear this consciousness for the rest of my life.

CHAPTER 14

Drunk with the Wine of Freedom

In 1946 I had no job, no education, and no material wealth, except for the few thousand Reichsmark I had saved as a soldier. On the black market the money would have bought a few loaves of bread; however, at a university, it bought a few semesters of education. Hence, the most reasonable course of action for me was trying to enroll at one of the many universities that gradually reopened all over the country. The trouble was that they were overwhelmed by thousands of former soldiers who also wanted to study. When I arrived at a university to enroll, it usually was already filled to capacity. Once I traveled to Bonn to seek admittance to the university where my wartime comrade, Paul, now missing in action, once had studied. However, as usual, I arrived too late. All I got out of the trip was a night in a former air raid bunker that teemed with lice and stank of urine and vomit.

In May 1946 I heard over the radio that the French military government was planning to reestablish the former University of

Mainz. This once-prestigious institution had existed during the Middle Ages, but was now history, except for the magnificent library that miraculously had escaped destruction. The new university, the French government announced, would bear the name of Johannes Gutenberg, son of the city of Mainz and inventor of the printing press.

Time was of the essence. First I had to apply to the French administration of Saarland for a visa to travel to Mainz. Since that city lay in the French occupation zone, the permit was granted without much fuss. The same day, I jumped on a train to Mainz. There I heard that the new university would be housed in some former air defense barracks that now were mainly rubble. But the military government left no doubt that it was determined to convert the ruins of the former instrument of war into an institute of learning. When I arrived at the pitiful future campus, I learned that most departments were already filled to capacity, but a few openings were still available in the department of science.

Up to that time, I had not seriously reflected about my future; indeed, I was not even sure whether I was qualified for an academic career. In the seven years since I had left school, I had forgotten so much that I would not have passed an ordinary high school exam. In fact, I was afraid that I had lost even the skill of learning, particularly in mathematics, where I seemed to have the greatest gaps. I theorized that mathematical skills, because of the abstractness of the subject, evaporate faster than knowledge in the more life-oriented disciplines such as history or literature. My suspicion grew when I noticed that I did not even know the difference between simple mathematical functions such as *sine* and *cosine*.

In this predicament, the spirit of my cherished high school teacher, Theo, came to my rescue. It reminded me of how happy I had been in his science class and how easily I absorbed scientific ideas when my mind was unencumbered by ideological ballast.

In this mood I enrolled as a student of mathematics and physics at the new Johannes Gutenberg Universität of Mainz. For the first time since the end of the war, I saw a glimmer of hope.

Not all buildings of the former barracks had been completely destroyed. Some were salvageable and quickly restored, though with such inferior material that they crumbled already a few years later. I was lucky to be admitted to the dormitory that was housed in the uppermost story of one of the refurbished buildings.

My two roommates, Are and Hel, had also enrolled in mathematics and physics. Are became a life long friend. Since my new friends were both younger than I, they had seen military service only in the last few months of the war. The three of us formed a little club that lasted almost to this day. Using the first two letters of our three family names, we dubbed it the MaMaBa club. We also arranged the six letters into a logo that became our trademark. We were always together, whether attending lectures, doing homework, chasing girls, going to dances, listening to concerts, swimming in the Rhine, or stealing cherries from the orchards in the vicinity of Mainz.

We also developed a little routine designed to receive an extra meal at the canteen. As we were standing in line and the first of us was almost ready to surrender his coupon, the third caused a little commotion. The second then exploited the diversion of attention by offering his coupon before the first had surrendered his. This way we saved one coupon for an extra meal. We dubbed the method "iteration" after a mathematical procedure that enhances the accuracy of a calculation by running the result repeatedly through the same routine.

Most of the other students were of my age and had seen combat during the war. Many had been wounded, some were crippled, and a few were still nursing their wounds. They were the lucky ones who had survived the war. Now they were trying to reconstruct their lives. As students, they were unusually mature and serious. Most of them studied as diligently as their under-nourished bodies would permit. There was hardly an incorrigible Nazi among them. While a few had learned to hate all politics, most had embraced the ideals of democracy, though they were unsure how to turn them into reality. It was an atmosphere of good will, restrained skepticism, cautious optimism, and a nag-ging awareness of our political inexperience.

Studying in those days was not easy, to say the least. The main obstacles were hunger, lack of heating, unavailability of books, scarcity of consumer goods such as paper and pencil, evaporation of knowledge during the war, and the fact that we were required to spend one hour per day clearing away rubble. Of these hard-ships, hunger was the most debilitating. Not only did it rob us of the energy to pursue our studies—I was so emaciated that I sometimes could not climb the stairs to the dormitory—it also deprived us of the time to study, by forcing us to spend valuable hours in pursuit of food.

As I had suspected, I lacked the energy to follow the lectures in mathematics. Severe undernourishment already would have sufficed to guarantee failure, but the substantial gaps in my high school education proved almost as crippling. Most other students of mathematics found themselves in the same predicament. To alleviate the situation, the faculty instituted so-called bridge courses which offered intellectually impoverished former sol-diers the opportunity to bridge the gap between their present state of knowledge and an ordinary high school education. After having attended such courses for two semesters, I qualified for the regular lectures.

All faculty members had passed a denazification procedure by German authorities and an additional screening by the military government. Most of the professors of science and engineering were in their fifties and sixties. Since they had worked for the armaments industry during the war, they had not been soldiers.

The few younger professors either had survived combat or had been unfit for service. Naturally, there was a certain kinship between the former soldiers among faculty and students.

I have never seen a group of academics more dedicated to teaching and learning than the professors and students of my first few university years. The age-old dictum that war is the father of all things, probably an exaggeration and certainly a sad comment on human nature, assumes here a more conciliatory meaning. These men and women had gone through extraordinary hardships, both physical and mental. They had learned to take nothing for granted: neither their priceless freedom to think nor their precious daily bread; neither their protection from lawlessness nor their shelter from the elements. Though there was some bitterness and occasional cynicism, the predominant mood was a deep sense of gratitude for the opportunity to dispense or receive education, and a holy resolve to use it.

Two older physics professors had a strong influence on my further development. One, a theoretician, was the director of the Institute for Theoretical Physics; the other, an experimentalist, was the director of the Institute for Experimental Physics. Both were sincere democrats, and both, alas, were also mortal enemies. In spite of their lofty goals and convictions, they were not beyond jealousy and little intrigues. As I learned quickly, professional envy flourishes not only among cobblers and tailors, but even more so among intellectuals and academics. It was ironic to hear from the theoretician that Newton and Leibniz once were engaged in a vicious priority fight, and it sounded almost apologetic when he hastened to add that Einstein had never succumbed to the green-eyed monster of envy.

The theoretician was a competent scientist who had reached almost international fame. He worked hard and demanded the same of his students. I always thought that he overdid it, but I regarded him highly, and so did most other students. He would have been an ideal teacher, had it not been for his severity and lack of humor. Although I was not the best of his students, he took an early liking to me and furthered my academic career in many ways, such as providing me with coupons for textbooks, which were rationed, or nominating me for scholarships, which were in high demand. Before the currency reform, money was in ample supply, but thereafter it was as rare as virtue. Hence, without those scholarships, I simply could not have completed my education. The most prestigious and lucrative scholarship, which I owe to this professor, was the Johannes Gutenberg Prize of the City of Mainz.

This professor's specialty was quantum physics, but sometimes he digressed to Einstein's theory of relativity. I don't know whether he did this to gratify my personal wish to learn more about this branch of physics or without regard to me. But I recall having talked to him about the Judeo-German culture that was now destroyed. On one of these occasions, the professor remarked that Einstein was a cofounder of the quantum theory and also one of its most prodigious contributors. Therefore, he mused, even if Einstein had not written a single word about relativity, he still would have gone down in history as one of the greatest physicists of all time. Such enthusiasm was unusual for the professor, who prided himself on a scientific objectivity that bordered on dryness.

The refreshing outspokenness of the remark about Einstein touched a nostalgic nerve in me. It reminded me of my friend Paul and even more so of my cherished high school teacher, Theo. In general, however, the theoretician lacked Theo's ingeniousness, his willingness to listen to his students, and his attention to their special intellectual needs. He was a competent lecturer; Theo was a brilliant teacher.

The professor was an unusual man in more than one way. An inflexible patriot of the pre-Nazi era, an ardent pacifist, and a card-carrying member of the Social Democratic Party, he became a member of the Bundestag, the German parliament, after his retirement from academic life. In 1957, when I had long left the University of Mainz, I wrote him of my impending emigration to America. Though I was prepared for his disapproval of my leaving the country at this critical time, I did not expect the hostility of his reaction. I hoped he would invite me to a farewell visit, but he didn't. Instead, he sent a terse reply and a letter of introduction that was worded so coolly and matter-of-factly that it was more renunciation than recommendation. That was the end of a promising mentor-scholar relation that never developed into friendship.

The experimentalist did not have the theoretician's professional reputation. This was one reason, but not the only one, why he was under attack by his colleague. Yet I liked the man, and he liked me, primarily because we shared the same political inclinations, and also because he showed a special appreciation for former front soldiers. I enjoyed talking to him, as I liked conversing with the other professor, but their mutual enmity made a fruitful discussion with both of them difficult. I certainly would have come closer to both of them, had it not been for their internecine petty feuds.

I had become a socialist in the meantime, though I abhorred the dictatorship of Communism almost as much as Nazism. Thus, I was delighted when the experimentalist instituted a colloquium in which he propagated pacifist and socialist ideas. He called it the Seminar for European Reconstruction. This colloquium addressed the problem of the widespread destruction in Europe and the related issue of Germany's guilt. Since this subject had nothing to do with physics, some people saw the seminar as the professor's escape from academic duties, but I considered it a moral obligation, and so did the roughly one hundred students who attended it. There were about twice as many men as women. Almost all of the men were former front soldiers, and many of the women had served as nurses during the war. I have seldom seen a group of people as mature and sincere as the attendees of this seminar. Notably absent was the theoretician.

What I liked most about these people was that they openly discussed Nazi atrocities. In the years to follow, unfortunately, Germans became ever more reluctant to talk about the Holocaust. Today only the immediate postwar generation admits Nazi atrocities openly and completely. Ten years later, in America, I met many Germans of my generation and learned, to my dismay, that discussing the Nazi past was taboo. But in the early postwar years, the historical responsibility of the German nation was openly debated. I hungered for such discussions because I sensed that they helped heal my psychic wounds. The mental imprisonment had ended, but the inward wounds had not yet healed. That would take not only more time, but also a healer as resourceful as America.

The seminar was not the only non-science class I attended. I spent about half of my time in lectures on philosophy, literature, and the arts, which was one of the reasons—aside from the main reason of undernourishment—why it took so long until I graduated. Two of my literary loves were the letter-novel *Hyperion* by Friedrich Hölderlin and the collection of poems *Das Stundenbuch* (The Book of Hours) by Rainer Maria Rilke. What I sought in these poetic works was the purity and innocence which, I was afraid, had been ruined forever by the Nazis.

There were also diversions and amusements. At Lenten time people celebrated Carnival, which enjoyed particular popularity in the Catholic cities of the Rheinland. Most famous for their Mardi Gras activities were the cities of Cologne, Aachen, and Mainz. On the eleventh day of the eleventh month of the year, at 11:11 P.M., the key to the city was surrendered to the "fools," who then convened their famous "fools' sessions," which were known for their wit and candidness. The wittiest joker was decorated with the Order Against Animalistic Seriousness.

On the Monday before Ash Wednesday people abandoned their usual restraint: houses were open, partners were exchanged, and the fools ruled the city. There was even some Rhine wine. People danced and kissed in the streets, and some went further than that. When all was over, at Ash Wednesday, the fools marched to the Rhine River, where they washed their empty wallets, while shedding crocodile tears.

At the university, the pent-up hunger for merriment led to particularly orgiastic scenes. The great hall, the *Aula,* was reserved for dancing, kissing, and necking, while the cellar was the place for those who wanted more. There were even some beds to facilitate mating. The harder the times, the more furious was the hunt for pleasure.

The need for diversion was also felt at the MaMaBa club, which had been extended from three men to three couples in the meantime. The young women, who were slightly younger than Are and Hel, had completed high school shortly before the end of the war. Now they were students of medicine.

One day, the three young women invited us to the cellar, where they practiced anatomy by dissecting corpses. As we entered the cadaver cellar, one of them greeted me by hitting me over the head with an arm she had just severed from the cadaver of an old man. While I hated the smell of formaldehyde, I was not particularly disturbed by the dead man's hand in my hair, nor was anybody else. In fact, nobody minded the corpses and body parts that were lying around, since everybody was familiar with such scenes from the war. The women, who had served as fire fighters during the air raids, had seen more grisly scenarios.

But playing with corpses was not the main business of the extended MaMaBa club. The real purpose was dancing. The three young women and my friends Are and Hel were enthusiastic dancers, though I was not. Since I had no dancing experience, they dragged me to a dancing course so that I would catch up with the advanced skills they had acquired in high school, before the war had put an end to such pastimes. After I had passed their critical exam, we went to our first dance. I did not become a dancing fan, but I acquired a taste for the romance that goes along with it.

In the following months we went to many dances, under circumstances that were not exactly inviting. Plagued by hunger, surrounded by rubble, and dressed in unflattering clothes—I was still wearing my Billy the Kid outfit—we danced zealously, as if we had reason to celebrate a most enjoyable event. And maybe we had.

I have a particularly fond memory of one of these dances that took place during a starry summer night in the ruin of a commercial building next to the ancient cathedral. Except for a few remnants of the walls, the only part of the structure that had survived the war was the cement pavement that now served as a dance floor. The debris had been cleared to the sides and little islands in the middle to make room for the dancers, who circled around the wreckage. Birch trees had sprouted from the rubble and grown to the height of the collapsed roof. Now their branches reached across from one side to the other, shadowing the zealous dancers with a canopy of greenery. The light of the moon filtered through the quivering leaves and competed with the dancers' mercurial motion. We were in a remarkable state of enchantment. Our effusive mood would have been unusual under normal circumstances, but against the background of misery and rubble from the war, it was a miracle. The secret was the music.

The name Glenn Miller had heretofore been unheard of in postwar Germany, but his music caught on with the people from the moment it rang out. At this unforgettable dance among ruins, it infused the whirling couples with a sense of joy and optimism they had not experienced in years. "Don't lose heart" seemed to be the message of these rhythmic sounds, "better times are ahead." Indeed, from the happy faces of the dancers one could get the impression that better times had already begun.

The effect on me was even more mysterious. I was not quite as elated as the others, but rather pensive and retrospective. It was a strange feeling I can only describe as nostalgia, though I am fully aware that I had nothing to be nostalgic about. Had I been an American GI, my mood would have been understandable, but I had been . . . well, that was now past. Now I was breathing peace while being under the spell of a kind of music I had never heard before.

According to the English-speaking announcer, Miller had composed this music during the war, while serving in the U.S. Army. Maybe that is what bewildered me. Maybe I was bedazzled by the fact that Miller's music, even though it had been created during the war, did not contain the slightest trace of it. A nation, I thought, that can produce such music, while being engaged in a furious struggle, must have the innocence of a child. What kind of music did German composers offer during the war? With the exception of the sentimental ballad "Lilli Marleen," the propaganda machine of the Nazis had allowed only ideology-tainted songs of calculated bravura. Yes, it was the innocence that struck me. Oh, did I envy the Americans for that precious gift!

In the summer of 1946 I met a former colonel from the German army. His name was von Vahlen; at least, I thought it was. He was a student of medicine, but comported himself already like a medical doctor. During the war, the colonel had been wounded several times and now walked on crutches because one leg had been amputated up to the hip. The wound, which had not completely healed, required daily dressing and caused him considerable discomfort, though he never complained. When he cheerfully hobbled through the long hallway of the dormitory, one could hear the clatter of his crutches from one end to the other.

Colonel von Vahlen was the most mysterious individual I have ever met, which is why I called him *Graue Eminenz* (gray eminence). He relished the name and did his best to deserve it. Because of his undeniable leadership qualities, he was always surrounded by a group of students, mostly younger men and women. I referred to them as his disciples, and he did not object. Indeed, he would have liked to add me to his entourage, but that was not to my taste. I knew he was not a Nazi, but I was weary of his military demeanor, which was enough for me to keep a certain distance.

One thing I didn't like about the colonel was his inscrutability. I could not even find out when and where he was born. I was also critical of his political attitude. While he did acknowledge Nazi atrocities, he blamed Hitler more for his strategic blunders than his crimes. On the other hand, I respected him because, as the evidence suggested, he had been a brave soldier. For similar reasons, he valued me and wanted to recruit me for his cause; however, since he kept it under a veil of secrecy, I held myself aloof. Thus, we observed an uneasy fellowship that lacked one of the most important ingredients of true friendship: trust. I criticized him for his continued allegiance to Germany's military past; he blamed me for my flaming pacifism.

I probably would have severed relations with Colonel von Vahlen had it not been for one quality of his that made him valuable in a rather mundane sense: he provided a most welcome supply of food. The fact that I was attracted by something as prosaic as food may not speak well of me, but whoever has felt hunger gnawing at his guts as I have will understand. The simple fact is that the colonel rescued me from starvation.

When the colonel went on one of his frequent hoarding trips

through the agricultural villages that dotted the Mainzer Rhein plateau, I knew he would come back with a few loaves of bread and some eggs or bacon. I accompanied him on two or three of these food-finding expeditions, and I have never seen a more persuasive beggar. He knew how to touch the hearts and to open the hands of petty farmers who, only a few minutes earlier, may have chased away another food hunter. But he did not beg; he commanded. His war injuries and crutches certainly helped, but the secret of his success was his convincing manner and natural authority. When he cheerfully hobbled into a farmhouse and unabashedly stated his demand, people felt that they had no choice but to give to this extraordinary man.

What impressed me even more than the colonel's way of obtaining food was his manner of giving it away. When he had returned from a successful hoarding trip, he gathered his disciples in his room and, in a fatherly way, saw to it that everybody got his fair share. It was as if an eagle was feeding his young. Although I was not one of his regular followers, he often invited me to "the sharing of the loot," as he called it.

At such occasions he liked to tease me with my low military rank by calling me "Sergeant." I was itching to respond with "Yes, Colonel Sir," but that would have conflicted with my self-imposed rule to eradicate every trace of the military from my life. Thus, I addressed him with "Your Eminency," which he liked even better. Anyway, submitting to this kind of charade was a small price to pay for the precious food.

Colonel von Vahlen had interesting stories to tell from his service during the war. Though he may have been a little liberal with the truth, circumstantial evidence left little doubt that he had met Hitler. He always referred to him as *Gröfaz* and said that the unflattering sobriquet was common usage among staff officers. From this and other remarks it was obvious that he didn't like Hitler.

If I had to classify the colonel, I would say he was a civilized German militarist. Once he flashed a photograph showing himself in his colonel's uniform standing next to Admiral Wilhelm Canaris, who was the chief of German counter-espionage during the war. After the attempt on Hitler's life in July 1944, Canaris was arrested and later hanged. From these and other indications, I inferred that the colonel was no friend of Hitler, but his obsession with secrecy left some lingering doubts. Maybe he had learned the secrecy fuss from Canaris, who had played a somewhat murky role in the Third Reich. At any rate, the colonel was an admirer of military leaders, particularly those of the old school, but he was not a Nazi. When he was in the mood, he spoke in glowing terms of Field Marshal von Mannstein, General Guderian, and others. My former commanding general, Field Marshal Schörner, was not one of his favorites, maybe because he was Hitler's.

It was never clear to me why the colonel was enrolled as a student, for he never attended any lectures, but claimed to be a physician and also acted like one in emergency situations. He treated himself for his war injuries and seemed to have access to drugs. I had the impression that he was addicted to opiates. Once a month he observed what he called *dies erotica* with his mistress, a stunning blonde whom I met once. Toward my friends Are and Hel, he was haughty and dismissive, and he referred to the MaMaBa club as "the boy scouts."

Secrecy surrounded the colonel from the first to the last day of our acquaintance. Sometimes he hinted darkly at a mission he still had to fulfill. It was as if he wanted to prepare his "disciples" for his approaching demise. As it turned out, he was right. One day he disappeared without a trace. It was rumored that he had been caught crossing the border to Communist East Germany. Whatever may have been behind his disappearance, for him it was a fitting departure.

With the colonel gone, I was without an auxiliary food source. Fortunately, the cessation did not last long; relief was in sight. On a beautiful summer day I shall never forget, a motorcar with a loudspeaker on top announced that the American Mennonites would soon start a daily feeding on campus. The bulletin sounded like a message from heaven and caused incredible excitement. It meant relief from hunger for all of us, and for some it literally amounted to rescue from starvation.

The food from the good people of America was a nourishing gruel of corn meal, milk powder, sugar, raisins, and water. Every noon I joined a group of several hundred students who lined up at a battery of military field kitchens to receive this life-saving meal, and every night I dreamt of the next feeding. Since that time I have a fondness for grits and corn bread. About forty years later, on a car trip through the eastern United States, I had the opportunity to thank the Mennonites in person.

One noon, as I was sitting under a tree, eating the ambrosial gruel, I suddenly thought of the concentration camps. Before killing their prey, the emissaries from hell enfeebled their victims with hunger and cold. Although I was amply acquainted with hunger, I was painfully aware that I would never be able to comprehend the suffering of those whose souls were murdered before their bodies were destroyed. The Mennonites undoubtedly must have heard of this satanic killing machine, but now they sent their heavenly food to the country where it had been invented.

At about the same time an incident happened that would have been amusing in any country except Germany. At a prestigious place on campus stood a life-size replica of Michelangelo's Moses. One morning the nose of the sculpture was found blackened with shoe polish. Since the prank could have been interpreted as an anti-Semitic demonstration, it was a serious matter. The university president hastily convened a meeting with student leaders in the great hall, beseeching them to produce the culprit. But to no avail.

Now events escalated. The military government issued an ultimatum, threatening to close the university, whereupon students distributed handwritten leaflets of protest. Then police appeared on campus. Lecture halls were closed and a curfew was ordered. Some professors and students departed in anticipation of more serious disturbances. At the eleventh hour, student leaders organized a rally, in which they condemned the "senseless act" and petitioned the military government to abstain from drastic measures. Finally, the authorities relented, but only after every inmate of the dormitory had declared in writing and under penalty of perjury that he had nothing to do with the vandalism and that he condemned anti-Semitism in whatever form.

The miscreant was never found, but life at the university normalized. Most students and professors were convinced that the vandalism was the deplorable act of an immature prankster who did not know what he was doing. At the Seminar for European Reconstruction, we were satisfied that anti-Semitism was dead in Germany. Of course, that assessment was premature. Today some anti-Semitism does exist; however, the vast majority of the people reject it. Its few adherents are the usual misfits of society, who try to overcome their inferiority complex by declaring members of certain minorities, such as Jews or Blacks, as inferior. These freaks exist in all societies, and probably in the same proportion.

Sometime in 1947 I heard of a political event that would have a decisive impact on my future life. America had granted independence to the Philippines, and with this unilateral act, the superpower had honored a long-standing promise to forgo "the pearl of the Orient Sea," should the people of that country express their desire to live their own political life.

I was stunned. Even though I had been thoroughly cleansed of

Nazi ideology, I was not prepared for such an act of national self-denial. And for a good reason, for there was another superpower that did not show the slightest inclination to follow America's example. While the United States freed the Philippines, the Soviet Union subjugated several small nations in Eastern Europe. To top its European conquests, the Soviet Union, just a few days before the Japanese surrender, had declared war on that nation for the express purpose of snatching a few islands from the land-starved empire. In contrast, America lived up to the ideals of the Declaration of Independence. It must be a great nation, I thought, that relinquishes an island country of exceptional beauty and strategic importance at the very height of its own power.

This was the last impetus I needed to study the land of Jefferson and Lincoln. As a first step, I thought, I should read the American Constitution, but in the rubble of postwar Germany, that document was hard to come by. By sheer coincidence, I mentioned my problem to one of my professors. "Search the cellar of the library," he advised me, "it ought to be there." So I did, yet what I found, luckily, was not the Constitution, but the Declaration of Independence. Little did I know that the ideals of freedom and self-determination are expressed far more eloquently in Jefferson's words than in the legalese of the Constitution. When I carried the strange document from the cellar of the library to the light of day, I almost felt like an archeologist. And when I read it, I thought it could have been written for the Philippines as well as for the United States.

The Americans' act of granting independence to the Philippines and their Declaration of Independence changed my life. Drunk with the wine of freedom, I resolved to visit America as soon as the opportunity should arise. I also read Lincoln's Gettysburg Address. The pledge that "government of the people, by the people, for the people, shall not perish from the earth" struck me as a renewal—on the battlefield—of a commitment that is already implicit in the Declaration of Independence. The second redemption of that commitment—also on the battlefield—was the cleansing of this earth from Nazism.

It took a decade until I emigrated to the United States, and six more years until I became an American citizen. But in 1947, I still had years of study ahead of me. That was the time when I had a string of surprises, some happy, some not.

One day I was called to the manager of the dormitory, who was related by marriage to both the university president and the French military governor. This cozy relation was already known to me from the unofficial intelligence service of Colonel von Vahlen. Now I was about to receive a firsthand lecture in nepotism. As the manager announced to me, I had been selected to tutor the university president's daughter in mathematics.

She was a beautiful girl, highly intelligent, and infectiously vivacious. Soon we fell in love. As pleasant as this turn of events was, it also had unpleasant consequences, as I soon found out. One day her father surprised the girl as she was reading a letter of mine. The next day I was unceremoniously dismissed as her tutor, and the following day I was expelled without notice from the dormitory. The girl and I laughed heartily when we shared the news. Needless to say, the petty reaction of two old men did not affect our relation. A year later she enrolled as a student of art and literature at the university. Now I had even more reason to attend lectures on subjects other than science. It was a turbulent time, sometimes happy, sometimes not. The rest is private.

In the meantime, German currency had been reformed. If my memory serves me right, forty Reichsmark were exchanged against one Deutschmark. Almost overnight, the showcases of shops were filled with goods from food to clothes. But now I had little money to buy the cherished goods. Nevertheless, starvation had ended. I also received a decent suit from my aunt in America. Slowly I gained some pounds and lost my resemblance to Billy the Kid. Just in time to meet my future wife.

Renate and I met at the engagement party of Are's sister. It was love at first sight. A year later, we met again in Mainz and became engaged. Being seven years younger than I, Renate was living as a lay sister in a Lutheran convent. The "Stift," as it was called, operated a hospital and a kindergarten, in which Renate worked. Her father was a world-renowned specialist in dendrology, the study of trees. During the war, he had been director of the Palm Garden in Frankfurt. Renate was a teenager at the time, but when the bombs fell on Frankfurt, she served as a fire fighter and even pulled corpses from the rubble. On one such occasion, she rescued her own father from the debris. Luckily, he was alive.

After the Americans entered Frankfurt, they expelled Renate's family from their living quarters in the Palm Garden and confiscated some of their books and furniture. The books were later returned, still showing the stamp *beschlagnahmt* (confiscated) inside. Today they grace our bookshelves as token reminders of a time when even the most civilized people were not entirely immune to the temptations of absolute power.

CHAPTER 15

A Semblance
of Normalcy Returns

Renate and I were married in 1953 in Darmstadt, where her parents then lived and her father was director of the botanical garden. The church ceremony was performed in the convent where Renate had served as a lay sister and kindergarten teacher, while the rest of the celebration took place in her parents' home at the botanical garden. Since Renate had many friends from her time as a lay sister, and her father had even more acquaintances as president of the German dendrological society, the wedding was unusually elaborate and beautiful.

Also in 1953 I graduated with a diploma (roughly a master's degree) in theoretical physics, still under the auspices of my original professor. I then accepted the position of research assistant to the director of the Institute for Theoretical Physics at the Technical University at Aachen. Are, my friend from the MaMaBa club of Mainz, was already an assistant professor there. For the first time in my life, I began to earn some real money. At first,

Renate and I thought that it was plenty; a few months later, we felt otherwise.

Before our first child was born, Renate held a part-time job to make some extra money. Working as an interviewer for a commercial research institute, she went from door to door, asking people how they liked certain consumer goods. When our son Matthias was born, she quit the job. Fortunately, I was no longer a penniless student at the time, but a salaried employee.

The institute where I worked on a research project funded by the government had about twenty members, some of them first-rate physicists. The interplay of all this talent engendered many lively debates, mostly of a scientific nature. As a scientist, I profited greatly from these discussions; as a spiritual being, I was somewhat dissatisfied. What I missed was the broader intellectual framework in which all sciences have their place. Physics, in isolation, does not appeal to me. I need to see it in a wider philosophical context. The raison d'être of philosophy, I believe, is to provide a home for all sciences and religions. Specialization may be inevitable, but the mutual alienation that plagues the professional community these days is preventable, in my opinion, by the all-embracing spirit of philosophy.

The director of the institute was a competent physicist, but also a hard-nosed specialist who had scarcely any interest other than his pet scientific projects. A consummate workaholic, he was mainly concerned with pushing out one publication after the other. His hectic schedule left him little time for educational or social contacts. But he also had his positive sides. By procuring the government funds for the numerous research projects on which we worked, he was the engine that kept the institute going. Fairness commands me to acknowledge that I owe him the first paid job of my life.

Aside from my friend Are, there was one person who was keenly interested in the philosophical and religious issues that were raised by modern physics. This young professor was about my age and had served in the army roughly as long as I had, but was professionally far ahead of me. As a high school student, he had delivered to his teacher a treatise on quantum theory that had caught the attention of Werner Heisenberg, who was one of the theory's cofounders and the discoverer of the "uncertainty principle" named after him. After the war, Heisenberg maintained his interest in the young man, who had become an associate professor in the meantime. Some of his brilliant work found its way into the prestigious *Encyclopedia of Physics*.

I learned more from this young professor than from any other teacher, except for Theo, my unforgettable high school teacher. Our discussions, together with Are and a few others, ranged from physics to philosophy, politics, psychology, and even music. He was one of the few members of the institute who had a distinct interest in preeminent contemporary non-physicists like Sigmund Freud, George Bernard Shaw, or Jean-Paul Sartre. Unlike Theo, the professor had a great sense of humor and also a penchant for gossip. His favorite pastime was to beat up on a simple-minded student who made an irresistible target for his sharp wit. When the poor devil got caught in a web of contradictions, the professor roared with laughter.

I was hoping to discuss the Holocaust with this man; however, on that score, I was disappointed. Whenever I brought the subject up, he shrugged it off with a few words of regret. There was no real resonance, no kindred feeling. He loved to ridicule Hitler, but he did not abhor him, as I did. The whole subject of Nazi atrocities seemed to bore him. We also did not speak about our experiences during the war. All I knew was that the professor had been a soldier, but not where he served or whether he saw combat.

The professor's silence about the Nazi past was shared by virtually all members of the institute. Most of them had not seen

combat, either because of young age or because of physical handicap. Hence I could understand that they had no great desire to
listen to the usual war stories, but it pained me that they evaded
the subject of the Holocaust. This chapter of German history was
a tacit taboo.

As I see it today, this persistent silence had mainly two causes.
The first one was classic psychological suppression. This attitude
was typical of the majority of the German people at the time.
After the horrific revelations of the first two or three postwar
years, many Germans began to suppress the memory of the concentration camps. It must be said, however, that there was a new
wave of national self-examination about two decades after the
war, and there is another one today. On the other hand, Germans
of my generation still observe a stubborn silence about the genocide of the Nazis.

The second cause of the silence was the instinct for political
and material rehabilitation, which awakened in the same proportion as the national self-examination went to sleep. A few years
after the war, Germans were almost exclusively concerned with
reconstruction, education, starting a business, or building a
career and making money. A hint of the coming economic miracle was in the air.

There is a third cause, which, however, is not typical of the
man in the street, but mainly an academic phenomenon. It is a
combination of intellectual arrogance, faulty value judgment, and
exaggerated fear. My colleagues overvalued science and under-
valued their new—and unfamiliar—democratic civic responsibility. They concentrated on scientific achievements to the exclusion
of almost anything else. Obsessed with an ambition to become
first-rate physicists and fanatically resolved to conserve their
mental resources, they may have felt that admitting, once or
twice, that there had been Nazi crimes was all they needed to do.
Dwelling on undisputed facts, in their opinion, was a waste of
time.

It was not all work at the institute; there were also social activities. Dance parties, musical recitals, motorcycle outings, drives to nearby Amsterdam to enjoy Dutch food or visit the Rembrandt Museum, and other activities of this kind reinforced the slow ascent to normalcy. We travelled to meetings of professional societies where I saw a few giants of physics—Werner Heisenberg, Max von Laue, and Pascual Jordan.

My favorite pastime was visiting the ancient cathedral in Aachen. Dating back to about A.D. 800, the Aachener Dom is the burial place of Charlemagne, and its choir is famous for performances of old music masters, particularly Palestrina. It was here that I first heard the B Minor Mass of Bach. Rarely ever has a concert touched me as deeply as the performance of this particular work at that special place and time. The *dona nobis pacem* (grant us peace) gripped me with its striking actuality. Starting at a very low pitch in the male voices, it gradually rises, with the entrance of the female voices, the trumpets, and the timpani, to a heartrending plea for peace. At that point, I was so overcome with emotion that I had to rush outside, where I heard the final chord, followed by the audience's rapturous silence.

I dearly needed such experiences to overcome the depressing memory of the Nazi past. There were moments when I could not believe that I had fallen for an Adolf Hitler, nor could I believe that an entire nation had succumbed to his seductive lead. At the time, I had a worn-out book with photos from the Holocaust. I forgot its title. Whenever I opened it, I momentarily toyed with the thought that the gruesome pictures were not true. Yet the truth was worse. I knew it. There was no escape.

My general feeling was a certain intellectual loneliness. I was spiritually liberated, but unfulfilled and restless. I thought that the mental liberation should not be an end by itself, but a gift to be used. Deep in the recesses of my mind, I had the vague feeling that the spiritual freedom I now enjoyed would change my life someday.

The root of my problem was the Nazi past and the way the nation dealt with it. I was hoping for a spiritual conversion of the German people. I wanted them to play a radically new role in this world. For one thing, I was adamantly opposed to the rearmament, which the Western Allies had suggested and the German government was all too eager to accept. Germany, I thought, should be the first nation on earth to relinquish all weapons, renounce all violence, and rely exclusively on the protection of international law.

In later years, I had to moderate my radical pacifism. At the moment, however, it drove me into opposition to the foreign policy of Chancellor Konrad Adenauer. While I strongly supported his attempts to integrate the Federal Republic into the family of Western democracies, I rejected his plans to make the western half of Germany a member of the military alliance of NATO. I also resented Adenauer's assent to the nation's division into two countries. His eager acceptance of the de facto partition reminded me of his efforts during the 1920s to separate the Rhine province from the rest of the country and make it a buffer zone between Germany and France. Since that time, Adenauer's name was almost synonymous with separatism.

That said, I must add that there were also things I liked about Adenauer, such as his courage, his strict adherence to democratic principles, and his policy of reconciliation with France. Most important, I stood firmly behind his efforts to indemnify the Jews. When Adenauer traveled to Israel and was received by Prime Minister Ben-Gurion, I admired the chancellor's courage and the prime minister's magnanimity. There was hardly any other German who politically could have afforded this journey at that time.

Years later, when Chancellor Willy Brandt knelt at the Auschwitz memorial, I was deeply gratified and even proud that Germany had statesmen of such humility and nobility. However, I was disappointed that this gesture was not as popular with the German people as it should have been. I wanted the whole nation to kneel, if only symbolically, before the millions of human beings that had died at the hands of the Nazis.

Today, the younger generation of Germans confronts the wrongs of the past with an entirely different attitude. Uninhibited by feelings of guilt, yet keenly aware of their historical responsibility, they search for the truth with an almost religious zeal. They consider it their sacred duty to keep the memory of the Holocaust alive in the national consciousness. In that spirit, young Germans have transfigured the former concentration camps into shrines of atonement. On religious holidays, thousands of people pilgrimage to the places where brutality and horror once reigned.

There are several special groups that have made penance for the Holocaust their sole purpose of existence. One such group is the Ecumenical Sisterhood of Mary at Darmstadt. On the very day that Adolf Eichmann went on trial in Jerusalem, the sisters from Darmstadt opened the Israeli branch of their convent just a few blocks away. There are probably no people on earth who are doing more to atone for the sins of their fathers, in words and deeds, than the young Germans of today.

When I was still living in Germany, and also later in America, I regularly read the weekly *Die Zeit,* published by Marion Gräfin Dönhoff and Helmut Schmidt. I have never seen a more decent and responsible newspaper, not even in America. For several decades now, *Die Zeit* has been the voice of those intellectuals who want to discuss the sins of the past and the duties of the present. One of the weekly's main objectives was to make sure that the Holocaust will never be forgotten in Germany. To that purpose, every issue featured a special report on the fate of one particular Jewish individual or family.

One of these reports is particularly fresh in my memory. Significantly, it is one of the least violent accounts. Most of the other stories reverberate with pain and drip with blood. There is no blood in that account; however, the pain of the victim is appreciable only through the medium of a letter this woman received from a Nazi official. The letter is the focus of the whole story. Its gripping power resides in its language. Only a person with a fossilized soul can muster such language.

Shortly before the war, this Jewish woman of northern Germany sent her teenage son to England for safety. After the war, the young man returned to Germany in search of his mother. All he found was a letter from the local party official, which his mother had received shortly before her deportation. Here is what he read: "Your relocation has been ordered. You will report on day so and so at seven o'clock in the evening at the railroad station. You are allowed to bring twenty Reichsmark and ten pounds of luggage. You will surrender the key to your apartment at that time. Your property falls to the state."

Here we have the language of mercilessness. It is at once enriched and impoverished. Enriched, because each sentence says much more than the sum of its words; impoverished, because it says much less than a smile or a tear. The reptilian letter writer was a bureaucrat who conducted the Holocaust from his desk. His fanatical zeal to purge the last shred of mercy from his petrified soul, and his clinical desire to demonstrate his success to victims and superiors alike, has reduced his language to the poverty level of an anesthetized imbecile. No doubt, if the same party official had written a letter to his superior, it would have been in flowery bureaucratese. But since he was out to murder, he sharpened his language, as a butcher sharpens his knife.

Of course, there were thousands of such "desk murderers"; witness Himmler, Heydrich Rheinhard, and Eichmann. These were the sinister bureaucrats who planned the Holocaust and supplied the "camp murderers" with victims. Their brutality was matched only by their cowardice. I suppose every nation has potential "desk murderers" and "camp murderers" in its midst. But only in Nazi Germany were these individuals licensed to do their gruesome work. Without the evil ideology of Nazism, the extermination camps would never have been created, and the thousands of murderers they employed would have been safely tucked away in the recesses of society.

I was deeply grateful to Schmidt and Dönhoff that their newspaper chronicled the fates of hundreds of Jews with incorruptible fidelity. Helmut Schmidt, of course, was the later chancellor who continued the policy of reconciliation with France and Poland, which had been started by Adenauer, Brandt, and others. Countess Dönhoff pursued the same goal as a journalist. She was born in East Prussia. At the end of the war, when the Red Army was approaching and committing unspeakable atrocities, she fled on horseback to the West.

In 1955, I took the position of a development engineer at a turbine factory of Siemens, Germany's equivalent to America's General Electric. I had been recommended by my uncle who was an executive in the steel industry and had helped me ever since I had returned from the war. The factory was located in Mülheim-Ruhr, near Essen, the heart of the industrial Ruhr district. At the time, the city was not a pretty sight since much of it was still in ruins. There were no parks or flowers, the air was fouled by the newly revived heavy industry, and the Ruhr River was dead from industrial waste. When I visited the place thirty years later, flowers were everywhere, the air was almost pristine, and the river was teeming with fish.

I was interviewed by the manager of the division for the development of gas turbines, a huge man who was surprisingly soft-spoken and mild-mannered. As I soon found out, he was also unusually artistic and musical. A competent engineer and a renowned author and lecturer on gas turbines, the manager made more the impression of an orchestra conductor than an engineer. I took an immediate liking to him, and he seemed to reciprocate, as he hired me on the spot.

On closer acquaintance, I found out that the manager was a highly moral person with a slightly moralistic inclination. He also was almost completely without humor. A joke, even a relatively clean one, could make him squirm with embarrassment. In many ways, he was similar to Theo, my former high school teacher, who liked to smile, but never laughed.

The manager and I were kindred spirits in many respects, most importantly with regard to the Holocaust. Once he took me along on a duty trip in a company car. That's when we had our first extensive dialogue about the Nazi past. It turned out that we shared the same feelings. The massive, systematic genocide was as incomprehensible to him as it was to me. "I sometimes wake up in the middle of the night," he said, "and see the poor people marching toward the gas chamber." When I mentioned the picture of an elderly Jewish woman, with an infant on her arm and two children on her hand, treading unknowingly toward the gas chamber, he immediately said that he knew the picture.

The manager's reaction emboldened me to tell him about my Jewish war comrade, Röper, whom I had failed for fear of retribution. He listened closely and became increasingly pensive, yet he did not blame me. "We are all guilty, in one way or another," he murmured.

Once, during my employment at Siemens, the manager made a business trip to the United States. When he came back, he was full of praise and admiration. The Statue of Liberty and the Lincoln Memorial had made the deepest impression on him. But Manhattan had horrified him. "The Broadway is a den of vice," he whispered with his hand over his mouth, as some people do when they speak of the devil. When I left Germany for America and took my leave of him, his last words were, "Look at the stars, but always be aware of the gutter."

The possibility of immigrating to the United States came in 1957 with a letter from Hel, who was the third member of the MaMaBa club of Mainz. He had joined the team of German rocket scientists at the Army Ballistic Missile Agency (ABMA) at Redstone Arsenal near Huntsville, Alabama. The team leader was Wernher von Braun, the legendary space scientist who had directed the German rocket development program during the war. The now defunct rocket center was located at Peenemünde, a tiny community on a small island off the Baltic coast.

Hel had joined ABMA under "Project Paperclip," a program of the U.S. government designed to recruit German scientists for the armed services and industry. Now I used the same program to realize a dream I had nursed since I had broken the mental chains of Nazism, the dream of going to America. I cannot say that I consciously wished to become an American. That came later. At the moment, I only wanted to see the country that had impressed me with its strength, its fairness, and its love of peace.

A few days after I had applied with the Project Paperclip office in Frankfurt, a sergeant of the U.S. Army appeared at our apartment in Mülheim to initiate the recruiting and immigration process. Being friendly and helpful, he told us at the outset that he was a Jew, but did not hold any grudge against us. I still remember how patiently he answered our questions and how carefully, almost lovingly, he described the transoceanic flight in an air force plane. "Yes, you will be served food and drink. You probably will get a box with fried chicken." The prospect of a meal of chicken electrified us; although the period of starvation had ended roughly six years ago, chicken was still a luxury we could not often afford.

A few weeks later, I had to travel to Frankfurt for several interviews, including an interrogation and lie detector test by an intelligence specialist. The officer, a colonel of the U.S. Army, was a huge man with reddish hair who was fluent in German. As he was operating his strange machine in the quiet of the interrogation office, he spoke with a very low, almost hypnotic voice. Some of his questions were neutral or even irrelevant; others were aimed at my political past. Eventually, he came to the question I had been waiting for: "Have you been a member of the Nazi Party?"

Here is my answer: "When I completed my eighteenth year of life in June of 1939, I was a member of the Hitler Youth. According to Nazi law, I should have been automatically transferred to the Nazi Party. But since I became a soldier a few months later, on New Year's Day of 1940, I received neither a notification of admittance to the party nor a membership book and number. Thus, I don't know whether or not I was a party member."

"Yes," replied the officer, "you were a member, and your membership number was such and such." He knew this from the Nazi archives in Munich the Americans had seized in 1945.

The revelation of my party membership neither surprised nor upset me. I had never made a secret of my Nazi past; I did not do so then nor do I do so now. The party book is only a piece of paper. What counts is what I believed and what I did. As a boy I was longing to get close to Hitler and shake his hand. I never made it. There were always those millions of contemporaries standing between him and me who now claim that they never have been his admirers. I am not one of those.

The prospect of working for the U.S. defense establishment did not bother me either. The radical pacifism that I had embraced during the first few postwar years had long given way to a more realistic view of the world. I loved freedom and peace as much as ever, but I had learned in the meantime that the free world must be ready to defend its freedom. Ever since the United States had granted independence to the Philippines, I knew that America did not seek dominance over any other nation. At the same time, I became increasingly concerned about the threat from the Soviet Union to world peace and freedom. Hence I thought it was imperative that the United States was militarily as strong as possible. Therefore, I welcomed the opportunity of contributing to America's military strength.

Back in Mülheim, I received notice that my family and I would be admitted to the United States and that I would be employed by the Army Ballistic Missile Agency under contract with the U.S. Army. But there was one problem. Under U.S. immigration law, pregnant aliens were not allowed to enter the United States. And since Renate was carrying our second child, Bettina, she had to wait until the child was born. In the meantime, I was requested to report for duty in Frankfurt.

In September 1957, I reported to the recruiting office of the U.S. Army in Frankfurt, where I signed a contract and awaited air transportation to the United States. I would have loved to know my salary, and I was sure it was buried somewhere in the paperwork, but the contract, which was as thick as a book, was absolutely unreadable. I had always thought that the Germans were the world champions of bureaucracy, but when I saw this contract, I was no longer so sure.

This was the first time I was cured of a misconception about America, but there would be many more to follow. Most of them were as trivial as that one. They only proved that the American nation, by far the most complex and heterogeneous society on earth, incorporated all the little faults of the other nations and races that are its stock. The lessons that really counted came many years later. They were not corrections of misconceptions, but a chain of enlightenments, as I slowly became an American. They were not double negatives, like dispositions of preconceptions, but the slow and wondrous assimilation of positive ideas that are the essence of Americanism.

A few days later I received my first salary, some $350 for two weeks. Not much money by today's standards, but an incredible amount to my mind, particularly when converted into Deutsch-marks. I kept only a little of it and sent the rest to Renate for housekeeping.

At the Rhein-Main Air Base, I got another lesson about America. It was as trivial as the first one, but more charming. Up to that moment I honestly believed that food was free on U.S. government premises, certainly on military installations. Hence, I did not pay for my meals in the cafeteria until one day a sergeant gently tapped me on the shoulder, saying, "Sir, you forgot to pay." I doubt whether he earnestly believed my protestations that it was an honest mistake, but he took pains to make me believe so.

A few days later I took off for America. The stewardesses on the military aircraft were as friendly, and the chicken was as tasty, as the Jewish sergeant who had recruited me had predicted. The plane flew to McGuire Air Force Base, New Jersey, where I was officially admitted to the United States. Renate and the two children followed on the same route in March 1958.

If the official admittance to America at the air base was somewhat bureaucratic and colorless, the welcome in New York City was the more heartwarming. In the lobby of the Alamac Hotel, I was greeted in fluent German by Dorothy, the official envoy from the Army Ballistic Missile Agency. A stunning blonde, Dorothy was responsible for the care of the many German scientists who flocked to the missile program under Project Paperclip.

I could not have wished for a more hearty reception. Dorothy was as resourceful and knowledgeable as she was friendly and warmhearted. It turned out that she was the child of Jewish parents who had fled Germany under Hitler and now lived in San Francisco. But there was not a trace of resentment or reproach in Dorothy's behavior, and we became immediate friends. Fate was smiling upon me. A graceful Jewess welcomed me to America.

A dream had come true.

Epilogue

If I have learned one thing from my life under the Nazis, it is to listen more faithfully to that inner voice that exists in all of us and always tells us when something is wrong. I believe this moral voice is the faculty that makes us really human. It spoke to me at the most critical moments of my life. To my lifelong regret, I chose to ignore it and to listen to Adolf Hitler instead.

When I was very young, the voice was faint and gentle; as I grew older, it became louder and blunter. The first time I heard it, if ever so faintly, I was ten years old. My father cursed the Jews, while my mother tried to allay his rage. The discomfort I felt at that moment was the inner voice, trying to tell me that hate is ignoble. A few years later, when I attempted to rationalize the atrocities of Kristallnacht, the voice was already louder. And when I watched the frightened Jews in Berlin's S-Bahn, it scared me with its strident ring.

Why, then, did I succumb to the ideology of hate? To say that I was too young would be a cop-out. After all, there were others not much older than I who withstood the siren song of evil. For example, consider the young conspirators from the resistance group "The White Rose." I read their story long after the war, as an American, with tears in my eyes. A small circle of young men and women who were medical students at the University of Munich fought the Nazis in 1942–43 by distributing leaflets that called for resistance against the criminal regime. Here is the beginning of their leaflet:

> Nothing is so unworthy of a civilized nation as allowing itself to be governed without opposition by an irresponsible clique that has yielded to base instinct.

The group leader, Hans Scholl, was only three years older than I, and his sister, Sophie Scholl, was exactly my age. When the conspirators were caught, they were tortured, tried, sentenced, and beheaded within four days. In the night before his death, Hans Scholl wrote on the prison wall a terse sentence by Goethe that he had learned as a child from his father: "Hold out in defiance of all despotism." Why had I not known this saying? Why?

Reading the report by Inge Scholl, the surviving sister, was one of the most remorseful moments of my life. Viewing the photographs with the young, beautiful faces was almost unbearable. Following their lives from childhood to death, from Hitler Youth to the guillotine, filled me with an ineffable sadness. Ashamed and humbled, I asked myself a hundred times why I had not been one of them. Why?

I did not find the answer. I only know one thing: There is no authority on earth, no man, no government, no law, no scripture, that exempts us from the sacred duty to follow our own conscience, no matter what demagogues may preach, what public opinion may echo, or what fear may whisper. I have sinned against this sacred commandment, and so have millions of Germans of my generation.

Why did the Holocaust happen? Why in Germany? One can think of many causes; Hitler, certainly, was one of them. Other contributing factors are the endemic anti-Semitism of prewar Europe, Germany's defeat of 1918, the Treaty of Versailles, extreme economic hardship, the threat of Communist takeover, and so on. The trouble with all of these reasons is that they are not convincing. None provides an insightful answer to the crucial question of why Germans succumbed to Adolf Hitler. Why?

To find the deeper causes, it helps to look at another nation for comparison. I believe that America has something to teach us here. Imagine that there had been an American Hitler in the dark years following the economic debacle of 1929. Would America have fallen for the hatred he preached? Would the Holocaust have happened in the United States under conditions comparable to those that preceded the power seizure by the Nazis in Germany?

The answer is a flat "no." And the reason is the American spirit. This spirit is perhaps most vividly exemplified by Jefferson and Lincoln, but by no means restricted to them. It pervades the history and the psyche of this nation from George Washington to Franklin Delano Roosevelt. It is the conviction that freedom is a birthright of individuals and nations, as expressed by the Declaration of Independence; and it is the awareness that this freedom must be defended at all cost, as the country has demonstrated by fighting two wars of liberation on foreign soil. The American spirit is the belief that democracy is the only way for people to live with each other. It is the faith in the republic and the loyalty to the American Constitution. It is the conviction that the individual has certain fundamental rights, as expressed by the Bill of Rights.

Germans had the Weimar Republic and the Weimar Constitution, which were as republican and democratic as government and written law can be. Yet they didn't believe in them; indeed, they hated them. They lacked the spirit that inspired Americans to defend democracy at home and on the battlefield. Germans did not care for a democracy they had never experienced. All they wanted was deliverance from the injustice and suppression of the Treaty of Versailles. But they didn't see, or didn't care, that the very ideology they embraced meant much greater injustice and suppression of other individuals and nations. They were morally disarmed by their lack of faith in democratic ideals and their indifference toward freedom. Germans lacked the American spirit. That is the deeper reason why they succumbed to Hitler and his tyranny.

My explanation may seem simplistic, but I believe it goes to the heart of the problem. Again, America has something to teach us. There are dozens of examples in American history when the nation, caught in an immoral act or flawed with an unethical institution, corrected its wrongs by a self-induced process of spiritual renaissance. America freed itself, in the bloodiest war of its history, from the abomination of slavery. I believe that this readiness to repair its own faults is the source of the nation's miraculous moral strength. I have seen America stumbling more than once; but I always observed America getting up, and moving on.

I am well aware of the stains on the American shield of honor, such as the genocide of Native Americans, the lynch-murders by the Ku Klux Klan, or the internment of Japanese-Americans in 1942. These hateful acts only show that the American society, as every other nation, has a fringe element of misguided militants, who are always ready to persecute racial, ethnic, or religious minorities. But the question is whether the society has the moral fiber to fight these elements and to pay any price for rendering them harmless. It is the triumph of the American spirit that the nation always took up this fight, though sometimes after long delays, and rectified the wrongs committed by its radical fringe.

This remarkable self-correcting spirit radiates into every niche of society. It equips the well-meaning individual with an admirable immunity to the merchants of hate. Other nations are quick to malign America for the violence in its streets and schools. While this is certainly a moral and a social problem that needs to be solved, it also has technical causes such as the unparalleled availability of guns that stems from colonial times. As far as I know, no other nation has it written in the constitution that "the right of the people to keep and bear arms shall not be infringed." My faith in America tells me that this country's self-correcting spirit will solve this problem, too.

I recently read the diary of an American exchange student who studied in Leipzig in 1932–33, that is, before and after Hitler seized power. In general, the young man was generous with his praise and reserved in his criticism of Germany, but when it came to the Nazis, his judgment was unequivocally negative. The sweeping power of his rejection demonstrated total immunity to the appeal of Hitler's demagoguery. That was the American spirit.

This spirit has proved itself again and again in American history. I witnessed the civil rights struggle of the 1950s and '60s, the national unrest about the Vietnam war, the Watergate crisis, and other upheavals. Each time, I was amazed with how much reason, faith, dignity, and civility the nation admitted and corrected its faults. To me, these moments of crisis were triumphs of the America spirit.

I think the core of this spirit is the belief in the sanctity of the individual and the right to question authority. Along with this right goes the moral duty to oppose any authority when it indulges in criminal activities. Germans of my generation have sinned against this spirit, and so have I. In so doing, Germans helped the Nazis, knowingly or not, to do their murderous handiwork, and so did I. I shall bear this repentance for the rest of my life.

At the end of this book, I want to say a few very personal things. In writing my testimony, I attempted to tell the truth, even though I knew from the very beginning that it would be painful, particularly the memory of my father. But the Holocaust was an event so horrible and unparalleled in human history that it requires unparalleled and uncompromising actions. I wish my father knew that I always remember him as a good father and that the unpleasant task of recollecting his hateful preaching does not in the least diminish my love for him. Indeed, as his son, I take comfort in the thought that, having freed myself from the mental prison of Nazism, I also have freed my father, if only posthumously.

Now I am an American, and yet my German heritage continues to cast its spell over my life. On national holidays, I envy my fellow Americans who helped eradicate Nazism from the surface of the earth. They can be proud of what they did; I cannot. They are honored; I am not. Everything I did before and during the Third Reich, whether it was noble or ignoble, brave or cowardly, is branded with the negative sign of history. And yet, I don't want it any other way, for it tells me who I was and who I am now.

I wrote this book to make my contribution, however small, to the cause of preventing Nazism from ever happening again. I believe I owe this to the Jews and all the other victims of the cataclysm. To the survivors, I offer my apology. But I know that that is not enough.

I ask for forgiveness.

Bruno Manz was born in 1921 in Dortmund, Germany. There he attended high school until he became a soldier in the German army at the beginning of World War II. He fought in Finland at the Eastern front against Russia. At the war's end, he briefly became a prisoner of war of British forces in Norway and was released in November 1945.

Manz began his study of mathematics and physics at the University of Mainz in 1946. In 1957 he graduated with a Ph.D. in theoretical physics from the Technical University, Aachen, Germany. He was employed as a research scientist by Siemens of Germany from 1955 to 1957. In 1957 he immigrated to the United States.

Dr. Manz was first employed by the Army Ballistic Missile Agency at Redstone Arsenal, Alabama. In 1959, he accepted a position as operations analyst with the U.S. Air Force, first in Alamogordo and then in Albuquerque, New Mexico. He retired in 1988. He also taught physics, mathematics, and operations research for three universities: the University of New Mexico, Highlands University of New Mexico, and Chapman College.

In 1955 he married his present wife, Renate. The couple has four children, two born in Germany and two in America. Dr. Manz now lives with his wife in Albuquerque, New Mexico.